CITIZEN WARRIOR:

The Spirit World Battle for the Soul of Your City

Citizen Warrior:

The Spirit World Battle for the Soul of Your City

Creative Non-Fiction
by
MICHAEL K. MANCHA

Adelaide Books
New York / Lisbon
2020

CITIZEN WARRIOR:
The Spirit World Battle for the Soul of Your City
By Michael K. Mancha

Copyright © by Michael K. Mancha
Cover design © 2020 Adelaide Books

Published by Adelaide Books, New York / Lisbon
adelaidebooks.org

Editor-in-Chief
Stevan V. Nikolic

All rights reserved. No part of this book may be reproduced in any manner whatsoever without written permission from the author except in the case of brief quotations embodied in critical articles and reviews.

For any information, please address Adelaide Books
at info@adelaidebooks.org
or write to:
Adelaide Books
244 Fifth Ave. Suite D27
New York, NY, 10001

ISBN: 978-1-953510-55-6

Printed in the United States of America

For Elizabeth.

She loved me at the time of life when I felt most unlovable and that has made all the difference.

Contents

Preface **11**

Chapter 1
Seduced **13**

Chapter 2
Not for Self, But for Others **18**

Chapter 3
The Divine, the Devil, and You **23**

Chapter 4
The Spirit Realm **29**

Chapter 5
The Sixth Sense **38**

Chapter 6
Spirit and Soul **42**

Chapter 7
God's Book on You **48**

Chapter 8
The Soul of a City **60**

Chapter 9
The Hopeful Romantic **72**

Chapter 10
The Builder and Architect **76**

Chapter 11
Savannah Seeds **85**

Chapter 12
A Gifted Lady **93**

Chapter 13
The Lens of History **105**

Chapter 14
Symbolism and the City **127**

Chapter 15
A City of Great Importance **137**

Chapter 16
A Haunted Lady **152**

Chapter 17
The Paranormal **159**

Chapter 18
Two Kingdoms **171**

Chapter 19
The War in the Spirit World **179**

Chapter 20
Evil Strategies **201**

Chapter 21
The Walls and Gates of a City **215**

Chapter 22
Divine Order **225**

Chapter 23
Evil Presence **237**

Chapter 24
Ignorance and Strongholds **246**

Chapter 25
Lady Savannah and Greed **254**

Chapter 26
Enterprise Perverted **265**

Chapter 27
The Enslaved **278**

Chapter 28
Preservation of Our Cities **291**

Chapter 29
Legacy of Corruption **304**

Chapter 30
Vision and Compassion **319**

Chapter 31
Freeing the Captive City **325**

Chapter 32
The Seven Keys of the Kingdom **337**

Chapter 33
The Battle Plan **374**

A Final Word **381**

About the Author **383**

Preface

Let's begin with a few probing questions:

Is it possible that an invisible, spirit realm exists simultaneously with the visible, physical world?

Is it possible that within this spirit world is an ongoing clash between good and evil forces that influences the most fundamental aspects of our lives here on Earth, and our existence following our deaths?

And is it possible that the understanding we have and the actions we take concerning these spirit battles, determines whether good or evil prevails?

And what about our cities, comprised of a concentration of human population, how might they be influenced or shaped by the action or inaction of their citizens?

Is there an intended destiny for the cities that sprinkle the landscape of planet Earth?

With regard to the city in which you live, what human activities have taken place over the years that have contributed to present societal conditions?

And is there a means, a strategy, by which your city might fulfill her intended destiny?

Let's take a journey. A journey from the present, into the past, and then back again. Our steps will take us on a pathway that intersects two worlds. We'll meet flesh and blood personalities from past ages, and also encounter entities devoid of human flesh and bone that existed then and still wander the planet today.

The views and concepts presented in this writing are based on a thread of common belief that has spanned the course of mankind's history; that is during our lifetime on Earth, these opposing fundamental constants are in operation: good and evil, truth and lies, and moral enlightenment and ignorance. Reason would then dictate that two sources exist from which these extremes originate, generally referred to as God and the Devil. If what I propose in the pages before us is true, then so must the existence of these two entities.

As we embark, I want to issue a warning and a dare. If you read on, you do so at your own risk. In my research, I drew from many sources, including the Holy Scriptures. Various authorities within our western culture have characterized those that embrace such things as fanatical, intolerant, and irrelevant. I challenge you to suspend judgment and temporarily place that brand of hype on a backburner. If you will, you may just sense a stirring deep in your heart and impressions within, heretofore foreign. Perhaps, you'll experience a shift in how you view such ideas, and the emergence of a new perspective. That would be the rise of faith…miraculous and supernatural. It is the presence and work of the Divine as the human soul opens to new possibilities.

Here we go.

Chapter 1

Seduced

In selecting a city as the case study to apply my proposals, the choice was simple. Like many other readers, the images of Savannah, Georgia, painted with the deft strokes of author John Berendt in his 1994 release, *Midnight in the Garden of Good and Evil*, left me with the question: can a place like this still exist? Then came Clint Eastwood's 1997 big screen rendering of the book that fueled my curiosity all the more. It wasn't until seven years later that I first set foot on Savannah soil.

I recall that first visit to this little garden by the sea. It consisted of seven days of taking in the sights, sounds, and smells of the town via some trolley and much shoe leather, while toting ten pounds of photo gear. My wife, Elizabeth, and I flew back to California knowing that another trip was inevitable. Actually, we didn't have much choice in the matter.

You see, our visit yielded much more than the common getaway or escape from a routine of too much work and not enough play. It was an encounter with a personality, a life form embodied in a city shaped over time by an assortment of events, and by people with diverse gifts and diverse vices. Added to the passion of human nature and inspired innovation, were frequent relentless assaults by Mother Nature that brought Savannah to her knees and the cusps of extinction.

Our orientation to Savannah history revealed evidences of an ebb and flow of both destructive and constructive influences that for almost three centuries of time have forged the image and character of the town. In itself, this was not a surprise as all social communities of human beings are subject to these basic processes. However, the measure and intensity of the clash of these opposing powers in Savannah had been exceptional, and still is, as the extreme tug of war continues to this day. The competing forces are unseen, but the evidences of the ongoing conflict are clearly visible.

Our second visit to Savannah was one year later. Gestation had taken place over the previous twelve months and the purpose of the return was to stake out the right place to live. Within five days we found it and again returned to California. Within the next four weeks, we packed up, drove the two thousand, five hundred miles from west coast to east coast, and the population of Savannah then increased by two (five if you include our three dogs).

Savannah Mystique

The town can be likened to an onion in that it becomes increasingly potent with the peeling of each layer. Or, perhaps, a woman; more complex and intricate as one becomes better acquainted. The more you know *about* her, the less you *understand* her. The quintessence of Lady Savannah.

Without exception, when consulting a travel guide, a description of Savannah will include adjectives like beguiling or enchanting or mysterious. However, in my experience, I found these characterizations sorely lacking in capturing the essence of the town. The events she has been subjected to during the crucible of time, defy adequate analysis. There is a depth to Savannah that cannot be plumbed. And the mere arrangement of words on a page will only provide a peek at this conflicted lady. One must expose oneself to her charms…walking her streets, breathing her air, surveying with one's physical and spiritual senses, and then allowing time for the heart to digest the impressions. This is just the beginning of understanding. She defies rational explanation, but she is real, and her elusive, enigmatic persona, irresistible.

I believe Savannah *is* seductive because *she* has been seduced. It is likely that the sole way to grasp a measure of understanding is by coming under this spell she casts, to be drawn close enough to her passion fires to glimpse her soul, but with careful, measured steps to avoid too severe a burn.

At Her Mercy

As I begin this writing, I have lived in Savannah for one decade, a mere drop in the bucket of her complex, nearly three centuries of existence. Above my enjoyment of the history, natural beauty, music, and food, are the people. The town has been a classic melting pot of Earthbound humans since her founding. I remain fascinated by what seems to be the command the city has over her populace, if, in fact there is any distinction between the two. When talking with native-born or long-time residents of Savannah, you'll often hear how that person had moved away to a place like Los Angeles or New York to broaden their horizons, only to return with their tail between their legs. She is a lady walking a dog, only allowing so much leash until the dog is drawn back to her side.

Also common is the transplant from the west coast or northeast that waltzes into town intent on bringing Savannah "current". Inevitably, these mavericks meet with failure and slowly discover that he or she has been subdued; that in attitude and lifestyle have conformed to *her* image and are just added victims of her charms.

One cannot taste of Savannah's unique offerings for long without feeling they have been transported to a past era or have walked onto the set of *Gone with the Wind*. It's Antebellum Land at Disney World if they had one. But Savannah is the real thing. For certain, the bulk of this lady's influence is that she seems frozen in another time. The reasons for this state of being are as murky as the abundant marsh waters of the region. But perhaps this perplexing lady has been unknowable because we have attempted to filter her through the grid of human intellect and reason. Could it be that the key to unlocking the mysteries of Savannah lie in the application of spiritual principle and revelation?

Test Her Waters

There are many books available that highlight the various historical figures and events that have shaped this Lady. Most are accurate and draw from common sources and confirmed testimony. However, ever since Berendt blew open the flood gates, there has been a steady flow of publications focusing on ghosts and devils and hauntings that supposedly abound within the city limits. Accompanying this print phenomenon, has been a meteoric rise of ghost tour companies that spin tales of the underworld, each with differing versions of the same story, subject to the guide's embellishment. In lockstep has been a parade of television production crews led about by professional ghost hunters seeking contact with these spirit entities. Whether these entrepreneurs are motivated by a curiosity of the "unknown", or the known financial benefits is a separate issue.

Most every book offers at least one of the explanations that abound as to the identity and/or presence of these entities. Just as elusive is any consensus among local pros or members of the scientific community at large, whether lab geeks or the onsite paranormal "experts."

My approach is not to lay Lady Savannah on a couch and psychoanalyze her as defiance of rational principle is one of her stubborn attributes. This writing is an attempt to sift from her shadowy waters the key dynamics and factors that have contributed to the condition in which we presently find her. The intent is to consider what *powers*, mortal and immortal, may exist that have influenced and continue to shape her character and personality. I also put forth a strategy that if implemented will free Savannah to walk the pathway of her unique destiny.

I implore you to be opened-minded, to earnestly consider what is proposed, and to "test her waters" so that you might draw your own conclusions. In so doing, you may discover the means to the liberation of your own city.

In 1820 a city newspaper editor name John Harney published this declaration as he fled a stricken Savannah on the heels of one of several visitations of the dreaded Yellow Fever: "I leave you Savannah with the worst of all curses, to remain as you are." In response to that embittered pronouncement, it is my sincere hope that after nearly three centuries of continued embattlement, Savannah will be free of her shackles and realize her divine destiny.

Chapter 2

Not for Self, But for Others

Let's begin by looking at what people think about Savannah. What are their impressions based on what they have heard, read, or, personally experienced? Absent ulterior motives, a plurality of thought and feeling is usually a good means to assess a city's personality.

Using Facebook friends as a sounding board, I posted the following status:

I need your input. I am conducting some research for a project. In 50 words or less, please give a description of your immediate impressions when you consider the city of Savannah (in terms of her personality and reputation). It doesn't matter if you are a resident, tourist, or have never been to Savannah but have heard things about her. Don't be shy and thanks for your help.

These were some of their comments:

Lynn Bates – "I think of her beautiful squares, 'painted ladies', Bay Street, and of course St. Patrick's Day!"

Millie Hobbs – "The heartbeat, the breath, and the life blood of the South exemplified in Southern Hospitality and Graceful Beauty unsurpassed."

Marta Haley Fields – "Hot, humid southern beauty. Elegant, tired. Rich and poor."

Elaine McCoy – "Exquisite southern charm. Like no other city you have ever been in. Rich in culture and history and while there are some darker sides to the city – is lovely and welcoming."

Allison Vincitore Hill – "Beautiful, historic, charming, fun, happiness, good food, great people, and ghostly!"

Mark Brown – "Savannah is where the Azaleas bring the sweet smells of spring to life down Victory Drive, taking you to the beach to feel the spray of the ocean on your face with the sand under your feet."

Sheri Pizzi – "Southern charm and hospitality. Sweet sticky fragrance of flowers in the spring and summer along with high levels of humidity. Home to ladies and gentry. Charming with CLASS, Sweet Southern Traditions...PRIDE."

Sandra Holland – "Stunningly complicated city where the real ghosts hang out in the regrets and guilt of Old Savannah, the Nouveau riche and plain folk. The downtown is a historical masterpiece where transplanted trolley drivers lie to tourists about who slept where. The only real ghosts? Coffee breath."

Jeanette Maxwell – "Haunted!!"

Terry Tyson Stirling – "Savannah, she's like a slow-moving river, one can drift through her French styled parks filled with azaleas and live oak trees…a few may see a dirty face in this beautiful place, but she is strong, has weathered many storms. Savannah, she is the definition of southern charm."

Karen Thompson – "Savannah USED to have a reputation of being the epitome of the South. Class and mystery mingled well together. Politicians made reasonable decisions, but that is gone by the wayside. Folks from other areas have aptly named it 'Little Chicago'. Savannah, physically beautiful, but highly undesirable as it is now."

Bessie White Kicklighter – "Crime."

Johnnstacie Young – "At first, being from the west, we were awed by the history, but then you see the trash everywhere. The Saint Patrick's Day Celebration turned out to be a huge disappointment with the beautiful River Street turned into a gaudy display of drunks, junk beads and hats."

Brandie Pishny – "Savannah is a city filled with historical architecture, a charming commerce district, friendly souls, and cuisine of which all other dining experiences are compared and have no equal..."

Carol Tierney – "The squares seem to have a mystic quality... like they're from another time and place."

Jennifer Walsh – "Historic, civil war, ghostly, mossy, Muskogean, mysterious."

From these wide range of comments and descriptions of Savannah, it is evident that the city is complex in character and personality; "intriguing . . . crime-ridden . . . friendly . . . charming . . . a party-town . . . hospitable . . . elegant . . . tired . . . rich . . . poor . . . haunted," and so on. There is certainly no consensus of opinion or impression as the adjectives encompassed a vast spectrum of thought and emotion. To say this Lady is fascinating and enigmatic is an understatement.

Name and Identity

Now we'll take a rearview look at the names Savannah has been given in past times; names that have "stuck". These depictions of the city have survived the test of time and provide us a peek into the heart and mind of the Lady.

The following are the most prominent titles given Savannah by those she has courted:

"That gently mannered city by the sea," Margaret Mitchell, *Gone with the Wind* 1936

"The wickedest city in America," Billy Sunday, when preaching in Savannah during Prohibition

"That spot of spots, that place of places, that city of cities!" Robert E. Lee in 1865

"A beautiful lady with a dirty face," British Lady Nancy Astor in 1946

Again, quite a disparity in meaning, ranging from "gently mannered" and "beautiful, to "wickedest" and "dirty".

These are additional names ascribed to the city over the years that are unattributed to any one individual:

"The separate State of Chatham"

"Little Chicago"

"Venice of the South"

"The Hostess City of the South"

"The City Built on its Dead"

"The Most Haunted City in America"

These various impressions and thoughts about Savannah betray a long and, often, difficult historical path. But before there ever was this puzzling lady, how was she envisioned by those whose hearts were sparked by her possibilities?

Georgia's Founding Motto

The founding father of Georgia, James Edward Oglethorpe, along with the other twenty British trustees that nurtured the vision of the 13th American colony, adopted the motto, *Non sibi sed aliis,* or, in English, Not for self but for others. Their hope and intent were that the people who occupied the land would be marked by their willingness to serve and care for *others*. This is the opposite of self-serving. It is the giving of one's time, energy, and tangible resources for the purpose of meeting the needs of one's fellow man.

The spirit of self-sacrifice was at the heart of what Oglethorpe envisioned in laying the foundation of the colony. This was a lofty goal given the bents of human nature, and, sure enough, we'll discover how Savannah was seduced into becoming something contrary to the hopes of Oglethorpe and company.

Chapter 3

The Divine, the Devil, and You

Before we look closer at the subject of our writing, the Lady Savannah, I want to emphasize that while we will weigh the actions of those among her citizenry and the effects of certain events, we will primarily be assessing the influence and activities of forces that operate invisible to the naked eye; powers only fully perceived by the spirit of man. We must first establish a basic premise, a grid of understanding through which my proposals will be filtered. Let's do this by considering the legitimacy of the following three statements:

- God and the Devil do exist, propagating good and evil, respectively.
- The spiritual realm and the supernatural do exist.
- You and I are creatures fashioned with a spirit and a soul.

Sounds otherworldly? It's not. It is fundamental to our existence. The problem is that the physical world is so relentless and demanding of our attention that we seldom get around to considering the realm of spirit and how it might impact the natural sphere of our existence.

What I'm about to give you is a crash course in the history of the relation between the eternal Heaven and the temporal planet called Earth. This accounting is based on Holy Scripture, and whether you subscribe to it or not, you may find it interesting. The narrative involves the basic relationships between the three categories of intelligent living beings that have existed since the creation of the earth: God, Angels, and Mankind. There may have been or presently may be other forms of created intelligent life in existence; however, we'll restrict ourselves to what has been revealed and pertains to our sphere of living. Here's the chronology:

Creation of the Heavens and Earth – God (Hebrew word *Yahweh*, meaning eternal one, self-existent) forms the heavens (Hebrew word *shamayan*, meaning heights, elevated, or sky) and the earth (Hebrew word *Adamah*, meaning ground). These heavens consist of the atmosphere that covers and surrounds the earth, as well as the *outer* space of stars and other planets. The earth, simply, is the earth; the ground on which your feet and mine are planted.

Creation and Existence of Angels – When God created angels (Greek word *aggelos*, meaning messenger) is unknown; however, they exist in the heaven where God dwells. They are called the heavenly hosts because they are many. They are submitted to God and willingly acknowledge His supreme power and majesty.

Rebellion in Heaven – Lucifer (from the Hebrew word *helel*, meaning brightness), a high-ranking angel, leads an attempted mutiny against God, involving one-third of the heavenly hosts. Lucifer is cast out of God's heaven and exiled to planet Earth, not yet inhabited by mankind. He transitions from possessing fullness of life and dwelling in the glory of the eternal kingdom of Heaven, to a meaningless, wandering existence in darkness on a lifeless, uninhabited ball of dirt.

Creation of Mankind – God creates the first man, Adam, and the first woman, Eve, in his image (to reason, think, and rule) and places them in the Garden of Eden on planet Earth. They are given divine authority over the planet and all living creatures thereupon. Adam and Eve are to multiply and, through their offspring, extend the boundaries of the Garden until the whole Earth is filled with the light and life of God. This commission includes power and authority to subdue (restrain and suppress) the activities of Lucifer and the fallen angels. Mankind's rulership upon the planet would increase and advance only as they remained submitted to the rulership of God.

The Fall of Mankind – Adam and Eve are tempted by Lucifer, now known as *Satan* (Hebrew word meaning adversary) or the Devil (Greek word *diablos*, meaning liar, enemy, or false accuser), to disbelieve and distrust God. They choose to rebel against God, thereby violating God's divine Law. Mankind comes under the judgment of his sin and rebellion, which is physical death and eternal separation from the life of God. Adam and Eve are driven from the light of His presence, into outer darkness. This judgment is also upon every human being that would be born through their bloodline, in all subsequent generations of time.

Loss of Authority – By coming into agreement with the Devil, mankind becomes subject to his will. They are now slaves to the one who they have obeyed. Also lost is mankind's dominion, i.e., his power and control over the earth. The Devil is rightfully in charge according to divine Law.

Tyranny of the Devil – Mankind, separated from his Creator, dwells in darkness in the Devil's domain, without any hope or means of escape.

Heaven's Response – Jesus, the Son of God.

His Mission: Jesus comes to Earth to "seek and save that which was lost" (Luke 19:10).

His Birth: Jesus is born of a woman, thereby qualifying himself as human. However, being born of a virgin, he is not subject to the judgment of sin inherited by all those of Adam's "seed" and bloodline.

His Life: Although tempted throughout the course of his 33-year life, Jesus does not disobey or rebel, remaining in favor and communion with God the Father.

His Death: Jesus offers his life as payment in full for the debt of mankind's sin, as a ransom for those bound by its power. He sacrifices Himself, the innocent for the guilty. As a human, he bears the penalty and judgment for all mankind, past, present, and future, that required death, separation from the life of God.

His Resurrection: Jesus suffers a physical death and temporary separation from His Father while on the Cross. However, the grave has no power over Jesus following the death of the body. He remains pure in spirit and in righteous standing with the Father having never, personally, trespassed God's Law. Once expired, His body is raised from the dead by the power of the Holy Spirit. He enters again into fullness of life and union with the Father.

The Gift of the Holy Spirit: Upon His return to Heaven, Jesus sends the Holy Spirit to live within those who have trusted Him and those who will come to trust in Him. The Spirit will enable and empower all those who are sent into the communities of the world with the message of eternal salvation through Christ.

The Two-Fold Fruit of Victory

Remember, Jesus' mission in coming to Earth, according to the disciple Luke, was "to seek and save that which was lost." Mankind was lost. You and I were lost. Our commission as those in relationship with God our Creator, and the authority to accomplish that purpose, was also lost, forfeited through disobedience. Because of God's love and the sacrifice of His Son, the following was accomplished:

Restored Relationship with God – Mankind's judgment and punishment for sin has been satisfied through the sacrifice of Jesus. All humans are offered forgiveness through the shed Blood, the death of Jesus. In receiving that forgiveness, a man or woman passes from death, into life, and becomes a "new creation" (2 Cor. 5:17), alive in Christ. The sin issue having been dealt with, mankind is delivered from the grip and tyranny of the Devil, and relationship with God, the Father is fully restored.

Restored Authority to Mankind – The Devil is stripped of his dominion over the planet and the authority returned to mankind. Also, restored relationship with their Father through Jesus Christ, gives humanity total authority over the Devil and his wicked forces. The commission to subdue the Devil and bring order upon the earth is fully in force. But remember, our authority is dependent on our individual submission to God's authority.

Notice how human existence begins with fullness of life and the enjoyment of God's presence. Mankind is then subject to separation and death because of sin, and, finally, ushered back into God's presence and again made fully alive! The scriptural accounting of the creation, fall, and means of salvation is a simple history (His Story) of the human experience upon Earth. Relationship between God and His human creation is clearly the dominant theme.

But let's not miss the important subplot: Mankind's commission from God. From the foundation of knowing and walking in intimate relationship with God, we are tasked with something supremely important. The means to living life with maximum purpose and direction lie in the understanding of our partnership with God in subduing the Devil and dismantling what he has produced among humanity. God's intent from the beginning was to place mankind on the earth to multiply and fill the planet with those who would willingly honor Him and display His magnificence and splendor. Nothing has changed as this remains His desire and our Commission.

If this is all true, then why are the human societies that occupy this planet, still plagued with evil? Why does increasing darkness continue to manifest over the people of the earth? I am a lover of happy endings; however, this story is far from over. There remains much to be written as the Devil, according to Scripture, still roams the earth "seeking whom he may devour" (I Peter 5:8).

Chapter 4

The Spirit Realm

If what we just considered really took place, then it is safe to presume a spirit realm must exist; a world populated by unique beings, functioning within a structured government, a hierarchy of authority, and operating with specific purposes.

My primary contention, and running theme throughout this writing, is all that exists and consists in our individual human makeup as well as the elements of the physical world that surrounds us, has its origin in spirit life. As you move forward, keep that principle foremost in your mind.

A.W. Tozer, the brilliant mid-twentieth century theologian and author, writes in his classic, *The Pursuit of God*:

> The world of sense intrudes upon our attention day and night for the whole of our lifetime. It is clamorous, insistent and self-demonstrating. It does not appeal to our faith; it is here, assaulting our five senses, demanding to be accepted as real and final.

Remember, our five senses are only capable of receiving and assessing that which occurs in the natural, physical world. If there is a coexisting spirit world, then something beyond the abilities to see, touch, hear, smell, and taste must be in operation.

The Superior Reality

The Old Testament book of Ecclesiastes includes this statement, "He has made everything beautiful in its time. He has also set eternity in the human heart…". Every person shaped by the hand of God, possesses an inner witness to His existence, as well as their own eternal existence. However, the means to understand God and the supernatural will not be defined by the doctrines contained within the various religious ideologies and philosophies of mankind.

Religion is an attempt by man through an exercise of his natural intellect to understand and explain God and His workings. In fact, the word *religion* comes from the Latin word *re-ligare*, which means to re-bind, or to re-connect. The implication is that a bond that once existed with the divine is now broken and there remains a drive within the human for restoration. So, the activity of religion, in essence, is mankind's quest to find a way to *re-connect* with a higher, infinite power.

One of the fundamental claims of Christianity is that it is not a religion. It is God providing the means for that "reconnection". It is God, through Jesus Christ, transcending the divide between the heavenly and the earthly in order to bring saving grace to a race, wholly inadequate and powerless of saving themselves. Humankind is incapable of understanding their plight and the provided means of escape aside from divine revelation.

The nature of the spirit world is clearly defined through the Bible narrative. I call it the Supernatural According to God.

Within the pages, every need of mankind is addressed. In it we find the answers to the most fundamental questions pertaining to life in the present, and the hereafter: What is my origin? Why am I here? What follows the death of the body? Does Truth exist, and how can I know it? Does "spirit" exist? Does God exist and what is He like? What is good and evil? The Bible was produced and made available because God took the initiative to make sure that mankind is informed as to His existence, the supernatural, and the realm in which it operates. Why human beings reject what God has graciously revealed for their benefit, and invent their own explanations, is a deadly malady. However, a remedy *does* exist.

Bill Johnson in his book, *When Heaven Invades Earth*, refers to the spiritual realm, perceived only through the eyes of faith, as the "superior reality". He writes,

> The invisible realm is superior to the natural. The reality of that invisible world dominates the natural world we live in…both positively and negatively. Because the invisible is superior to the natural, faith is anchored in the unseen.

Tozer concurs,

> A spiritual kingdom lies all about us, enclosing us, embracing us, altogether within reach of our inner selves, waiting for us to recognize it. God Himself is here waiting for our response to His Presence. This eternal world will come alive to us the moment we begin to reckon upon its reality.

Reckon is another word for faith. It means to consider something as fact and then act upon it. It entails the involvement of both our mind and will.

When we exercise faith, we are tapping into the unseen.

What is Faith?

Relationship with God begins and is sustained by one thing: faith. The importance of possessing and exercising faith cannot be stressed enough. It is mandatory. It is non-negotiable. Scripture makes it clear that "without faith it is impossible to please God" (Heb. 11:6), and "the just shall live by faith" (Rom. 1:17). It is also practical, for "we walk by faith, not by sight" (2 Cor. 5:7). If we are to live wisely and productively, we must be people of faith.

Consider the following definition of faith found in the ancient letter written to the Hebrew Christian community of that day:

> Now faith is the assurance of things hoped for, the conviction of things not seen…By faith we understand that the universe was formed at God's command, that what we now see did not come from anything that can be seen (Heb. 11:1, 3).

If, in fact, there exists a source of power in an invisible realm responsible for the creation of the visible, physical world, then the unseen realm is *superior*. If we are, in fact, spirit beings and will live on following the death and deterioration of the physical body, then the invisible realm is, indeed, *superior*. The principle is set forth that any attempt to understand and interpret life on Earth solely through our physical senses, is sure to fail. It is *by* (and through) *faith* that we possess insight and understanding.

In effect, what is visible is the adversary of the invisible, the physical of the spiritual. Whether an adherent to Christianity, a nonbeliever, or a follower of one of the numerous existing religions, if we live according to the dictates of our physical senses and natural intellect, frustration and failure is guaranteed. We will remain blind to the spirit world.

Faith is the key that opens the door to the unseen world. As we exercise faith, our spirits awaken from their perpetual slumber and become acclimated to this greater, superior reality. It is the absence of faith, unexercised faith that makes us dead to spiritual truths. Faith will "take" from what exists in the invisible realm and make it a reality in the natural, physical world.

The Initiative of God

This prompts another, vital question: How do I come to possess faith?

The human being born into this world is lost and dead. Each is the by-product of two human beings that are of the bloodline of the first two human beings, Adam ("the first man") and Eve. Upon their *seed* rests sin's judgment. It is by being supernaturally transferred out of Adam's seed, into the seed of the "the second man", Jesus Christ, that we pass from death into life, and from the tyranny of fear, to the possibilities of faith.

The Apostle Paul, in his letter to the early church in Corinth, elaborates concerning those born of Adam and those provided the way to rebirth in Jesus Christ,

> The *first man* was of the dust of the earth; the *second man* is of Heaven. As was the earthly man, so are those who are of Heaven. And just as we have born the image of the earthly man (Adam), so shall we bear the image of the heavenly man (Jesus Christ) (1Cor. 15:47-49).

In his book, *The Power of the Blood Covenant*, author Malcolm Smith explains,

> We need a second man to restart the human race, another Adam who can set right what the first Adam brought to destruction and then take humankind to the intimacy with God he had been created to enjoy. We need one who can represent us to God saying the yes to Him that the first Adam failed to say, and in that yes lead us all to the destiny for which we were created.
>
> God the Father in His great love for us determined to send His Son who, without ceasing to be God, would take to Himself our humanity and become flesh. The Son in love for us agreed to come and as a true human live out our human life, face our hardships and temptations, and finally offer Himself to die as and for us. He would rise from the dead, having put away sin and achieved the reconciling of the world to God.
>
> Whereas we *do* inherit the fallen nature of our earthly parents, we do not inherit the faith and salvation of our parents. It is our individual choice to receive what God requires to save us from our sin, so we may be "born again" (John 3:3) into the family of God.
>
> Because all human beings come into this world bound in darkness, we are blind, deaf, and dumb to the things of spirit. We cannot figure out what pleases God by applying our brainpower to the problem. We are "dead in sins" (Eph. 2:5), according to the Scriptures. Therefore, not only are we powerless to remedy the malady of our souls, we are without any awareness that a problem even exists!

The fact of the matter is that our fleshly, human nature opposes the things of the spirit. It is convinced that all that exists in our Earth-suits of flesh and bone, is the mind, and we can rely upon our intellect to figure out any meaning or purpose of life. The Apostle Paul wrote of the *enmity*, or, hostility between the spirit and the flesh. They are opposed to one another in their essence.

Not only do we need a savior to deliver us from this inherent condition, we require a higher power to begin the process of persuading us that we are *in need* of a savior. This is the role of the Holy Spirit, the Counselor and Guide, in the life of the human.

In turn, any correct or *right* thought that we may have *about* God, is an *act* of God stemming from His heart of compassion, to not leave us in our desperate state of need. We are wholly incapable of producing that kind of inspiration. We are completely reliant on the Spirit of God to take the *initiative* to bring our thinking to light, to move us along the pathway that leads to a decision to receive the gift of salvation.

The Eyes of Faith

Yes, we are solely dependent on God's initiative to bring us to an understanding of Truth. However, there is a proactive way we can accommodate the working of God's Spirit in our lives. What, then, is our role in this faith process?

The answer is a simple one. The key to developing conviction about "things not seen", is to spend time in the presence of God.

The "eyes" of faith are resident in our hearts, the seat of our affections and center of our moral consciousness. The Scripture directs us to "look not at the things which are seen, but the things which are not seen" (2 Cor. 4:8). We must command these inner eyes and direct them upon God. When we choose to fix the gaze of our hearts upon God, who is invisible to the natural eye, we are exercising faith. We are acting upon the witness of God's Spirit, to our human spirit that God does indeed exist, and that "He is a rewarder of them that diligently seek Him" (Heb. 11:6).

This is faith in action. As we continually look upon God, our inner, spiritual vision becomes increasingly acute. When we ignore or resist the draw of the Holy Spirit, our hearts become hardened and we remain blinded to spiritual understanding and Truth. I'm reminded of the lyrics to a song by the late Keith Green, "it is so hard to see, when my eyes are on me." So true.

Paul, in his letter to the Corinthians, penned "Eye has not seen, nor ear heard, neither have entered into the heart of man, the things which God has prepared for them that love him" (1 Cor. 2:9). If we do not read on, we are left with an attitude that God and His ways are unknowable. However, the next thing Paul wrote was this, "But God has revealed them to us by his Spirit, for the Spirit searches all things, yes, the deep things of God" (1 Cor. 2:10). Did you catch that? *Revealed to us! The deep things!*

This is the remedy for the malady we referred to earlier. In any developing relationship, whether family members or friends, the more time we spend with the person, the more we know and understand their thoughts, attitudes, and feelings.

It is no different with God, our Father. It is in hungering and thirsting to know Him, and pressing in while guided by His Spirit, that we are enlightened and convinced of spiritual realities. This comprehension only comes by the exercise of living, personal faith. And the Scriptures also inform us that God has fashioned each of us with "a measure of faith" (Rom. 12:3), so we already possess what is necessary to prime the pump and initiate our faith journey into the spirit realm!

Chapter 5

The Sixth Sense

As we enjoy relationship with our Heavenly Father, He shares His life and His heart with us. He imparts wisdom and revelation. The eyes and ears of our souls grow attuned to the spiritual world in which "We live and move and have our being" (Acts 17:8). We become increasingly discerning of what is occurring in this unseen realm. We learn how our own actions play a crucial part in the outcome of eternal matters. Discernment is simply the ability to "see" that which is taking place in the spiritual realm. However, having discernment without an active response will not change a thing.

John Dawson, missionary and author of *Taking our Cities for God*, writes regarding the gift of spiritual discernment:

> Exercising discernment is an act of the will and an act of faith. It takes a childlike humility to act upon the impressions that the Holy Spirit brings. This kind of unsophisticated vulnerability is needed if we are to see any supernatural manifestation of the Lord's power.

The Spirit of God gives us insight to what is taking place in the unseen sphere so we will act in a way that is in accordance with His will and purpose. We aren't enlightened to only *know* and then spectate, but to also *act*. We are to cooperate with God so what exists in the spirit realm can be manifested in the physical world and have its intended effect.

This truth is set forth in the narrative of an incident that occurred 2,800 years ago, involving a prophet of God named Elisha, his servant, and a dreaded enemy. Waking one morning, the prophet and servant found their city about to be routed.

> When the servant of the man of God got up and went out early the next morning, an army with horses and chariots had surrounded the city. 'Oh no, my lord! What shall we do?' the servant asked. 'Don't be afraid,' the prophet answered. 'Those who are with us are more than those who are with them.' And Elisha prayed, 'Open his eyes, Lord, so that he may see.' Then the Lord opened the servant's eyes, and he looked and saw the hills full of horses and chariots of fire all around Elisha (2 Kings 6:15-17).

In this account, there are several elements that contributed to the opening of the servant's eyes to the superior spirit world that encompassed him:

- Initially, the servant limited his assessment of the circumstances to only the *physical evidence*. As with most people, His natural tendency was to base his expectancy of the outcome solely on what was physically present.

- The presence of this formidable foe prompted a *reaction of fear and dread*. This is the inevitable emotional reaction of one who believes that he or she is alone and without help when threatening circumstances surface in life. Bear in mind that this servant was no novice. For some time, he had served and traveled with the prophet Elisha through whom God had parted the Jordan river and raised the dead, among other miraculous events. This servant had witnessed God's intervening presence and power.

- In addition to trepidation, his response to the challenge was in the form of a question, "what shall we do?" This was an admission of his desperation and an inability to meet this threat in his own power. This question needed to be asked and answered. Surely doubt and faith were wrestling within him, contending to influence the choice the servant would make. Would he yield to unbelief and run, or would he stand firm in the confidence that God was present and able? Would he become an enlightened, vital participant in the spirit battle or remain a carnal bystander, paralyzed with fear?

- Elisha got right to the point. The servant was challenged to *reject fear and exert faith* in the One who exists and operates beyond the limits of this natural world. Our adversary, the Devil, attempts to keep us ignorant and blind to the greater reality that exists in the unseen realm. God works to open our eyes so that victory is assured when we put our trust in Him. God's angelic warriors were poised and ready to subdue any earthly army regardless of size or weaponry. However, their release into battle would be triggered only by a response of faith from Elisha and his servant.

- Notice the key element within Elisha's response to the circumstances. His assessment was accurate and his response, immediate. As a prophet of God, this man walked with an acute sensitivity to the spirit realm. He could assess situations and circumstances present in the natural world based on his awareness of what was occurring in the superior spirit world. He stood his ground, *confident in the outcome.*

- Lastly, Elisha did more than just watch and wait. He prayed. He showed compassion for the plight of his servant. His was a *faith response* as he turned to the only One who could influence and change the limited perception of his servant. In doing so, God opened the eyes of the servant's heart, enabling him to see that his enemies, both human and spirit, were vastly outmatched by angelic warriors poised to protect and deliver. This caliber of prayer life on behalf of others is to mark the true servant of God.

As both Elisha and his servant were enabled to see into the spirit realm, the importance of the life ruled by confidence in the unseen was underscored. With an ironic stroke, God took the physical eyesight from their enemies and struck them with blindness! Not only were they without the supernatural ability to perceive God's forces formed against them, they were now without that on which their subjective reality was based! So utterly complete was their defeat!

We are crafted by the hand of God with the intention to partner and co-labor with Him. We are His children, intimately related to Him and being raised by Him to become wise and discerning. Our role is crucial in the outcome of life and death issues played out in this world but determined by what exists and takes place in an invisible one. Those who rise to this challenge will discover the walk of faith the ultimate adventure!

Chapter 6

Spirit and Soul

For us to better understand the essence and operation of faith, it is necessary to know how the human is put together, enabling the man or woman to receive and process that which God communicates. Let's take a look at the "moving parts" of our internal being and, to some degree, the manner in which they function.

Mankind at Creation

We will now transport ourselves back in time to the beginning, when the first man and woman were created and placed on this astronomical ball called Earth.

The Bible account of the human creation claims the following: "And the LORD God formed man of the dust of the ground and breathed into his nostrils the breath of life; and man became a living soul" (Gen. 2:7 AKJV).

This verse succinctly states that the soul of man is a result of God's initiative to breathe (*ruach*, the Hebrew word for spirit) life into a natural body, formed from earthen soil, that results in a "living soul". The spirit is not a feature or possession of man, but *is the man*, and, along with his soul, *is his essence*. Also addressed is the answer to the age-old question of origin: where did we come from? The answer has always been simple, perhaps too simple for our intellect, alone, to consider: the human soul is the by-product of spirit life that proceeds from God. God conceived man in his heart and breathed him into existence!

For us to understand the dynamics involved in the developing of human personality and character, as well as the cities in which we live, we need to look at the concept of soul and spirit. What are the two? Is there a distinction, and, if so, what is the difference in their functions? Also, how does the idea of *soul* relate to the city and urban life?

If we are to live out our days on Earth with maximum purpose and direction, it is necessary to clearly define what God had in mind in the first place when He fashioned our being. In understanding *who* and *why* we are, we can then understand the nature of our relationship to other human beings and to the communities in which we have been placed.

The spirit of man and the soul of man are the two components that make up every human being. They are distinct in their fundamental nature yet operate in conjunction and union with one another. The Bible, God's Word, is clear in explaining the nature and function of these two aspects of our being.

I will also quote extensively from *The Spiritual Man*, penned by Watchman Nee in 1968. It is the most profound, yet understandable commentary I've come across regarding the definition and function of the human spirit and the human soul.

Nee writes,

> It is imperative that a believer knows he has a spirit, since, as we shall soon learn, every communication of God with man occurs there. If the believer does not discern his own spirit, he invariably is ignorant of how to commune with God in the spirit. He easily substitutes the thoughts or emotions of the soul for the works of the spirit. Thus, he confines himself to the outer realm, unable ever to reach the spiritual realm.

Paul lays the biblical foundation for this truth:

> The natural man receives not the things of the Spirit of God: for they are foolishness to him; and he cannot know them, because they are spiritually judged (1 Cor. 2:14 AKJV).

Spirit

Scripture teaches that the human spirit is comprised of three elements, or functions: conscience, intuition, and communion.

Nee states,

> The conscience is the discerning organ, which distinguishes right and wrong; not, however, through the influence of knowledge stored in the mind but rather by a spontaneous direct judgment.

King Solomon said, "The human spirit is the lamp of the Lord that sheds light on one's inmost being" (Prov. 20:27). Man, therefore, is the creature with a conscience that receives light and illumination from God and is man's resident "judge" weighing attitudes and actions.

With regard to intuition, Nee writes,

> Intuition is the sensing organ of the human spirit . . . Intuition involves a direct sensing independent of any outside influence. That knowledge which comes to us without any help from the mind, emotion or volition comes intuitively. We really 'know' through our intuition; our mind merely helps us to 'understand'.

The Apostle Paul also wrote to the Corinthian church, "For who knows a person's thoughts except their own spirit within them?" (1 Cor. 2:11). The operation and action of intuition is highlighted in the life of Jesus when he was said to have "perceived in his spirit" (Mark 2:8 AKJV), or "was deeply moved in spirit" (John 11:33).

Intellect must exercise its faculty to produce thought results. When the Spirit communes with our spirit, the product is of inspiration, instantaneous, and complete. We must resist filtering the voice of God's Spirit through the grid of our intellect. Truth must be received without applying human criteria.

We must allow the Spirit to sensitize our inner being to recognize and discern spirit communication. Alone with God, in quietude is the one means by which to develop this precious ability.

The capacity of man's spirit for communion, or worship, is clearly put forth throughout the New Testament. Luke in his Gospel quoted Mary, the virgin mother of Jesus who declared, "My spirit rejoices in God my Savior" (Luke 1:47). John the Beloved chronicled the words of Jesus, Himself, "The true worshipers will worship the Father in spirit and in truth" (John 4:23). And the Apostle Paul said, "I will sing with my spirit" (1 Cor. 14:15).

Nee concurs,

> Communion is worshiping God. The organs of the soul are incompetent to worship God. God is not

apprehended by our thoughts, feelings or intentions, for He can only be known directly in our spirits. Our worship of God and God's communications with us are directly in the spirit.

Soul

In addition to our spirit, we each possess a soul. Our souls provide us with the awareness that we exist, that we have "being". The soul is the seat of our mind, emotion, and will (volition), and encompasses that which defines our humanness, our personalities. The ability to think and reason, to aspire; the capacity to love, to know joy or fear; the process of deciding or choosing, are all functions of our souls.

Nee, defines these three functions in this way,

> *Mind*, the instrument for our thoughts, manifests our intellectual power. Out of this arise wisdom, knowledge and reasoning. Lack of it makes a man foolish and dull. The instrument for our likes and dislikes is the faculty of *emotion*. Through it we are able to express love or hate and to feel joyful, angry, sad or happy. Any shortage of it will render man as insensitive as wood or stone. *Volition* is the instrument for our decisions, revealing our power to choose. It expresses our willingness or unwillingness: 'we will', or 'we won't'. Without it, man is reduced to an automaton.

The Unregenerate Spirit

Because of the fallen condition of the human being born into this world, the spirit doesn't function in the ways previously detailed. From conception, the spirit lies in a darkened state and is dead to God because of sin, absent of God's light and life. The soul, on the other hand, continues to function and dominate the man without the guiding influence of his spirit in union with God's Spirit. Without the moral compass of intuition and conscience, the soul alone drives the man. The unity of the created being is disrupted as the soul is intended and must be in a submissive position to the spirit. This leaves the human subject to the preying tactics of the Evil One.

When one is brought back into relationship with the Father through the sacrifice of His Son, the human spirit is regenerated to life, similar to a jump charge of a car's dead battery. The Holy Spirit, now fused with man's spirit, begins the cleansing and purifying work of converting the soul, influencing and shaping the mind, emotions, and will of the man or woman. The conversion of the soul into the likeness of Christ is in process. The human will must be receptive and responsive to follow the light of Truth that emanates from his spirit if the soul is to prosper.

The Scriptures exhort us to pursue and seek His righteousness. What does this mean? In a nutshell, it means choosing to bring the attitudes and actions of one's life into alignment with God's moral law. Be certain, we are wholly inadequate to advance in this pursuit if left to our own human nature and devices. However, we are wholly capable if the nature of Christ has been implanted within us through the gift of salvation and the regeneration of our spirits. Paul wrote to the first century church in Philippi, "For it is God who works in you to will and to act in order to fulfill his good purpose" (Phil. 2:13).

Chapter 7

God's Book on You

Up to this point, we have looked, primarily, at the functions of the human spirit and human soul. I have attempted to present, in accordance with scriptural revelation, how the spirit and soul were intended to function according to God's design. We noted that the operation of the soul, involving mind, emotion, and volition, in effect, makes up the personality of the individual. Now, let's consider another feature of the soul that reveals the depth of the Designer's tender love and care over each of our lives.

Fate and Destiny

Fate is usually thought of as a predetermined course of events beyond human control. A belief in the concept of predestination promotes resignation with regard to the issues of life, and an attitude of "que sera, sera", "what will be, will be."

This fatalistic view was prevalent among the ancient Greeks who believed in the Three Fates: Clotho, Lachesis and Atropos. These were the mythological goddesses reputed to be the personification of destiny; the weavers of fate who determined all that would occur in the life of every human being, from the time of birth, to the time of their death. The thread of human life is woven by Clotho (beginning of life), measured by Lachesis (length of life), and then cut by Atropos (ending of life). An imaginative view but lacking in substance.

It is true that God is sovereign and that His master plan for creation will be accomplished. Nations will rise, and nations will fall in accordance with God's timetable. The history and fate of mankind was prearranged and predetermined by God's providence. What we do or do not do won't change the outcome regarding the "big picture". The seventh century BC prophet Isaiah made this clear when he wrote, "I foretold the former things long ago, my mouth announced them, and I made them known; then suddenly I acted, and they came to pass" (Isa. 48:3). The humorous Yiddish proverb puts it this way, "Man plans, and God laughs!"

However, regarding you and me as individuals, the concept of destiny has a much different application. We have often heard the words, "God loves you and has a plan for your life." This is true, but there is no guarantee we will see His plan come to pass. Because we are equipped with free will, the direction and outcome of our lives are fluid, influenced by our continuous choices and actions.

The biblical idea of *destiny* and its actual outworking are two different things. To what degree we experience God's intentions for us is based on our submission to Him. I agree with the Greek philosopher Heraklitos, who wrote "Ethos Anthropos Daimon", or, in English, "A man's character is his fate." Another ancient proverb states, "A man's own folly ruins his life, yet his heart rages against the Lord." We can't blame God, or fate, when our own choices bankrupt our lives.

The course of our lives can be likened to one in a motor vehicle, negotiating a mountainous highway, with an intended destination. For the journey, we have been provided a roadworthy vehicle, a sufficient gas supply, and a paved roadway with signposts along the way to keep us going a safe speed, and in the right direction. Although there are some bumps, twists, and turns along the way, we have adequate ability to steer the vehicle. Our arrival at our destination is guaranteed if we stay awake, heed the signposts, and employ our skill to operate the vehicle. In fact, the more diligent we are to execute our responsibilities, the more interesting and satisfying the journey.

Your Appointed Path

Inherent in every human being is a blueprint etched by the finger of God. The design includes the creation of your physical body, and His breath of spirit life into that body of flesh and bone, that defined your unique personality.

If that isn't sufficiently marvelous, then consider this: *before* you existed physically or spiritually, you were already intimately in the heart and mind of God. As He considered you, He foreknew and foresaw what circumstances and issues you would face during your walk on this earth. Into His design for you, He prearranged encounters and experiences that would work for the highest good in your life, mindful of the freewill choices you would make along your personal, *appointed path*!

Nearly 3,000 years ago, David, the psalmist and King of Israel, wrote this:

> My frame was not hidden from You when I was made in secret, when I was woven together in the depths of the earth. Your eyes saw my unformed body; all the days ordained for me were written in

your book before one of them came to be. How precious to me are your thoughts, God. How vast is the sum of them (Ps. 139:15-17).

There is nothing that has occurred or will occur in your life that can take God by surprise. As the Alpha and the Omega, the Eternal One, He has already "visited" the days of your past, this present day, and all the days yet to come. With that, He has provided all you will ever have need of, both in the physical aspect, and spirit aspect of your existence.

A contemporary of David's, the prophet Jeremiah recorded what God spoke to him about his own life,

> Before I formed you in the womb, I knew you, before you were born, I set you apart; I appointed you as a prophet to the nations (Jer. 1:5).

So, it is also clear that God's book on you involves an appointed station or vocation in which you are designed to function. This implies specific purpose and actions, many times referred to as *works* in the Bible.

One half of a millennium later, when a man named Jesus walked the earth, he often would change the name of someone who, prior to their encounter with Jesus, was going through the motions of a humdrum experience in life. The name-change reflected God's intended vocation and influence for which they were created.

Consider the man, Simon. The name means *he has heard*. Immediately, upon his introduction to Simon, Jesus said to him, "And I tell you that you are Peter" (Matt. 16:18 NIV), which means *the rock*. In time, Peter would be transformed from an emotional, "reactionary" who would *listen to and believe* anything, to a solid, uncompromising "revolutionary" who would be instrumental in building the church of God.

This kind of tender-loving attention is not just reserved for the heroes of history but is true of every person ever born into this world. We are each uniquely fashioned by Him; in physical appearance, personality, and with regard to the plan and purposes we are to fulfill. In discovering our personal, appointed path, and conducting our lives, accordingly, is how deep, inner fulfillment and satisfaction will be realized. And just as important, this is how we can make significant, lasting contributions to our communities and to the world!

God is the Author of your life, and there is no epilogue in His book about you!

Identity Seekers

It is presented in Scripture that we are incapable of discovering our personal identity aside from the Spirit's work of revelation. We willingly, yet unwittingly, yield to others and adopt their version of who we are. If truth be known, we don't really conform to the view of others concerning us, we conform to what we *think others think of us*. Our self-consciousness tricks us into believing that all eyes are on us, when, in actuality, others are too preoccupied with worrying about what others think of them! This is the natural man's malady of gravitating toward other people, rather than God, for input as to our identity and self-worth. We look horizontally, when we should be looking vertically.

Today, take a few moments to note the appearance and actions of those you encounter in the public places of life. Look at each age group. Isn't it interesting how those within the group similarly portray themselves? The manner of dress, the choice of words, and the overall attitude is strikingly the same. Why is that? It is because they have compared themselves with themselves and have allowed that to be the criteria by which they shape and present their lives. This kind of pursuit only tends to feed our individual pride and envy and cause greater division, not unity, among the masses of humanity.

We all want to believe that we are special; that we are unique among the 7.5 billion people that inhabit this planet. However, we struggle with discovering the inherent identity that separates us from the throngs of other identity seekers. In the hunt, we tend to conform in thought and actions to the images presented by our society through entertainment or sports or we pattern our lives after some pop cultural hero or heroine. This is no different than putting on a face mask of, let's say, Brad Pitt or Angelina Jolie, and then going about our life pretending to be him or her. We will always know we are not, as will others, and this pretend game only leaves us void of self-worth and self-esteem.

Churchgoers are subject to the same entrapments of human nature as those who deny Christ. Hero worship, in a subtler form, is rampant within these religious bodies as many attendees seek to conform their lifestyle and self-image to the "super spiritual" among them, becoming followers of man rather than followers of God.

Knowing how God has uniquely fashioned us in both physicality and personality, and how he intends to use our lives as a constructive force, will make us confident and satisfied people.

Individual Gifting

In His crafting of every person, God has included a special endowment of capability; a talent that is unique to the individual. Your gift or talent is intended as support and assistance in accomplishing the purposes He has designed for your life.

It exists to benefit you, and others, within the community of people you live among.

It is made clear in God's Word that first and foremost our hearts are to be devoted to Him. Following on the heels is we are to love our neighbors as ourselves. From the well of walking in close communion with our Heavenly Father we will draw an understanding of the nature of our relationships with our fellow humans, and how we have been uniquely equipped to serve them.

Often a person's gift lies dormant within their being, undiscovered and untapped, or simply neglected. In Paul's letter to his protégé, Timothy, he encourages him, and us, to "fan into flame the gift of God which is in you" (2 Tim. 1:6). This is meant as a kick in the pants to summon into action our unique abilities. Action is the "trigger" that releases the power for your gift to have its intended influence and effect.

So often we have the inclination, desire, or passion to express that which we feel from deep within. Then our inner voice of doubt kicks in, *But, what if I fail? What will others think of me?* We then dismiss the prompting as silly or a passing fancy without ever acting on it. I encourage you to step out and take the risk! What you are experiencing is the bud of your talent seeking the daylight of outward expression, so it may bloom and be the fragrance to others for which it was intended.

The Greenhouse Effect

I have learned of two intangibles a person must possess if their faith is to flourish, and a discovery of their unique giftings, realized. Neither are optional. They are:

- The willingness to move outside of your personal comfort zone.

- The willingness to come into the light of God's presence.

For a 10-year period of my life, I was involved with what is classically referred to as foreign "missionary work". Actually, my belief is that anyone who professes to have a vital relationship with the Creator, will be involved in "missions". One is commissioned by God and is on a mission from God if, in fact, one is rightly related to God. And that mission is for us to *live* and *speak* the Truth in whatever walk of life we find ourselves. Our personal mission field may be in our neighborhood, place of employment, school, or, for some, in a remote part of the earth while immersed in a foreign culture. Time is short, the laborers are few, and we must get about the Father's business is what the New Testament clearly espouses.

My missions experience during that decade of time took me to several different parts of the world and involved working with teams of young people, typically, fresh out of high school. These eager beavers were charged with energy and ideals, and ready to make their lives count regardless of the cost it could exact. The program they signed up with ran for about 5 months, and included an initial three-month teaching phase, designed to instill team purpose and unity, followed by a two to three-month commitment to live and work in a part of the world determined to be much in need of God's truth and love.

Typically, the student-adventurer was from a middle-class upbringing, raised in comfortable suburbia, and conditioned to having what they wanted, on demand.

The teaching phase usually generated considerable turmoil within the student as each was encouraged to sit still under the searchlight of Truth. It was an intense time of weighing motives and attitudes while in the presence of God. For those who persevered in this process, it was a transforming time as both the humility and strength of Christ's image came forth in their lives.

Then came the outreach phase. As expected, some of what was experienced during this time exacted a toll on the physical body and emotions, as well as the mind. These young people were not in Kansas anymore. Some found themselves in remote provinces of China, others in rural parts of the former U.S.S.R., and some in mountain villages of the Dominican Republic, among other obscure places. It was a mix of highs and lows as the experience of bonding with the precious indigenous people brought joy and enlightenment, while the demands of assimilating into a thoroughly foreign culture invaded their personal comfort zones. These young people endured these challenges for the singular purpose of bringing to unreached people, what they knew would radically change their lives.

What they didn't expect was a reciprocal experience.

Not only did it transform the lives of many to whom they were sent, more so was the surge of growth and vitality in the lives of these young people. You see, they were thrust into situations they never would have experienced back home or couldn't easily avoid. Each participant found themselves flexing their "soul muscles" in ways they had previously only dreamed! The discoveries were priceless, the ground gained, eternal!

The experience was similar to the plant that is placed in a greenhouse; an environment where it is exposed to intense sunlight and absorbs the heat generated by that light. The effect is that the plant is removed from hindrances of growth and subjected to that which produces rapid growth.

I challenge you to step out and take a risk. See what you will discover about yourself and about your God!

God the Gambler

The gifts given by God come in many forms. Some require that we exercise a degree of sacrifice and responsibility, such as the blessing of a good job or financial wealth. Others are not the result of commitment or obedience as they are inherent in nature, built into us at conception. These inherent giftings are given for a lifetime and are irrevocable.

God is the ultimate risk-taker. God has gambled in allowing us autonomy and permanence with regard to these innate giftings, distributed among mankind. The gift or talent is neutral in and of itself, so the risk lies in how we will exercise and apply these precious possessions during our lifetimes.

The proverb puts forth that "A man's gift makes room for him and brings him before great men" (Prov. 18:16 AKJV). As we exercise and develop our inherent talents and abilities, "doors open" and opportunities arise for significant influence.

If we present these possessions back to God with a commitment that they be used to serve others and to further His purposes in this world, then the potential for good is unlimited. If we view these possessions as our own personal triumph and exploit them for selfish gain, then the opposite applies, the potential for destructive affect is great.

People are the vehicles through which both God and the Devil advance their agenda here on Earth. They vie for control knowing the influence of just one person, whether for good or evil, is immense.

We must not be ignorant concerning the potential power that our gifts can exert over the lives of others.

The Devil's intention is to twist, distort, and corrupt your personality and the unique deposit of talent that He has invested in you. The Devil is the original pervert and all that we associate with that word, and much more, has its origin in him.

As we will soon see, there are many gifted men and women who found their way to Savannah and exercised their talents. Some contributed to the vitality and vibrancy of the city's persona and influence abroad. However, history reveals that others applied themselves in ways that crippled the Lady's potential for positive and constructive inspiration.

Blessing or Cursing

I believe Nurse Jackie in the 2009 TV medical drama was spot-on when she said, "the people with the greatest capacity for good are the ones with the greatest capacity for evil."

Within every gift and talent lies the potential for either blessing or cursing. A blessing brings goodness, mercy, and a measure of prosperity to a human life, whereas cursing brings destructive influences upon the individual. God bestows these inherent abilities with the intention that they bless; however, whether good or evil comes from them will be dictated by the nature of the moral values embraced by the individual.

When you consider the people who have had dramatic and profound influence in this world, who comes to mind? You may gravitate to the arena of politics or the arts or, perhaps, the entertainment world. The following is a short list of renowned individuals who possessed the same gift, but with far different application and influence among society.

Leadership: George Washington / Adolf Hitler. Will the leader raise the banner of righteousness or wickedness?

Songwriting: John Denver / Snoop Dogg. What message will be put to music that will captivate the human soul?

Novelist: Fyodor Dostoevsky / Stephen King. Will the novel or poem inspire faith or fear?

Cinema: Frank Capra / Quentin Tarantino. What message will the film deliver, one of redemption or despair?

Comedy: Jeff Dunham / George Carlin. Will the material dispense the medicine of good humor, or sink to vulgarity?

Athletics: Tim Tebow / Wilt Chamberlain. Will the sports hero promote a lifestyle of temperance or decadence?

I often think with admiration of Eric Liddell, the early twentieth century missionary and track athlete. He recognized his inherent gifts and used them to honor God. In doing so, he discovered the secret of possessing true joy, and the path that leads to a fulfilled destiny. His words express this insight, "God also made me fast. And when I run, I feel His pleasure . . . If you commit yourself to the love of Christ, then that is how you run a straight race."

King David also understood what was required for him to find his appointed path. Over his lifetime, he had experienced the ups and downs of his own right and wrong choices. He concluded that it is in the choosing of good, rather than evil, that results in a life of joy, prosperity of body, soul, and spirit, and realization of destiny. He put it in simpler terms when he wrote, "The steps of a good man are ordered by the Lord, and he (the good man) delights in his way" (Ps. 37:23 AKJV).

You will discover God's plan and a release of talent as you commit yourself to honor and serve Him. The abilities with which you have been uniquely gifted are then empowered and directed by His Spirit. The results will amaze you, and those with whom you come into contact.

But what does this have to do with Lady Savannah and the other towns and cities that sprinkle our planet?

Chapter 8

The Soul of a City

A city will take on a corporate identity based on the contributions of the individual members of the populace. The collective nature of these individual contributions will shape the personality, character and define the values of the society. It will also define the contribution the city will make to the greater whole of human society. How these individuals steward their God-given time, energy, and abilities will define their offerings to the whole of society.

Author John Dawson writes concerning the make-up of the city,

> A city is a human institution, and like all institutions it develops a 'creaturehood' or personality that is greater than the sum of its parts. Each metropolis has unique characteristics when compared with other cities.

Neil Johnson, Arts Columnist for *The Times* in Shreveport, Louisiana, wrote about the influences of one segment of their population, the artisans of Shreveport,

Our soul is not defined by a single person or acting troupe. Or a band or choir. It takes a community of artists, each adding their own voice to the chorus. And, yes, through generations. They don't have to be living to have contributed to our soul.

So, the soul of a city, her character and personality, is the collective representation of her citizens. Her soul is formed by the activity and conduct of many people over the course of many years. Decades and even centuries of time may be involved, and, as such, this molding process is fluid and subject to both the *positive* and *negative* input of its citizenry. Because each is a part of the whole, every person will impact the outcome in one way or another.

Robert Leger, Opinions Editor of the *Arizona Republic* newspaper, touched on this idea when he wrote,

> There's more to a city's soul than its buildings. The 'soul' is wrapped up in the sense of place. Boston's history. New York's bustle. Washington's self-importance. San Francisco's mystique. Phoenix's self-doubt. One can't help but 'feel' and 'sense' these elements of urban 'soul' when moving across the landscape and among the populace in any given town or city.

The "sense of place" referenced by Leger is comprised of the prevailing characteristics of the city's soul, the product of the collective contributions of her people. These city traits are profoundly impressed on residents and visitors, alike. They are felt and *perceived* in the very atmosphere encompassing the people.

The people *are* the city, and the city *is* the people. Although the city is shaped by her populace, she has a reciprocal power to influence her citizenry. And what the city gives back will be more complex than our individual contribution, given her soul is formed by many.

Simply put, a city is comprised of a concentration of human population. Within that society, men, women and children each exercise their skills, ingenuity, beliefs, and moral perspectives within their own families, and as part of a larger family community.

As the human soul involves the capacities of mind, emotion, and will, so does the soul of a city. The mind is primarily *expressed* through the various institutions and community organizations that play a major role in shaping *public opinion* and the formation of social *creeds*. The emotion is reflected in the *mood* among the populace and can be *felt* in its very atmosphere, whether it be depression, joy, anger, guilt, or optimism or pessimism. And the will is primarily *exercised* through the courts, elected politicians, and law enforcement agencies, that enforce the prevailing *mindset* of the society. The city's soul is a collective representation of her people.

These elements of the city's soul are a clear "barometer" of what has transpired and what is presently taking place in the spirit realm. They are directly related to the nature of the spirit powers that contend for influence and, ultimately, control over the populace.

A Lady Seduced

Savannah is not evil. Savannah, like any other city, possesses a distinct *potential*; a possibility of expressing the inherent ugliness of evil. In this precise way, so does Savannah possess the potential of flourishing with goodness and displaying her intrinsic beauty.

The word *seduce* is derived from the Greek word *planao*. It means to be led astray. As we previously pointed out, Savannah is a beguiling, seductive Lady. Her soul emanates this magnetic, fascinating quality because she has been led astray; *she has been seduced*! She has wandered from the pathway of promise, as if lost in the dense woods that cover much of her ground.

During her visit to the city in March 1946, another Lady, Astor of Britain, made this observation, "Savannah is like a beautiful woman with a dirty face." Supposedly, her comment was about the littered streets. However, I contend that she perceived the potential of Lady Savannah, and saw past a repulsive exterior, to the beauty of her intended destiny.

So, what is the starting point in this spirit war and the battle for our communities?

The Battle For You

The battle for the soul of your city, begins with a battle for you! As we have seen, the city *is* the people, and the people *are* the city. What we choose to believe and act on will define the soul of our city.

As God and the Devil wage war, they target the human mind. Your thinking is the desired prize; what you will believe is worthy of your time and attention is the primary target. In this contest, God will dispatch the Spirit of Truth. The Devil will employ lying spirits. Both pathways of influence lead to the moral quality of the choices you will make, and, in turn, will define your city.

Author Miguel Angel Ruiz put it this way, "People like to say that the conflict is between good and evil. The real conflict is between truth and lies." This is accurate in the respect that good *is* good and evil *is* evil, and always will be. There is no controversy as both are unchanging in nature and character. The real issue that will decide the course of our lives is what *we choose to believe and act on*: the truth of good, or the lies of evil.

The outworking of our choosing is displayed in how we conduct ourselves as we engage in certain walks of society, including our interpersonal relationships, religion, profession, and politics. Ultimately, the battle is for control and possession of all that comprises our physical and, more importantly, spiritual existence. And, as we have learned, the vitality of the city's soul is a collective representation of the values embraced by her citizenry.

The Inside-Out Principle

So, how does one avoid being seduced by the evil lies of the Devil?

The proverb urges us, "Above all else, guard your heart, for everything you do flows from it" (Prov. 4:23). The idea is that the external conduct of an individual is dictated by that which has influenced the internal heart, the soul of the individual.

As you choose what will comprise the basis for your moral attitude and conduct, the essence of those principles is "stored" in your heart. Eventually your heart is full and will then brim over and flow out from your being influencing the various situations, circumstances, and people within your sphere of life.

Jesus said it this way,

> A good man brings forth things out of the good stored up in his heart, and the evil man brings evil things out of the evil stored up in his heart. For the mouth speaks what the heart is full of (Luke 6:45).

This is the *inside-out* principle at work. It demonstrates that which is decided in the invisible realm of spirit and soul, will determine what comes forth in the physical sphere of our existence.

Let's apply it using the analogy of gardening. Both God and the Devil will attempt to sprinkle their "seed" upon our hearts, the seat of our affections and the center of our moral consciousness. The seed that we accommodate becomes planted and lies dormant within. As we make choices in accordance with the nature of the seed, it will germinate and grow. If continued nurturing takes place, that which had been concealed within will become openly manifested in the person's attitude and conduct. The person is now known by this fruit borne as that is what will define the attributes of their character. In turn, the person will have the potential to influence the production of life or death in others. Bear in mind, every living thing produces after its own kind.

The Devil attempts to sow into our lives the things that keep us blind, unforgiven, and from eternal life in God's kingdom. In yielding to God's Truth, or succumbing to the lies of the enemy, an individual determines whether life or death is at work within them. The Devil knows what will precipitate God's judgment on an individual or a whole city, and he works so the choices we make keep us separated from God's life and subject to His divine, righteous judgment.

A basic study of once-great empires, including the Babylonian, Persian, Macedonian, and Roman, clearly demonstrates the inside-out process at work. These societies were not conquered by foreign powers or external forces, they crumbled because of an internal state of moral corruption. It was the self-destructive bents of the fallen, human nature, and its proclivity to pursue personal status, material wealth, and social power that spelled their undoing. The leaven of sin prompted by human weakness and the deception of the Devil was a cancer that ate at the fabric of society and resulted in eventual, total outward collapse of these civilizations.

These same enemies lurk within today's cities and nations, including the United States, as she has fallen away from her "first love" for God, and like the ancient pagans, has embraced various forms of idolatry. It is interesting to note that America's founders and the U.S. Constitution refers to the threats of both "foreign and domestic enemies." We seldom think of these domestic threats as the outworking of the evil motives and desires simmering within the hearts of her own citizens.

When we speak of the battle for the soul of Savannah, or any other city, we are really speaking of *who* will prevail as the primary entity, the Spirit of God or the Devil, that will influence and control the society of people, and ultimately the nature of that city's contribution to the rest of the world.

What is Truth?

So, it is crucial that we guard our hearts and assess the moral nature of what we embrace.

But how do we weigh whether an attitude or action is good or evil, or morally right or wrong? How do we evaluate morality?

This is not as difficult a subject to address as most presuppose. It is simply a matter of whether or not you believe there exists one God who created the heavens and the earth and all living things. If you say you do believe this, then God would be the one source to consult in order to understand and evaluate all that exists, including principles of right and wrong human behavior and that which defines good or evil human character.

If you say you do not believe God exists, then you are also saying there are no absolute standards by which to evaluate morality and are leaving the judgment open to public opinion. As such, there will be a plethora of thoughts, ideas, and philosophies, with the impossibility of consensus. This puts human societies on an inevitable collision course. It pits man against man, and, collectively, people groups against other people groups. We all want to, in the words of John Lennon, "give peace a chance"; however, our selfish proclivities disable us from complying with the process.

The proverb of Solomon makes it crystal clear, "There is a way that seems right to a man, but the end thereof are the ways of death" (Prov. 14:12 AKJV). The mantras of the 1960's, including "Do your own thing", and the Woodstock slogan, "If it feels good, do it", didn't work then, and won't work today. These kinds of coined, failed human attitudes are still propagated in today's world under the more sophisticated guise of "diversity", "inclusiveness" and "tolerance". The message is the same: any and all lifestyle practice is acceptable and will not be subjected to some narrow criteria of ethics. It is no wonder that Christianity is the one belief system under such vicious secular attack, given its absolute, clearly defined principles of right and wrong and good and evil. That it also claims to offer the sole means of eternal salvation doesn't add to its popularity.

Regarding the contemporary, political ideology behind *tolerance*, Dr. D. James Kennedy warns,

> Tolerance is the last virtue of a depraved society. When you have an immoral society that has blatantly, proudly, violated all of the commandments of God, there is one last virtue they insist upon: tolerance for their immorality.

Calvin Coolidge, the thirtieth President of the United States stood firm with his declaration,

> Men do not make laws. They do but discover them. Laws must be justified by something more

than the will of the majority. They must rest on the eternal foundation of righteousness.

God's character is the bedrock of moral truth, which is the foundation of divine law. He is the Righteous One, always just and "right". He is moral purity, without flaw or blemish. God does not need to answer to anyone, or consult any other source outside His own being, for, as A.W. Tozer puts it, "God is His own self-existent principle of moral equity."

Jesus said, "I am the way, the truth, and the life; no man comes to the Father, but by me" (John 14:6 AKJV). If we reject the existence of God, then we reject the existence of an absolute moral code directing us in the way we are to live, and the truth by which we may understand the meaning of our existence. If we acknowledge and commit ourselves to God, then we will know the Way, based on Truth, that leads to eternal Life.

Because God never changes, neither does what is morally sound. Morality is never moved by the fickle winds of human intellect or opinion. All mankind is accountable to His moral criteria, and we don't need to worry about the rules changing in the middle of the game.

Man, void of the influence of God's Spirit, considers truth as *fluid* and *relative*; that it should take the shape of what is trending societally, at any point in the passage of time. However, the confidence and security of today's man or woman can be founded on the fact that what God requires of them, is exactly what he required of yesterday's man or woman.

A culture molded by embracing the latest fad, message, or movement, may temporarily exude a degree of excitement and purpose, but, inevitably, the train on which that society rides will derail, leaving its passengers stranded, hopeless, and alone. The foundation upon which an individual life or a society of lives must build is that of God's unchanging, righteous law.

The Power and Evidence of Truth

By the working of God's Spirit, and the activity of our conscience, moral truth is impressed upon the human heart. It penetrates deeply and compels a man or woman to decide whether they will come into the light of Truth or remain in the darkness of ignorance. It is an issue of whom one will choose to serve, God or the Devil. The decision is the critical element as it will determine what eventually comes to fruition in one's life, determining destiny and impacting others in either a constructive or destructive way.

Matthew Henry, in his commentary on the Bible, writes of the power and evidence of truth in the spirit world and upon the human heart:

> The work of the ministry is a spiritual warfare with spiritual enemies, and for spiritual purposes. Outward force is not the method of the Gospel, but strong persuasions, by the power of truth and the meekness of wisdom. Conscience is accountable to God only; and people must be persuaded to God and their duty, not driven by force. Thus, the weapons of our warfare are very powerful; the evidence of truth is convincing. What opposition is made against the Gospel, by the powers of sin and Satan in the hearts of men! But observe the conquest the word of God gains. The appointed means, however feeble they appear to some, will be mighty through God. And the preaching of the cross, by men of faith and prayer, has always been fatal to idolatry, impiety, and wickedness.

Truth commands, it conquers, and it sets free as it marches forth. Saint Augustine of Hippo rightly observed, "The truth is like a lion. You don't have to defend it. Let it loose. It will defend itself."

The Outcome Decided

A heretical view of the correlation between the existence of God, and that of demons is the idea behind *dualism*. This theory spins that God and the Devil have separate existences, independent from each other, and that the fate of the human race is being contested between two equal powers. The fact is ignored that all created beings, human and angelic, must answer to God, as Creator of all things.

Of this we can be sure: the battle between the forces of good and the forces of evil does not involve two equal combatants. In the battle between good and evil, the Devil, especially in the contemporary entertainment mediums of television and motion pictures, is depicted as a formidable opponent, if not the favorite. God is presented as an equal combatant, at best, if He bothers to show up at all. The danger in this outlook is that it breeds paranoia and fear as the individual waits for the Devil to strike. The flipside is to underestimate or ignore the Devil's power which leaves us unguarded and vulnerable to his influence and attacks.

While both extremes should be avoided, we have been given specifics about his present abilities and his future destiny that allow for a balanced view and understanding of the Evil One.

Of foremost importance, is that the Devil has already suffered a humiliating defeat at the hands of the Divine. His sway and power over mankind trapped in spiritual darkness, abruptly ended when Jesus gave His life as a ransom and then rose from the dead as evidence of His victory and triumph over the power of sin, and all the evil powers of darkness.

The problem of the Devil's free-wielding autonomy in manipulating and deceiving a race of beings under divine judgment because of their sin and natural bent toward rebellion, has been forever resolved. Mankind is no longer bound to a death sentence but is freely offered eternal life and peace because of Christ's victory over the Devil, death, and the grave.

The future of all evil has already been decided. Because *all authority* in Heaven and on Earth belongs to the Lord, He will allow the enemy only so much leash to operate, and for a short season; just enough to accomplish His purposes. Then, the dismal, tragic destiny of the Evil One will be consummated.

The present problem among humankind is an issue of *unbelief*. This resistance to come into the light of Truth perpetuates a darkened lack of understanding. Unbelief springs from a root of *pride*; an unwillingness to confess one's need, humble one's self, and accept the gift and benefits of Christ's sacrifice. Pride is insidious, cunning, deceptive, a deadly beast perpetually poised to spring and consume its human host. Multitudes lead arrogant-driven lives then choose to go to their graves rather than exercise humility. Again, Saint Augustine offers the way of escape, "It was pride that changed angels into devils; it is humility that makes men as angels."

Contrary to the Devil, the future of the believer who has received Christ is one of glorious promise. The man, woman, or child that receives forgiveness, is ushered into the family of God and becomes a recipient of Christ's divine authority. Each is promised to be *more than a conqueror* in this world. This includes victory over the lure of the world, the destructive bents of human nature, and the deceptions of the Devil and his minions.

This is the crux of the battle waged in the unseen realm that will determine the destinies of every person who walks the earth, as well as the cities in which each live.

Chapter 9

The Hopeful Romantic

When my wife, Elizabeth, and I first moved to Savannah, we visited a church on Skidaway Island. At the conclusion of the service, we moved toward the back door where the pastor stood greeting the parishioners in the traditional manner. We introduced ourselves and briefly expressed our appreciation for the rich teaching just received. With a hint of a smile and penetrating eyes, he said, "Yours is the romance of Heaven." Without really understanding what that meant, my wife and I said thank you, and left the church.

When the pastor spoke those words, I discerned they were alive with spiritual insight and had reached their intended destination: myself and Elizabeth. Although I appreciated the affirmation at that time, there was much more to be gleaned from his statement.

The Romance of Heaven

Apparently, God is a Hopeful Romantic, for romance is at the foundation of God's creation of the earth and mankind;

a setting for the love story and a companion with whom to engage in intimate relationship.

God created man, made in His image, with the capacity for intelligence, and in possession of free will, so He would have those to whom he could demonstrate His tender, lovingkindness. But this was not to be a one-way relationship. Because we understand God to be flawless, and, if at all objective, we know ourselves as prone to error, we conclude there is very little we can offer God. We also conclude God possesses everything He could ever need, and His efforts to redeem man were solely for our benefit. While it is true God has no lack, there is one thing He desires that He has no control over: the affections of our hearts.

During his exile on the isle of Patmos, John, one of Jesus' disciples, had a vision during which he glimpsed God enthroned in Heaven. He wrote down what he observed and heard as God was being worshiped by a multitude of created beings: "You are worthy, O Lord, to receive glory and honor and power: for you have created all things, and for your pleasure they are and were created" (Rev. 4:11 AKJV).

We exist not only to enjoy God's goodness and mercies, but to return His love with gratitude and obedience; to give Him pleasure! The satisfaction and meaning for which relationships exist is experienced when there is an exchange of commitment and a total giving of one's self to the other. God's joy is full when you and I choose to devote ourselves to Him with our whole heart, soul, strength, and mind. Hence, He has fashioned us in such a way that each of us have a choice to either gladden or sadden the heart of our Heavenly Father.

As it was when He created man, so it was when He redeemed man: God desired to demonstrate his love, and to be loved. Salvation is the restoration of a broken relationship.

Love motivated God to send His Son. Even God's justice that demands judgment and punishment for those that defy and break His divine law, speaks of divine love and care.

The attitude of our Heavenly Father is never a cold, legalistic reaction of "you did it, you pay", as many would charge. Divine intervention has a divine purpose. It is a rescue mission. It is to dissuade us from engaging in destructive behavior that will separate us from sharing intimacy with our Heavenly Father. The proverb says, "The Lord disciplines the one he loves, and he chastens everyone he accepts as his child" (Prov. 3:12).

God's intention and hope for mankind is that we would *choose* Him above all other personal relationships, that we would value His presence and companionship more than anything else in life, and, in doing so, would know the love of One whose motives are pure and true.

Any human effort, including those of Christian organizations, to subdue the Devil and his dark forces, are futile if we are not foremost in a love relationship with our God. We are not enabled to love our fellow man until we have first received the love of God. It is His love in us that qualifies us.

The morning that the pastor said those few, but potent words, he was really saying, *The two of you have discovered the same love that motivated God to send His Son into this world, a love that isn't expended on self, but is expressed in a commitment to do whatever is necessary to meet the needs of the other, for the shared pleasure.* The Romance of Heaven.

Recognizing and receiving this kind of love from the heart of God and returning that love in devotion to Him and His purposes, is what will set you and me free! And should a society of people commit themselves to this brand of selflessness, then the influence is multiplied and the potential for good, unlimited.

The Garden and The City

Earlier, we briefly looked at the place that the first man and the first woman inhabited.

It was a garden.

It was a place where God walked with the couple "in the cool of the day" (Gen. 3:8 AKJV).

It was a location selected by God, with boundaries, and with specific purpose.

On that earthen soil, man and woman would derive the benefits of knowing in ever-increasing measure, the nature and character of their Creator. While growing in the knowledge of God, man would gain wisdom and understanding of the plan and purpose for their existence. The balance and order that prevailed in the garden, would spread beyond its boundaries and eventually cover the entire earth. Literally, there would be a paradise on Earth under mankind's authority. This perfection would be perpetuated, potentially, forever, if human beings acknowledged their God and remained submitted to His authority.

We also discussed mankind's forfeiture of dominion over the earth because of their rebellion against their Creator, and then looked at the mercy and grace of God as He took the initiative to deliver humankind from the grip of the Devil.

Nothing has changed with regard to God's original intention. Today, the same scenario is being played in every city that dots the planet. God has placed groupings of people in various marked out "gardens" throughout the earth. The potential exists for each community of humans, as they daily acknowledge and walk with Father God, to spread the fragrant knowledge of Him to others far beyond the physical boundaries of their towns and cities.

Chapter 10

The Builder and Architect

It is written concerning the patriarch Abraham, "He was looking forward to the city with foundations, whose architect and builder is God...for He has prepared a city for them" (Heb. 11:10,16). Abraham, by faith, was perceiving the city that God has built for those who have entrusted to Him their lives, an eternal home in which they will abide with Him forever. In fact, some specifications of the "blueprint" for this eternal city are listed in the Book of Revelation, chapter 21, verses 10-27!

The Supreme Architect also prepared an earthly city, a temporal abode for Abraham and his offspring, that was to be named Jerusalem. The Hebrew word is *shalem*, derived from *shalom*, meaning Abode of Peace or City of Peace.

God is no less concerned about our pre-Heaven residency during the days we spend on this planet. I believe God has participated in the founding of our cities from their inception. This includes prompting human agents with vision of the city's purpose, the geographical location, and the moral nature of law that will govern society. In the process, the peace of God will permeate the populace. This is the providence of God in action; His superintending care and guidance in bringing you, me, and our cities into that which was divinely predetermined.

Divine providence was certainly evident among the Hebrews who were miraculously delivered from their bondage in Egypt, then led by a cloud by day and a pillar of fire by night to the Promised Land where they were to settle. And who would argue that the men and women of Nottinghamshire, England were not under the guidance of the "hand" of God when they boarded the Mayflower in 1620 and boldly sailed to a new world?

What was it that distinguished the Hebrews and English Separatists that brought about the founding of their favored societies? It was their deep conviction and desire, despite their human frailties, that they be governed in accordance with God's law. This was the foundation stone on which their cultures would be built. The building blocks would consist of their acts of obedience, demonstrated over time that would prove their allegiance to God and His law.

A society that seeks God's favor, will experience the blessing of His presence as His Spirit fills their land, bringing increased enlightenment and influence upon the human mind and will. Where God is present there is protection, peace and prosperity, as well as creative power that will mold and shape the society according to His design and plan.

Tales of Two Cities

Solomon's proverb puts forth the theme of this book in one pithy sentence, "Righteousness exalts a nation, but sin condemns any people" (Prov. 14:34). Whether it be an individual human being, a family, a city, or a nation, pursuing and practicing righteousness; "rightness" with God, will result in prosperity and prominence.

A righteous city is a powerhouse for God. Its influence and affect are far-reaching. A city that is morally right with God will stand as a beacon of light amidst a lost and dying world. "For the eyes of the Lord run to and fro throughout the whole earth, to show himself strong in the behalf of them whose heart is perfect toward him" (2 Chron. 16:9 AKJV). The larger the number of people, the greater the force for propagation of godliness. The city is the primary candidate.

Since the fall of mankind, there has never existed a paradise on Earth. Man has attempted to organize and strategize to bring about a utopian society where peace and good will prevailed; however, it has never been accomplished. Mankind, without the blessing of his God, does not possess the "stuff" to live in harmony with his fellow man.

A city or nation without blemish is not a realistic expectation; however, there have been seasons of time wherein the presence and blessing of God has been keenly manifest among a people. This is true of both Israel and the U.S.A. In fact, throughout Earth history, few societies have experienced this kind of significant and sustained visitation of God's presence.

So, what is it that has made Israel and the United States exceptional and unique? Let's look a little closer at these two nations and try to identify what has contributed to their prosperity.

Bound or Free?

At the center of our experience on Earth are these two most fundamental questions pertaining to the quality of our existence: Will we live free? Will we be at liberty to express the human rights given by God, so we may find fulfillment during our days on Earth?

Freedom and liberty are not the same thing. Freedom speaks of being free *from* something, while liberty speaks of being free to *do* something.

God created us to be free, to have no oppressive rulership over our lives. We are also equipped with free will to choose how we will conduct our lives within or outside the boundaries of His moral laws. Ideally, a man or woman would have liberty to think and act and would prosper in accordance with the quality of those attitudes and actions.

Oppressive rulership can impact us in both the internal and external aspects of our being. One may have been freed by Christ from the guilt and weight of their sin and the exploitation of their fallen nature by the Devil, but still live in a society controlled by a system of government that restricts or forbids individual liberty to express that freedom. That person is free in an inward sense, but not in an outward sense. The soul has been set free but is not necessarily at liberty to express in their daily living what has been accomplished in the inward aspects of their being.

On the other hand, one may live in a society such as the U.S.A. that does not forcibly restrict one's rights to "life, liberty, and the pursuit of happiness" and its various forms of outward expression, but their inward state of being may be oppressed and bound by unconfessed sin and the manipulations of the Devil.

One may have freedom, but in this world will have to contend for individual and collective liberty.

Jesus said those that would come to know the truth, would be set free. He spoke of the internal aspects of our being, spirit and soul. For those who have committed their lives to Christ, the challenge before them is in confronting a world system predominantly governed by fallen mankind, that is under the jurisdiction of the Devil. It is firstly a process of addressing the human need for forgiveness and release from their sin, and, secondly, allowing the outworking of that inward transformation to influence the fabric of society, including the various institutions that often regulate the liberties of the citizenry.

It is the man or woman who has been freed from the bonds of sin and the tyranny of demonic oppression that is in a position to take that message of deliverance to those chained in spiritual darkness. As a city becomes increasingly populated with those devoted to the One true God, the light of His presence progressively invades the land. It is only then that a city, and, potentially, an entire nation can enjoy the liberty to live life the way God has intended.

This is the nature of the fight for the soul of any individual, city, or nation. And the battle is waged in the spirit realm, where God works to free the souls of mankind, while the Devil strives to ensnare and bind.

Tales of Two Visitors

Although the U.S.A. and the state of Israel have experienced outpourings of God's favor during the course of their existence, both have been profoundly affected by the issue of freedom versus bondage. America's darkest days were marked by her enslavement of fellow human beings, while Israel was subject to the chains of bondage by foreign oppressors.

Usually, to get the straight "scoop" about something or someone, the best means is to find an objective source, someone from the "outside" that has not been influenced by exposure to local opinion or process.

This was the case with one who ventured to America from a faraway shore, and one who journeyed to Israel, also from a distant land.

Alexis de Tocqueville

The Frenchman, de Tocqueville, came to the United States in 1831 for the primary purpose of determining what lay at the core of the prosperity America was experiencing. The experiment that is America was only 55 years in progress at the time of his visit. His hope was that what he might discover, could be carried back to his homeland and transplanted. De Tocqueville's observations and analysis of American society and government was chronicled and later published in his 1835 classic, *Democracy in America*. In that work, he summarizes that "America is great because America is good, and if America ever ceases to be good, America will cease to be great."

It was De Tocqueville's observation that "Liberty cannot be established without morality, nor morality without faith." Reverse the order of those elements and we have faith, morality, and liberty. The theoretical element of believing and trusting in God, coupled with an active lifestyle in which that relationship is exercised, results in the ultimate expression of the human soul.

De Tocqueville also referred to this fundamental truth as "liberty regulated by law", God's law, as expressed in the Judeo-Christian principles found in the Scriptures, on which the founders had based the rule of American law. American citizens would be free from despotic oppression, but their liberties would be defined and regulated according to God's perfect moral law.

Bear this in mind: America was not founded as a Christian nation. America was founded as a *free* nation; a society wherein freed men and women would live out their days on Earth with the liberty to pursue personal fulfillment and contentment.

Another of de Tocqueville's conclusions was that "Christianity is the companion of liberty in all its conflicts . . . the cradle of its infancy, and the divine source of its claims." In other words, if one is to experience any degree of individual liberty and its benefits, one must first embrace Christianity. De Tocqueville recognized that the fruit of liberty, manifested among American society, was a result of adherence and practice of the morals and ethics resident within the Christian faith. This implies that in the absence of the practical application of Christian ethics, true liberty cannot exist, and the people of that society will not prosper.

The theme that dominated de Tocqueville's observations was the vitality and prosperity that marked American society was derived from honoring God's righteous law. Citizens were not strong-armed into obedience but exercised the liberty to collectively determine what laws would govern the whole of society. America prospered because the Christian message took root in the hearts of her people, and the blessings of God were uniquely manifested throughout the land.

Queen of Sheba

Let's now consider our second sojourner, the Queen of Sheba. Just who was she? History records that she was the queen of a south Arabian kingdom in the geographic area that is now Yemen. Per the biblical narrative, in about 1000 B.C., she traveled to Jerusalem and met with King Solomon who was renowned for his wisdom in the then civilized world. Let's pick up the narrative in the Old Testament book of 1 Kings, vs. 1 - 9:

> When the queen of Sheba heard about the fame of Solomon and his relationship to the Lord, she came to test Solomon with hard questions. Arriving at Jerusalem with a very great caravan—with camels carrying spices, large quantities of gold, and precious stones—she came to Solomon and talked with him about all that she had on her mind. Solomon answered all her questions; nothing was too hard for the king to explain to her. When the queen of Sheba saw all the wisdom of Solomon and the palace he had built, the food on his table, the seating of his officials, the attending servants in their robes, his cupbearers, and the burnt offerings he made at the temple of the Lord, she was overwhelmed.
>
> She said to the king, 'The report I heard in my own country about your achievements and your wisdom is true. But I did not believe these things until I came and saw with my own eyes. Indeed, not even half was told me; in wisdom and wealth you have far exceeded the report I heard. How happy your people must be! How happy your officials, who continually stand before you and hear your wisdom! Praise be to the Lord your God, who has delighted in you and placed you on the throne of Israel. Because of the Lord's eternal love for Israel, he has made you king to maintain justice and righteousness'.

It was a discerning Queen that observed God's providence among Israel in placing Solomon over the people, and God as the Source of Solomon's "wisdom". But perhaps her understanding is most noteworthy by her recognition that the outworking of that wisdom, maintaining "justice and righteousness", resulted in "wealth", i.e., Israel's prosperity and influence among the nations.

About two-hundred years later, Israel fell to the Assyrians and was taken into captivity, as a succession of her kings failed to honor God and His Law. The prophet Isaiah saw the despicable and desperate condition of his beloved city, Jerusalem, and urged her to contend for the destiny from which she had strayed. He wrote, "Shake off your dust; rise up, sit enthroned, Jerusalem. Free yourself from the chains on your neck, Daughter Zion, now a captive" (Isa. 52:2). Again, freedom or bondage is at stake.

God has a specific destiny and purpose to be fulfilled, a calling to be answered for this world's cities. Too often that call is drowned out by mankind's clamoring attempts to forge his own path, in his own way, and God's gift to the city lies buried under the rubble of wayward, failed human effort.

Solomon sums up the issue with two succinct conclusions, "Unless the Lord builds the house, the builders labor in vain. Unless the Lord watches over the city, the guards stand watch in vain" (Ps. 127:1).

Chapter 11

Savannah Seeds

The City's Gift

If the city does possess a soul, then similar to the human being, it, too, is designed with a gift, a unique, divine endowment intended to bless its citizenry and others among mankind. John Dawson concurs, "Our cities have the mark of God's sovereign purpose upon them. Our cities contain what I call a redemptive gift." To understand this potential, we must seek to see beneath what appears a harsh or daunting veneer, to the potential for good and blessing that has eluded that society of people.

If this is true, then identifying the gift, i.e., discerning the nature of God's design for my city and yours, is of the utmost importance. In so doing, as engaged citizens we are enabled to cooperate with God in his plan and purposes. Remember, God will share His secrets with His own, so we may assist in bringing about His will here on Earth.

As we commit ourselves to this partnership, He will impart the necessary understanding and insight of His strategy to prosper our cities. The prayers of the heart and work of the hands in accordance with the will of God are highly effectual.

That leaves each of us with the responsibility of answering these questions:

What is the gift that God has imparted to my city?

How can I identify the gift?

What am I contributing as a citizen to help my city reach its potential?

The truths we look at in the following pages are relevant and applicable to every town and city that exists or has ever existed on planet Earth. Regardless of where your city has been in past times or where she is now, we can each make a difference in what she will become.

Now let's plumb deeper into the object city of our study, the Lady Savannah. As we are enabled to identify how she has become who she is, we will also discover who she is intended to be!

The Shaping of the Founder's Vision

Earlier, we touched on what was in the heart and mind of the primary personality who founded America's 13th colony, James Edward Oglethorpe. Let's now look closer at what led him to the vision and commitment he possessed.

James Oglethorpe was born on December 22, 1696 in London, England. There is little known about Oglethorpe's early years, other than he was one of ten children born to Eleanor and Theophilus Oglethorpe. Apparently, he was well provided for as his father was the owner of considerable properties in various parts of the country.

In 1714, Oglethorpe attended Corpus Christi College at Oxford University, but did not graduate having left school to join England's military and their fight against the Turks who had invaded Europe. Following a victorious return, Oglethorpe was elected to the seat in the House of Commons, previously held by his father and one of his older brothers. Oglethorpe focused on the domestic and international policies of England.

In 1728, at the age of 32, Oglethorpe had an experience that profoundly affected his life and set him on a course that would eventually define his legacy. Oglethorpe arrived at London's Fleet Prison to visit a close friend, Robert Castell, who had been jailed because of his debts. During that visit, Oglethorpe was powerfully moved by the deplorable living conditions within the institution and the inhuman treatment of those incarcerated. Castell died soon thereafter having contracted smallpox.

This spurred Oglethorpe to act to remedy the problem, apparently, something that his predecessors failed to do. Thaddeus Mason Harris, in this excerpt from his biography on Oglethorpe, continues the narrative,

> Shocked by the scenes he witnessed, he determined to expose such injustice; and if possible, prevent such abuse of power. With this view, he brought forward a motion in the House of Commons, 'that an inquiry should be instituted into the state of the gaols (jails) in the metropolis'. . . The investigation led to the discovery of many corrupt practices, and much oppressive treatment of the prisoners; and was followed by the enactment of measures for the correction of such shameful mismanagement and inhuman neglect in some cases, and for the prevention of severity of infliction in others.

The heart and mind of Oglethorpe was being enlightened as to his mission and greater purpose. What really set him apart was his readiness and willingness to take the necessary steps to transform vision to reality.

Running With the Vision

Although Oglethorpe did fuel the engine of prison reform, the greater issue of how to help the multitude of England's destitute needed to be addressed.

Again, Oglethorpe took the bull by the horns and brought together several colleagues from the jails committee, including John Percival, later the first earl of Egmont. Oglethorpe's group began ruminating over the idea of founding a new colony in America purposed to assist England's "worthy poor". They believed that if given the opportunity, these "misfortunates" could develop into skilled, contributing members of the new society. For these crafters of this venture, it was of the utmost importance to avoid the formation of the same class distinctions that troubled English society. Therefore, slavery would be forbidden as the settlers would be required to work their own soil.

This group of men then launched into a four-year period of lobbying wealthy potential donors, including the congregations of the Church of England. Probably the most difficult aspect of their task was convincing the governmental powers that the enterprise would increase the wealth of England. In due time, their persistence was rewarded and on April 21, 1732, King George II would sign the charter for the new colony, and his namesake, Georgia.

Once approved, the Trustees set about selecting those that would engage in the adventure. Initially, six-hundred men were interviewed and after a three-week process, the list was paired to 100 men. The final selection included thirty-five families and resulted in a total passenger list of one- hundred fourteen, including Oglethorpe.

On November 17, 1732, the chosen ones boarded the 220-ton galley ship, Anne, weighed anchor and sailed from Gravesend, England. After a 61-day voyage, during which two lives were lost, both infants, the Anne arrived in Charles Towne, South Carolina on January 17, 1733.

Location, Location, Location

Prior to the arrival in what would become the settlement of Savannah, the group briefly stopped in Port Royal. From there, Oglethorpe ventured along the Savannah River and discovered the site.

On February 10, he wrote in his personal journal,

> I went myself to view the Savannah River. I fixed upon a healthy situation about ten miles from the sea. The river there forms a half moon, along the South side of which the banks are almost 40-foot-high and upon the top a flat which they call a bluff… Ships that draw twelve-foot water can ride within ten yards of the bank. Upon the riverside in the center of this plain, I have laid out the town.

On February 12, two days after his journal entry, Oglethorpe and his people set foot on Savannah soil and began the arduous task of transforming a wilderness into a city.

As with Abraham, Moses, David, Peter, and Paul, God saw in Oglethorpe a man with a heart set on trusting and pleasing Him. In response, God spoke to him and faithfully led him forth. All that God requires in order for you and me to live lives of significance, is that we rise up, shake off the dust that has settled upon us, and take the sometimes-risky steps of faith that lead to powerful, effective living. The providence of God will be evident to those that seek first His kingdom and His righteousness, as well as the good and welfare of others.

The Words of Others

Robert Southey, in his 1820 work, *Life of Wesley*, wrote concerning Georgia,

> No colony was ever established upon principles more honorable to its projectors. The conduct of the trustees did not discredit their profession. They looked for no emolument (fee, salary, profit) to themselves or their representatives after them.

The following appeared in an evening London newspaper on Saturday, February 18, 1733,

> James Oglethorpe, Esq., one of the Trustees for establishing the Colony of Georgia, is gone over with the first embarkation at his own expense. To see a gentleman of his rank and fortune visiting a distant and uncultivated land, with no other society but the miserable whom he goes to assist; exposing himself freely to the same hardships to which they are subjected, in the prime of life, instead of pursuing his pleasures or ambition…at his own expense, and without a view, or even a possibility of receiving any private advantage from it; this too, after having done and expended for it what many generous men would think sufficient to have done; – to see this, I say, must give everyone who has approved and

contributed to the undertaking, the highest satisfaction; must convince the world of the disinterested zeal with which the settlement is to be made, and entitle him to the truest honor he can gain, the perpetual love and applause of mankind.

Edwin L. Jackson of the University of Georgia wrote,

> Living up to the motto of Georgia's Trustees – Non sibi sed aliis (Not for self, but for others) – Oglethorpe worked tirelessly on behalf of the colony during the initial months. Sometimes violating Trustee policy, Oglethorpe permitted Jews, Lutheran Salzburgers, and other persecuted religious minorities to settle in Georgia. On the matter of importing African slaves from any source, Oglethorpe never wavered in wholly opposing slavery in Georgia. With regard to Georgia's Indians, he had an enlightened policy, always respecting their customs, language, and needs. Land cessions were always agreed to by treaty according to proper Indian custom. Also, Oglethorpe actively sought to protect the Indians from unscrupulous white traders.

Reverend Johann Martin Bolzius of the Lutheran Salzburger immigrants that Oglethorpe settled in nearby Ebenezer, journaled this:

> So far as we can include from a short acquaintance with him, he is a man who has a great reverence for God, and his holy word and ordinances; a cordial love for the servants and children of God, and who wishes to see the name of Christ glorified in all places. So blest has been his presence and undertakings in

this land, that more has been accomplished in one year than others would have effected in many.

It is evident that Oglethorpe believed what the Apostle Paul wrote, "God shall supply all your need according to His riches in glory in Christ Jesus" (Php. 4:19). When one is convinced that God is personally involved in their interpersonal relationships and business matters, there are no reluctances in being generous; no fear of want or lack, for when the coffers are near empty, God refills them to overflowing.

Oglethorpe's Gifts

This was the heart of the Founder and Father of Georgia, James Edward Oglethorpe. He was a bold visionary, a wise servant-leader of people in both word and deed, a man marked by generosity, compassion, and mercy, who placed the needs and welfare of others above his own.

In summation, Oglethorpe's vision for Savannah is that she would be a community of people united in their belief that individual responsibility and mutual goodwill would bring about prosperity within their society, and to others beyond their borders. Probably, of primary significance is that his firm resolve to promote human liberty stood in direct opposition to the dark, rising tide of his day that threatened to engulf human civilization: the evil of slavery.

We all have the potential and promise of contributing to the righteous reign of God the Creator over the earth and among mankind. Ask, seek, and knock, then watch God open the doors for effective change and influence to take place in your sphere of life.

The cultivation of Lady Savannah was off to a good start.

Chapter 12

A Gifted Lady

Oglethorpe and his fellow Trustees envisioned Savannah as functioning in the following three basic ways:

- A City of Benevolence
- A City of Innovation
- A City of Defense

This was what James Oglethorpe perceived in his spirit as the potential for Savannah. The three-pronged *Oglethorpe Vision* is as pertinent today as it was in the early 1700's. Just as God's plan and destiny for you and I never change, so it is true of our cities.

Bringing forth the potential of the underprivileged, stimulating innovation and inventiveness within the citizenry, and standing as a defense against the advance of oppressive enemies are areas in which Savannah has achieved much success, but, at other times has experienced much failure. Not only are there clear evidences of these elements of activity over the past decades of her existence, they are still acutely evident today.

Michael K. Mancha

A City of Benevolence

This aspect of Savannah's potential is most clearly represented by those led by Oglethorpe to America and those that followed. Remember, the initial flow of immigrants consisted of misfortunates, the poor, and the persecuted of England and other parts of Europe. A second chance was being extended to these settlers who would have an opportunity to discover and realize their God-given gifts and potential. This was not a government hand-out program, as great perseverance and patience would be required if they were to achieve their dreams.

These immigrant settlers included the Austrian Protestant Salzburgers who were expelled from their country by Archbishop Firmian for following the teaching of Martin Luther, the persecuted Moravians from eastern Saxony, Germany, and Portuguesa and German Jews seeking freedom in the New World. These jarred open the flood gate that eventually saw the entrance of more than three thousand hopefuls during Oglethorpe's trusteeship from 1732 to 1752. The ethnic groups included English Londoners, Rhineland Germans, Lowland Scots, Sephardic Jews, French-speaking Swiss, Irish convicts, and some Piedmont Italians and Russians, all pursuing the hope of a better life.

This benevolent spirit of Oglethorpe found immediate kinship with that of the indigenous people of the southeast, the local Creeks, also known as the Muscogee people. It was Chief Tomo-Chi-Chi of the Yamacraw tribe who welcomed Oglethorpe and his "tribe" to American soil and graciously gave the settlers the land on which Savannah was to be raised.

This was a rare cooperation between European settlers and the native Americans, who, up to that time, had only shared bloodshed as the settlers blazed their paths into the new world.

This spirit of generosity was maintained through the ensuing years as numerous charitable societies, associations, and foundations were birthed. They included The Union Society (1750), The Savannah Poorhouse and Hospital (1809), The Savannah Free School Society (1816), The Dorcas Society (1816), The Widow's Society (1822), The Savannah Benevolent Society (1829), The Georgia Infirmary (1832), and The Massie School (1855). Also, many benevolent organizations were formed by various trade, ethnic, and religious groups to assist those within their social strata who were without the basic material needs in life.

Mary Telfair

None exemplified the spirit of benevolence more than Mary Telfair (1791 – 1875). Born into wealth and the daughter of Georgia's governor, Edward Telfair, Mary was an educated, intelligent, woman of conviction, unacquainted with the concept of compromise. Only five feet tall, Mary towered above the peers of her day while making her opinions on national and world affairs known.

In his entry to the New Encyclopedia of Georgia, Charles J. Johnson wrote,

> Hers was a mind of deep sensitivity that revered beauty and truth and abhorred pretension and show, as well as greed and insincerity. Telfair was frequently ill in an age plagued by illness. A member of the Independent Presbyterian Church in Savannah, she found comfort in her strong Christian beliefs and managed to cope with adversity.

Upon her death, Telfair bequeathed her Regency-style home, located on Savannah's St. James Square (renamed Telfair

Square in 1883), along with the books, furniture, and works of art, to the Georgia Historical Society. The society opened the house to the public in 1886.

Among her many gifts to the people of Savannah is the Mary Telfair Home, an institution committed to housing widows with families of small children that opened its doors in 1883 and functioned until 1953 when it was demolished.

In her will, Mary also provided funding for The Telfair Hospital for Females, built in 1884. When it merged with Candler General Hospital in 1960, the facility had distinguished itself by becoming the longest-operating women's hospital in the country.

Also testifying of Mary's philanthropy are the Telfair Museums in Savannah—the Telfair Academy, the Owens-Thomas House, and the Jepson Center for the Arts. They comprise the oldest public art museum in the South. They house permanent collections of works dating from the 1700's to the present, as well as temporary exhibitions that showcase national and international artists.

Realized Potential

The idea of benevolence dovetails with the concept of personal destiny. You see, the act of benevolence is an expression of kindness, generosity, and compassion toward those in need. It is an expression of goodwill, in that it is offered with the desire that the basic needs of the recipient will be met, and from that place of stability he or she can grow and reach their optimum potential in life.

While Savannah would be the object of God's benevolent compassion, her responsibility would lie in imparting that same spirit of giving to those she would encounter. The prosperity of the city would hinge on her willingness to freely and joyfully give, as readily as she would receive. It is the continuous fountain flow of which we earlier spoke. God would be faithful to supply, and Savannah would be accountable to disperse those good gifts locally and abroad. This is the intended beauty of the Lady Savannah!

A City of Innovation

Since the initial breaking of ground in Savannah, the idea of *originality* has been on display. Oglethorpe's innovative city plan consisting of 24 community squares, which we will examine later, attest to that. His intent that the unique inherent talents of the first immigrants come to fruition, would be exemplary of what would follow. From her inception, the identity of Savannah was marked as a society that would perpetually showcase the creativity of men and women, under the inspiration of the Spirit of God.

Savannah was the last of the original thirteen Colonies upon which the nation would be established. There's significance in the placement of Savannah as *last* of the *first* thirteen. In God's sovereign providence, He often saves the best for last, as if to say, *my supply and quality is inexhaustible! You thought that the thirteenth would be subpar in quality and value to the first. No, I saved the best for last!* Jesus further confirmed this principle when he said, "So the last will be first, and the first will be last" (Matt. 20:16). And during the initial decades of the nation's existence, Savannah was the birthplace of much of what shaped its economic and social identity.

The Lady's contributions include those of renowned individuals in the field of politics (Joseph Habersham, ratified the U.S Constitution, and Edward Langworthy, signor of the U.S.

Articles of Confederation), Law (Supreme Court Justices James Moore Wayne and Clarence Thomas), Invention (Eli Whitney, the Cotton Gin), community organization (Juliette Gordon Low, founder of the Girl Scouts of America), Literature (Pulitzer Prize winner Conrad Aiken, and Flannery O'Connor), and Music ('Ragtime' pioneer Tom Turpin, and Songwriter Johnny Mercer).

Pioneers of enduring religious institutions have been many in Savannah. The contributions of John and Charles Wesley of the protestant Methodist denomination, the forty-two Sephardic Jews that founded the Congregation Mickve Israel, and George Whitefield, founder of the Bethesda Orphanage, are just the start of a long list of individuals whose contributions shaped American religious culture.

The works of the world's greatest architects of the eighteenth and nineteenth centuries, including the Englishman, William Jay, are on display throughout the Historic District. The various styles include Federal (The Davenport House), Georgian (The Olde Pink House), Gothic Revival (Temple Mickve Israel), Greek Revival (First Baptist Church), Italianate (Mercer Williams House), Regency (Telfair Museum of Art), Romanesque Revival (The Cotton Exchange), and Second French Empire (Hamilton Turner House), a true melting pot, reflecting the diversity of the Lady's culture.

A study conducted by the reputable and esteemed Historic Savannah Foundation, found that of twenty-five hundred buildings catalogued in Savannah, forty percent have architectural or historical significance.

SCAD

The foregoing accounting of Savannah's cultural heritage is far from complete. The intention is to quickly qualify the city as key in the growth and formation of our nation and as a model for other cities that would rise on the landscape of this planet.

Of the various organizations and institutions of Savannah that have inspired and produced positive societal growth, none have been more instrumental than the Savannah College of Art & Design (SCAD), which opened its doors in 1979.

This college offers over forty art and design degree programs that were previously unavailable in southeast Georgia. SCAD also maintains campuses in Atlanta, Provence (France), and Hong Kong. Well over ten-thousand students are enrolled in the four campuses. The institution employs over fifteen-hundred individuals, and is recognized, nationally and internationally, for its education of entrepreneurs and future leaders in the vast world of the arts and design.

SCAD is a vital, multi-faceted expression of Spirit life that empowers the attendees, and a source of inspiration for the various recipients of their honed gifts and talents. SCAD is a product of God's grace for Savannah. It is one of His merciful counteractions among society, to the inroads of the Devil.

This leads us to the third prong of the Oglethorpe Vision.

A City of Defense

The nature of war is this: To be in a state of hostility or rivalry; to contend; a condition of antagonism or contention. War is an absence of peace. It is an inability for parties to co-exist within rightful boundaries. War between factions of population; arising out of religious, class, or racial differences, involves acts of aggression based on the desire to dominate and control. War is a quest for power, for supremacy, for one to rise above all others. And at the root of war is the familiar human nemesis, pride.

War is at work in every human being and begins at our biological conception. Our human bents are derived from our mothers and fathers, whose natural bents were derived from theirs. It is in our "seed". Every generation of men and women have "inherited" the rebel nature that fell upon the first man and woman as a result of their disobedience to the will of their Creator. This separation from God also leaves us in contention with all other human beings. We are at war with ourselves, a hostility between spirit and flesh, and as a by-product, we war against each other.

The battle is evident within the womb, as demonstrated by Esau and Jacob, the twins that tussled for control and dominance within Rebecca (Gen. 25:19-24). This is the onset of a lifetime of attempting to harness a beast driven and absorbed in *self*. Millions are made, and millions are spent on trying to teach the human to be "good". We buy books, we attend seminars, we warm the couches of shrinks, and, in the prison system, periods of isolation and contemplation are required with the hope that the criminal bents in mankind can be rehabilitated. But history dictates that the nature of mankind is such, that peace cannot be manufactured in the individual or among society. The answer is simple and mocked by the majority: The tide can only be reversed by a *rebirth* through Christ, into the family of God, wherein each is planted a new nature marked by genuine love and concern for others.

Savannah Wars

Except for the immediate period following the creation of the first man and woman, there has never existed a time on Earth during which external human conflict has not been present. So, this was true at the time Savannah was conceived. Therefore, the Lady was designed to be a City of Defense.

This intent existed even before Oglethorpe and the first settlers boarded the Anne and embarked on their adventure. We know the trustee's plan was driven by the desire to give new beginnings to England's destitute. But for the royals of the nation, there had to be more. In North America, the British were engaged in a tense geo-political chess match with the Spanish who already occupied the Floridian panhandle, and were intent on expanding northward, threatening the English colony of Charles Town. The new colony would serve as a deterrent and buffer against the advance of this arch enemy.

Not only was Savannah intended to provide a defense for the northern colonies, so was a nation being formed to be a protector and defender for those populations of the world under attack from both domestic and foreign aggressors. Once again, Savannah was a "first", a forerunner of what God purposed for the growing and prospering American colonies, and, soon to be, the United States of America.

In the context of sports, we've heard the expression, "The best defense is a good offense." The original application of this adage is with relation to the concept of war. It is known as the Strategic Offense Principle. It is based on the philosophy that, if one wants to ensure one's own safety, the most effective means is to aggressively engage one's enemy, forcing that foe into a defensive posture, rendering them incapable of mounting their own offense.

From the inception of Savannah, the colony trained to be battle-ready. Many of those who sailed the Atlantic for the hope of liberty in America, had fought for the freedom of their native land. Many had been subject to the cruelty of tyrants and the smothering oppression of despots. As Savannah continued to develop, they would take in the likes of the Scots and the Irish who were the products of past generations weaned on war.

Oglethorpe, also a proven British warrior, would lead the charge of the first generation of settlers, as the General stayed true to his call to protect Savannah and the developing American colonies. More than once, he stood against Spanish troops and repelled their northward advances.

Savannah was a key participant in the Revolutionary War, fought between April 1775 and September 1783. The Liberty Boys of Savannah, an offspring of Samuel Adams' the Sons of Liberty, and their protest of the Stamp Act, helped fan the sparks of rebellion that erupted into full-flamed war against British rule. Renowned combatants such as Marquis de Lafayette (French), Casamir Pulaski (Polish), and the Sheftall family (German Jews), fought on Savannah soil to secure the freedom of the colonists. One of the bloodiest encounters of the conflict, known as the Siege of Savannah, resulted in the death or wounding of over five-hundred men. The sacrifice of these and others have served as an inspiration to future generations of men and women who have fought for the freedom of Americans and other nations abroad.

The Civil War was also hotly contested in and around Savannah, as she served as a bastion of defense against the inroads of Northern troops onto the sacred ground of the South. Following his torching of Atlanta, Savannah was highlighted in General William Sherman's March to the Sea, while en route to South Carolina, where the final battles of the conflict were to be waged. It is interesting to note that the people of Savannah, led by their mayor, laid down their arms and surrendered, with the hope their city would not suffer Atlanta's fate.

General Sherman spared the Lady and in his December 22, 1864 telegram to Abraham Lincoln, he wrote, "I beg to present you as a Christmas gift the city of Savannah with one-hundred fifty heavy guns and plenty of ammunition and also about twenty-five thousand bales of cotton."

During the twentieth century, Savannah played hostess to the founding and development of several military operations that were committed to the protection of the United States and other nations targeted by foreign bullies. Instrumental in America's involvement and eventual victory in World War II was the Mighty Eighth Air Force, organized in 1942. It was the largest deployment of air forces into northern Europe. Savannah is also the home of Hunter Airfield located on the south side of the city, a military base that supports nearby Fort Stewart, home of the 3rd Infantry Division. It is the largest Army installation east of the Mississippi River.

Spiritual Battle and Spiritual Weaponry

The original colony was envisioned and purposed to be a buffer against flesh and blood enemies. However, the greater purpose lay in the design that she would be a wall of defense against mankind's spirit enemy, the Devil and his demonic forces. The city was, and is, intended to model a reliance on God as their Protector and the One who trains the hands of the citizenry for war. Spiritual war. This feature of the city is to be gifted to other American communities and others throughout the world!

The principle is that our *real* foe is not the flesh and blood tyrant, or invading armies that tote guns and bombs, but are unseen spirit entities that incite hostility, violence, and other evil lusts within the human heart. If the oppression of the spirit enemy is dealt with, then the oppressed man or woman is also disarmed. As we are freed, so is the city of which we are a part.

The planting and ongoing presence of Savannah's many churches give silent testimony to her call, not only as a fortified defense against the onslaughts of the Evil One, but also an *offensive* battering ram against the gates of Hell. The intention is that from within the churches would rise a spiritually united and equipped fighting force, that would with authority and spiritual discernment, infiltrate the Devil's camp and set at liberty those held captive in the realm of darkness and ignorance.

We will learn more in later chapters about how this is accomplished.

Chapter 13

The Lens of History

Earlier, we discussed the involuntary human bent to interpret circumstance and occurrence through the grid of intellect and reason. In a world defined by science, the concept of *spirit* has no place. It is the square peg, round hole scenario. It just doesn't fit. Again, this is mankind functioning without consideration of the activities within the spirit world and the nature of the spirit entities committed to controlling what is manifested in the physical world. Because of this powerful inclination, mankind has often been as clay in the hand of the Devil, to mold and shape at his will.

Today, as in every yesterday since the dawn of time, the Devil will stop at nothing to sow destructive seed into the life of an individual or a community of people. Savannah has been high on the Evil One's radar from her inception and he has been relentless in his quest to pervert God's design for the city. If he succeeds, there will be evidence of a twisted, distorted version of the intended purpose. This goal of the

Devil is accomplished by sabotaging the contributions of the individual citizens and those of the various city institutions.

Clues to what God has purposed for your city are best determined by observing what has presented itself over the course of her history. What has come forth that has stood the test of time and are the identifiable attributes of her character? These features will, to varying degrees, depict the design of God. However, as good and evil wrestle for control, the image of what God intended is often blemished and marred.

Referring back to Lady Astor's "beautiful woman with a dirty face" pronouncement, encapsulated within her words we find this whole idea of a city's gift that has been distorted. This quote has become a prominent portrayal of Savannah that continues to be applied to this day. It is a sobering declaration of aborted hope and of lost promise.

Viewing Savannah through the lens of history is key to identifying what took place that shaped her soul. If we "read" the past with discernment, then we will be enlightened as to how our cities have become who they are today. The past, indeed, defines the present, but doesn't have to define the future.

Let's get a sense of Lady Savannah by taking a tour to see who and what is memorialized by the existing city squares, monuments and other edifices within the Historic District. These enduring fixtures bear silent testimony of significant past figures and events.

City Squares

The uniqueness of Savannah was immediately evident as the plan for the city unfolded. The concept of a community laid out in *squares* was unprecedented. Exactly how and where Oglethorpe adopted this idea is speculative. Some believe it was derived from his military background and the grid design of encampments, while others attribute it to concepts contained in the book, *Vilas of the Ancients*, written by his ill-fated friend, Robert Castell.

Oglethorpe's original city plan consisted of twenty-four squares. Each square was situated at the center of a larger section of land called a *ward*. It is within the squares that the community activities took place. The institutions of the community, including the church and school, were built on two large lots situated on the east and west sides of each square called *trust lots*. The land on the north and south sides of each square were sectioned into twenty *tithing lots* that were part of a land grant of fifty acres, given to each original settler for farming. A lane was cleared through the middle of each lot so people could pass through. These lanes of passage became the streets that extend through the present-day historic district of Savannah.

These various squares marked out the area where those within the community would live and grow. It was upon that soil the identity of the city would be formed over time. The early history of Lady Savannah was forged by what happened on and around the squares.

Between 1733 and 1736, Oglethorpe oversaw the development of the first six squares, including what are now named Johnson Square, Wright Square (originally named Percival Square), Ellis Square, Telfair Square, Oglethorpe Square and Reynolds Square. The remaining 18 squares developed in the later years of the eighteenth century and throughout the course of the nineteenth century. Those include Franklin Square, Warren Square, Washington Square, Liberty Square, Columbia Square, Greene Square, Elbert Square, Orleans Square, Chippewa Square, Crawford Square, Pulaski Square,

Madison Square, Lafayette Square, Troup Square, Chatham Square, Monterey Square, Calhoun Square and Whitefield Square. Two of the squares, Elbert and Liberty Squares, were eventually replaced by a freeway and a courthouse, respectively.

Each of the people and events for which the squares are named represent a significant contribution to the makeup of the soul of the city.

Monuments

As we approach many of the city squares, our attention is immediately focused on the monuments that rise from the ground and pay tribute to a renowned figure in Savannah history. It is convenient for the tourist or citizen to pause before any one of the statues, give a cursory glance up, maybe read a bit of the inscription, and then move on. But if the souls of our cities are to be appreciated and understood, then it is necessary to consider how the activities of the heroes, *and* the villains, marked the society during their brief appearance on the scene. As we do, we're all the richer and wiser for it.

As we move through these brief bios, consider this question: Did the substance of their life establish a greater degree of divine or demonic presence over the area?

James Oglethorpe

In the center of Chippewa Square stands the nine-foot, bronze figure of James Oglethorpe, the collaboration of once preeminent sculptor Daniel Chester French, and architect Henry Bacon. The duo also applied their talents in the construction of the Lincoln Memorial.

The Oglethorpe monument, dedicated in 1910, depicts the Georgia Colony founder in full British military dress, ready with sword drawn. He stands facing south with a wary eye on any advance of the Spanish. A palmetto branch, symbolic of victory and peace, lies at his feet.

On the corners of the statue base are four lions holding shields that represent Oglethorpe's coat of arms, the seals of the Colony of Georgia and the City of Savannah. Engraved into the pedestal are words from the British Parliament's original charter granted in 1732.

From the Oglethorpe Monument historical Marker:

> Erected by the State of Georgia, the City of Savannah, and the patriotic societies of the state to the memory of the great soldier, eminent statesman, famous philanthropist, General James Oglethorpe, who in this city on the 12th day of February AD 1733 founded and established this colony of Georgia.

Tomo-Chi-Chi

Arguably, without the cooperation of Tomo-Chi-Chi, Chief of the Yamacraw Indians, the colony of Savannah may have remained just a good idea. His receptivity to the proposals of Oglethorpe and the friendship that developed between the two leaders, was of the utmost importance in settling and advancing the colony. Without the allegiance of Tomo-Chi-Chi, and the influence he exerted over other territory tribes, much blood surely would've been spilled, adding to that which had stained the soil during previous European advances into the region.

The Tomo-Chi-Chi Memorial, a massive granite boulder, stands in the southeast corner of Wright Square. The original

Tomo-Chi-Chi Monument was a pyramid of stone which was placed over his burial site in the center of Wright Square. However, at some point it was decided that Tomo-Chi-Chi's burial place was the best place for William Gordon's monument. Tomo-Chi-Chi's gravesite was bulldozed in the early 1880s and the monument to William Gordon erected in its place.

It is said that Gordon's widow felt bad about the desecration of the Indian Chief's grave and worked with the Colonial Dames of the State of Georgia to obtain a granite boulder from the Stone Mountain Monument Company to memorialize his life and death.

For a man whose cooperation with Oglethorpe and the first settlers of the colony paved the way for the foundation of Savannah (and Georgia) to be laid, you would think he'd be honored with more than a big rock.

John Wesley

The statue of John Wesley can be found in the heart of Reynolds Square, close to where his parish house once stood, and where Wesley held the weekly services of Christ Church. According to Wesley, "The first rise of Methodism was in 1729 when four of us met together at Oxford. The second was at Savannah in 1736 when twenty or thirty persons met at my house."

The statue, sculpted by Marshall Daugherty, was dedicated in 1969, and consists of a rectangular granite pedestal, inscribed on all sides, supporting a bronze statue of John Wesley, who is depicted as a young man attired in his Church of England vestments. In the sculptor's words,

> The monument is as he looks up from his Bible toward his congregation, about to speak and stretching out his right hand in love, invitation and

exhortation. In contrast, the hand holding the Bible is intense and powerful-the point of contact with the Almighty.

Wesley accompanied Oglethorpe on his second voyage to America and served as his secretary. He then served as rector of Christ Church for about two years, after which he and his brother, Charles, returned to England. We'll see later that it was more of an escape back to England.

Casimir Pulaski

This is another man for whom I hold great respect and admiration.

The Casimir Pulaski Monument can be found standing tall in the center of Monterey Square. General Pulaski left his native Poland to come to America to join the revolutionaries in their fight for independence.

On October 11, 1853, a solemn ceremony was conducted as the monument was placed in the square. William Bowen read the following tribute:

> To the memory of Brigadier-General Count Pulaski, who fell mortally wounded by a swivel shot while on a charge at the head of a body of cavalry before the British lines, at the Siege of Savannah, on the ninth day of October seventeen hundred and seventy-nine.
>
> Count Casimir Pulaski was born in the province of Lithuania, Poland, in the seventeen hundred and seventy-seven, and volunteered his service to the American Government in the great and glorious cause of Liberty and Freedom from British tyranny

– received a commission from the Government as Brigadier-General of Cavalry and fought gallantly in the battles of this country at Brandywine, Germantown, Trenton, Charleston, and Savannah. Aged 33.

In his letter to the Pulaski Monument Commission, the designer of the statue, Robert E. Launitz of New York, described the significant aspects of his work:

> It is perceived at the first glance that the monument is intended for a soldier, who is losing his life fighting. Wounded, he falls from his horse, while still grasping his sword . . .The love of liberty brought Pulaski to America; for love of liberty, he fought; and for liberty he lost his life – and thus I thought that liberty should crown his monument and share with him the crown of victory. The garlands surrounding the column show that Liberty is now a young and blooming maiden, surrounded with fragrant flowers.

Nathaniel Greene

On Johnson Square you'll find the Nathanael Greene monument. Brigadier General Nathanael Greene (1742-1786), who was outranked only by George Washington, demonstrated his heroics during the entire span of the American Revolutionary War.

General Greene led revolutionary forces in the Northern Campaign, on the battlefields of Trenton and Princeton in New Jersey, and Brandywine and Germantown in Pennsylvania. As the leader of the Southern Army, he took charge of an outmanned and outgunned group, and methodically wore down the British forces at Eutaw Springs, Guilford Courthouse, Hobkirk's Hill, and Ninety-Six, with surprise, quick-strikes.

Following the war, Greene and his family settled in Mulberry Grove Plantation in Savannah, which was given to him by the state of Georgia as a show of appreciation for his service and sacrifice. He died within a year from heat stroke and was buried in Colonial Park Cemetery. In 1902, his remains, and those of his son, were transferred to Johnson Square and interred at the base of the monument built in his honor. The 50-foot, white marble obelisk, designed by the well-known architect, William Strickland, was completed in 1830.

The original cornerstone was laid at a dedicatory ceremony in Johnson Square on March 21, 1825. The distinguished Marquis de LaFayette, another renowned Revolutionary War General, honored his old friend with these words:

> The great and good man to whose memory we are paying a tribute of respect, affection, and regret, has acted in our revolutionary contest a part so glorious and so important that in the very name of Greene are remembered all the virtues and talents which can illustrate the patriot, the statesman, and the military leader.

William Jasper

In Madison Square is a life-size monument made of bronze, crafted by New York's Alexander Doyle, and dedicated in 1888. The monument depicts the South Carolina born William Jasper, a non-commissioned officer that distinguished himself with singular acts of bravery during the American Revolutionary War.

Sergeant Jasper initially displayed his courage during the Battle of Fort Moultrie on Sullivan's Island when he left a protected position to rescue a South Carolina flag that had been sheared off and lay outside a wall of the fort. As the battle raged during the Siege of Savannah in October 1779, Jasper, in another brazen attempt to plant the South Carolina "colors" (flag) was struck by enemy fire and died at the age of twenty-nine years.

The William Jasper Monument, displayed just a few yards from where he perished, depicts him holding the flag of the Second Regiment of South Carolina Continentals during the conflict. In his right hand he clutches his cavalry sword as he presses his wounded side. To his right lies his bullet-ridden hat.

South Carolina's southern-most county is named after their celebrated hero, as are seven other counties in the nation. In 2018, the 194th Sergeant William Jasper Memorial Ceremony was conducted in Madison Square at the monument site.

Street Memorials

In most towns or cities, you'll find streets named after someone significant in its developmental stage, or who in some way marked or contributed to the identity of the city. Although the squares and monuments in Savannah honor men and women whose contributions were positive in nature, this rule does not hold entirely true in relation to the Lady's thoroughfares. Here are a few city streets whose namesake didn't have the best interests of Savannah at heart:

Reynolds Street. Named after John Reynolds, First Royal Governor in 1754, a self-serving individual who opposed the will of the people.

Lamar Street. Named after Charles Lamar a slave trader who defied Federal law, and operated the slave ship, The Wanderer in 1858.

Gibbons Street. Named after Thomas Gibbons, a corrupt politician of the 1920's and 1930's, and former mayor of Savannah.

Bouhan Street. Named after John Bouhan, a corrupt politician and mob boss who ruled Savannah during the mid-1900's.

Talmadge Avenue. Named after Eugene Talmadge, a four-term governor of Georgia and a White Supremacist.

Houses of Worship

As we continue to walk the streets of the Historic District of Lady Savannah, you can't help but notice the many and varied representations of her religious history.

It is simple logic that the larger the city, the more churches you'll find. The larger the population, the more expressions of religious devotion and worship there will be. Why? It is because what "religion" represents is mankind's inherent desire to understand his origin, his present purpose, and his future destination. It is an issue of mankind's need to *know* and to be *secure*.

For a smaller city, both in land area and population, Savannah boasts some big numbers with regard to her enduring and influential houses of worship. In fact, the history of Savannah, largely, was shaped by the leaders and people that made up the existing churches and synagogues.

Dissimilar to today's common assembly, these were not just places where people showed up on Sunday, engaged in small talk, fulfilled their religious duty, and returned to "real life". Life happened *in* these gathering places. The future of the city was often in the balance, and the stance that their leaders and members assumed, would dramatically influence the outcome.

Purpose and destiny for your and my city can be understood by what has been spoken and pursued by the *faith leadership* within the community. God's people are recipients of *vision* pertaining to God's purpose and intention for our cities.

The following provides some history pertaining to several of the more prominent early assemblies and leaders that exerted profound influence in the formation of Savannah. These assemblies are still in operation today:

Christ Church

Immediately upon laying out the squares for the new colony of Savannah, Oglethorpe set aside a prime trustee lot where the settlers could meet and worship, and where the first church of the colony would be erected. The first congregation met in February 1733 and an Anglican service, in accordance with the Church of England's teachings, was conducted. It was an open-air gathering as the first of the three buildings that would become Christ Church had not yet been built.

From 1736 to 1737, the congregation was under the pastoral oversight of John Wesley, founder of Methodism. Wesley conducted the first Sunday School class ever held in North America at Christ Church. In 1737, Wesley also published the first English hymnal in America, entitled *A Collection of Psalms and Hymns*.

Wesley was succeeded by George Whitfield, the fiery itinerant preacher, who served at Christ Church from 1738 to 1740. Also during that time, Whitfield established the colony's first orphanage, the Bethesda Orphan House, that presently operates as a boy's home and school. Whitfield was a major influential figure in The First Great Awakening that was to sweep through the colonies during the 1740's.

After the original church structure was destroyed in the Great Fire of 1796, and later, the second building was demolished having been found structurally unsound, the third building was raised in 1838. The Greek revival structure was designed by the St. Simons Island planter, James Hamilton Couper, and still stands today on Bull Street, the central thoroughfare of the Historic District.

First African Baptist Church

The Baptist movement is believed to have originated from within the English Separatist movement during the sixteenth to eighteenth centuries when Protestant Christians separated from the Church of England. The First African Baptist Church (FABC) in Savannah is known as the oldest continuous black church in North America and possesses a rich and powerful history.

The seeds of the FABC were planted in 1774 by George Liele, a Virginia born slave who, with the permission of his master, preached to slaves at plantations along the Savannah River. In May 1775, as the black believers united and grew in number, Liele received his ordination to the ministry and organized under the name Frist Colored Church of Savannah.

Among these slave converts was Andrew Bryan. Upon Reverend Liele's exodus from Savannah with the British in 1782, Bryan continued to organize the new believers in the face of intense opposition from both secular and religious authorities. In 1788, the group was officially recognized by Reverend Abraham Marshall, a leader in the Baptist movement in the South, and Bryan was ordained as their first pastor.

In May 1794, the congregation built a permanent structure on land purchased by Rev. Bryan the previous year and named the church Bryan Street African Baptist Church. In 1802, the name was changed to First African Baptist Church, as the growth of membership necessitated the formation of the Second and Third Baptist churches at separate locations. At the time of Bryan's death in 1812, he had seen the FABC grown to over 700 members. By 1831, there were over 2,700 members.

In 1859, FABC, while led by their third pastor, Andrew C. Marshall, secured the land upon which a permanent sanctuary would be built. The church construction was completed in 1859 while under the guidance of its fourth pastor, William J. Campbell, and continues to hold services to this day.

During the Civil War years, the church was a "stop" on the Underground Railroad, which was a network of secret routes and safe houses, used by slaves as a route for escape into free lands. The runaway slaves housed there were hidden in a 4-foot space beneath the floorboards of the sanctuary. Holes were made in the flooring so those hidden would have sufficient air to breath. The breathing holes presently still exist.

About 100 years later, the church continued the tradition of advancing the cause of liberty as it served as a weekly meeting place for blacks and whites involved in the 1960's Civil Rights Movement.

In 1979, Reverend Bryan was the first African-American to be commemorated with a historical marker. The text provides some detail about Reverend Bryan, following his ordination in 1788,

> The Reverend Bryan moved from place to place with his congregation and was even imprisoned and whipped for preaching during a time when whites feared any slave gathering as a focus for rebellion.

He persevered and finally bought his and his family's freedom and purchased this lot for his Church.

Second African Baptist Church

Originally named the Second Colored Baptist Church, the fellowship was founded in 1802 by members of the First African Baptist Church of Savannah. The process was orchestrated by the Savannah River Association, a local organization of Baptist churches that believed forming another local church would further their cause. At the time, the First African Church was 850 members strong, so two-hundred members were syphoned off to form the Second Colored Church. Reverend Bryan was also instrumental in the founding, and the Reverend Henry Cunningham, also a former slave, was installed as the congregation's first minister.

The name was changed to Second African Baptist Church in 1823. The original wood and stone structure was replaced in 1925 by a more refined building that was later destroyed by fire. It was rebuilt and, today, occupies the same ground on which the church was first founded. The original pulpit, prayer benches and choir chairs are still utilized in today's services.

In 1864 the church was graced with the presence of Secretary of War Edwin M. Stanton and General William T. Sherman. It is believed that General Sherman stood on the steps of the humble building and read the Emancipation Proclamation to the people of Savannah, that included the gifts of "40 acres and a mule" to more than 1,000 newly freed slaves. About 100 years following Sherman's departure from the territory, Dr. Martin Luther King, Jr, ascended the pulpit and spoke the words he would later preach during the powerful March on Washington, D.C., in 1963,

> Free at last, free at last, thank God Almighty, we are free at last!

Independent Presbyterian Church

The Independent Presbyterian Church is known as the mother church of Georgia's Presbyterians. The roots of Presbyterianism lie in the Reformation fueled by Martin Luther in the sixteenth century. The congregation in Savannah organized in 1755 and a church was constructed on land deeded to the colony by King George II. His desire was that the people would worship in accordance with the teachings of the Church of Scotland.

The first building was also a casualty of the Great Fire of 1796. A second structure designed and built by John Holden Greene in 1800, and praised for its beauty, also met its demise by fire in 1889. A duplicate of that church building was raised and rededicated in 1891, and still stands to this day.

The interior has been preserved in its original presentation and condition. The marble baptism font that found its way from New Jersey to Savannah, and was unscathed in the Great Fire, remains a fixture amongst today's congregants.

Lutheran Church of the Ascension

In 1734, following on the heels of Oglethorpe, were about 300 immigrants from Salzburg, a territory of the Holy Roman Empire at that time. They were a band of Lutheran believers who refused to recant their protestant beliefs and were expelled from their homeland by Archbishop Leopold Anton von Firminan. They settled along the Savannah River, about 30 miles north of Savannah, in an area they named Ebenezer.

As the population of Savannah increased, so did the efforts of the Salzburgers to nurture and organize Lutheran believers in Savannah. Under their leadership, a church was formed in 1741. The church property on which the present sanctuary is situated, was purchased by the congregation in 1771.

During the Civil War years, the church was utilized as a hospital. The sanctuary pews were used as firewood. The pew cushions were turned into beds for the sick and wounded. The building itself was spared any significant damage, although major interior renovations were performed following the conflict.

As the church continued to grow in both the number of congregants and its identity, it entered an aggressive period of rebuilding and expansion during the 1870's. Part of the remodel included the installation of a beautiful stained-glass window designed by George B. Clarke. The window, positioned above the altar, depicts Christ rising to Heaven with the disciples at his feet. It came to be called the Ascension Window. The people embraced the theme and they became the Evangelical Lutheran Church of the Ascension.

A supporting cast of additional stained-glass windows that present scenes from the life of Christ, and extend from either side of the Ascension Window, were added during the 1930's.

The Cathedral of St. John the Baptist

One of the "must-sees" during a visit to Savannah is this Roman Catholic cathedral that sits on the east side of Lafayette Square. Built in the French Gothic style, its twin spires rise to 214 feet above the Historic District. It is the Mother Church of the

Roman Catholic Diocese of Savannah that was established by Pope Pius IX in July 1850.

In 1799, French Catholic emigres who had fled Haiti during the slave rebellions, organized the first church, and were joined by free blacks from Haiti during the early 1800's. The believers first church, Le Congregation de Saint Jean Baptiste, was built during that time period and stood on Liberty Square. The building of a larger sanctuary on Lafayette Square was later completed and consecrated in 1839.

The construction of the present Cathedral of St. John the Baptist began in 1873 and its dedication took place on April 30, 1876. The twin spires were later added in 1896. Tragedy struck as the church was gutted by fire on February 6, 1898. In response, the congregation rallied and in less than two years celebrated the 1899 Christmas Mass in the restored building. Eighty-one stained-glass windows depicting biblical events were installed in the early 1900's and additional restorations were made as the century progressed.

Wesley Monumental Church

The Wesley Monumental Church pays homage to the Wesley Brothers, John and Charles. John was the driving force behind the birth of the Methodist denomination, while Charles served alongside John and was prolific in his composing of more than five thousand hymns, including the Christmas standard, *Hark! The Herald Angels Sing*.

The church was designed by architects Dixon and Carson in the Gothic Revival style and was completed in 1890. The inspiration was derived from the Nieuwe Kerk, a fifteenth century church in Amsterdam, Holland. Two majestic spires, 136 and 196 feet in height, tower above the main structure. Interior highlights include windows of European stained-glass depicting influential past Methodist leaders. The magnificent "Wesley Window" includes life-sized busts of the Wesley's and faces the pulpit from the rear balcony. At the top of the window is a globe displaying John Wesley's motto, "The world is my Parish."

Savannah's first Methodist Church, Wesley Chapel, was established in 1807 and located at the corner of Lincoln Street and Oglethorpe Avenue. Over the course of time, the congregation purchased a lot on Telfair Square and built the Trinity Church. In 1862, Wesley Chapel joined with Trinity Church.

In 1866, under the leadership of A. M. Wynn, Trinity Church founded a city mission to provide for the spiritual and material welfare of those in need. Two years later, the mission organized into Wesley Church. In 1874, plans were made to build a new church on a lot facing Calhoun Square, that Trinity Church also owned. It would be a monument to John and Charles Wesley. The congregation broke ground in June 1875, and in December, the South Georgia Conference of the United Methodist Church passed a resolution approving the erection of a monument to John Wesley in the form of "a beautiful and commodious edifice" to be called Wesley Monumental Church. Construction was slowed because of difficulties posed by the Reconstruction Era and a devastating Yellow Fever epidemic. It wouldn't be until May 1890 that the sanctuary would be built and dedicated. Since funds were solicited and contributions were received from many areas of the world, it has been said that Wesley Monumental Church belongs to all Methodists.

Saint John's Episcopal Church

The Episcopal beliefs are closely related to Anglican doctrine, which has its roots in the Church of England. Saint John's

Episcopal Church was founded in 1841 by former members of Savannah's, Christ Church, and intended to increase the Episcopalian presence in the region. Its first rector was the first bishop of the Diocese of Georgia, Stephen Elliott. Bishop Elliott was a strong opponent of secession and used his pulpit promote his views.

St. John's first sanctuary was built in 1843. As the congregation grew, Calvin N. Otis of Buffalo, New York, was commissioned to design a new sanctuary which he oversaw the building of between 1852 and 1853. The structure is in the neo-Gothic style and resembles a traditional British parish house. The sanctuary is renowned for the display of intricately created stained-glass windows that depict events from the New Testament.

In December 1864, with his arrival in Savannah, General Sherman completed his March to the Sea. Up to that point, he had fulfilled his proclamation to "make Georgia howl". However, upon discovering that Confederate forces had evacuated Savannah and a "red carpet" was rolled out by Mayor Richard Arnold and his aldermen, he relented and spent the Holidays with his feet up, preparing for his assault on South Carolina.

Immediately upon arrival, Sherman was provided with one of the finest mansions, owned by British cotton merchant Charles Green. On Christmas day, Sherman was in attendance at nearby St. John's Episcopal Church. Bishop Elliott, probably with some degree of validation, relinquished the pulpit to Captain George Pepper of the 80th Ohio Infantry, who preached the sermon that day.

Professor Derek Maxfield of Genesee Community College writes,

> 'Our Military Santa Claus,' as the *Chicago Tribune* dubbed him, enjoy a sumptuous Christmas

dinner at the Green mansion with his staff. After attending church service at St John's Episcopal church near his headquarters, Sherman and his staff attended to army matters until evening when about twenty officers, plus Mr. Green, gathered around the table to enjoy roast turkey, 'a splendid chicken pie, cold slaw, celery, sweet potatoes, turnips, champagne' and many assorted desserts.

Following the war in 1892, the Green mansion was sold to Judge Peter W. Meldrim, and in 1943 was purchased by St. John's Episcopal Church. It is presently utilized as a parish house and is a favorite tourist attraction.

Temple Mickve Israel

Temple Mickve Israel represents the third oldest Jewish congregation in the United Stated. The Gothic-style synagogue is situated on Monterey Square and in 1980 was entered onto the list of the National Register of Historic Places.

The onsite museum includes a display of items pertaining to Jewish culture in Georgia. Of special interest are the temple's original fifteenth century Torah and letters to the congregation from Presidents Washington, Jefferson, and Madison.

Text from the Temple Mickve Israel historical marker reads:

> *The oldest Congregation now practicing Reform Judaism in the United States, Mickve Israel was founded by a group of Jews, mainly of Spanish-Portuguese extraction, which landed at Savannah, July 11, 1733, five months after the establishment of the Colony of Georgia.*

Michael K. Mancha

The Congregation was incorporated in perpetuity by a special Act of the Georgia Legislature on November 20, 1790. After having worshipped in various temporary quarters for almost a century, in 1820 the Congregation built its own Synagogue – the first in Georgia – at the Northeast corner of Liberty and Whitaker Streets. The present Synagogue was consecrated on April 11, 1878.

In 1789 the Congregation received a letter from President George Washington which stated in part: "May the same wonder-working Deity who long since delivering the Hebrews from their Egyptian oppressors, planted them in the promised land – whose providential agency has lately been conspicuous in establishing these United States as an independent nation – still continue to water them with the dews of Heaven and to make the inhabitants of every denomination participate in the temporal and spiritual blessings of that people whose God is Jehovah."

Chapter 14

Symbolism and the City

You may remember these words from the 2006 motion picture, *The Da Vinci Code,* based on the novel of Dan Brown,

> Symbols are a language. They can help us understand our past. Understanding our past determines actively, our ability to understand our present. So, how do we sift truth from belief? How do we write our own histories, personally, or culturally, and thereby define ourselves? How do we penetrate years, centuries of historical distortion to find original truth?

Great questions.

Another question for which we must provide an answer is this: Do I believe there is a destiny, a pre-determined plan and purpose for my city? Whether we do, or do not, the answer lies within the *history* of your and my city. In seeking to discover "original truth" about our cities, the handprints of both God and the Devil will be clearly evident.

Frequently, God can't trust human lips to speak the words that bring recognition and acceptance of His existence among men. So, He orchestrates the building and placement of *things* that announce His presence and purpose. These *things* can also speak of the invisible conflict being waged for the soul of the city!

On display in almost any city, providing clues about the past and present, are more than monuments and memorials, statues and plaques. All cities possess structures such as buildings, bridges, and churches that silently speak of what has effected change among the populace, and what presently defines the city.

You see, the intent of the human crafter of the edifice is one thing; however, to find the deeper, more significant message and meaning, one must seek to understand *God's* intention, His "original truth" concerning the making of the structure. In His providence, what does He desire to communicate to the people? In other words, we must seek to hear the Voice of the past that speaks true understanding to discerning ears in the present, so that our own histories may be written in accordance with God's plan to prosper the individual and the community.

Remember, what is decided in the spirit world will eventually be manifested in the natural realm, whether things that speak of the presence and nature of good or of evil.

I've identified several of these tell-tale structures in Savannah, two of which are considerably instructive at this point in our study. One is quite revealing with respect to what God desires for the Lady. The other betrays the conduct of past generations that have caused stagnation and regression within the city.

Forsyth Park and the Fountain

When standing on Bull Street facing south toward Forsyth Park, one is greeted by an unforgettable and astonishing sight:

The Forsyth Park Fountain. A brick foot path, lined and canopied by tall, Spanish Moss-laden oaks, provides for a reverent approach to the historic landmark. Let's take the walk.

The ground on which Forsyth Park presently sits has played a significant part in the history of Savannah. During the Revolutionary War, the American and French allied forces camped on the land in their failed attempt to halt the advancing British army. The battle, known as the Siege of Savannah, is recorded as one of the bloodiest conflicts of the war.

As Savanah enjoyed more prosperous times during the early nineteenth century, city leaders envisioned the development of a central park that would reflect the prosperity and beauty, as well as the hospitable nature of the city.

On the website ExploreSouthernHistory.com, the chronology of the park and the fountain is detailed,

> The park began in the 1840s when 10 acres were donated for public use by William Hodgson. Using this core of land as a starting point, planners expanded the available acreage to 30 acres with a donation of land from Georgia Governor John Forsyth that tripled the size of the planned park. In 1851, in recognition of his contribution to the future of the city, the park was named in Forsyth's honor.
>
> With the original plan of Savannah as designed by General James Oglethorpe now filled, city leaders dreamed of a park that would expand the city to the south. It would become a center point for residential areas that would radiate out from the beautiful common area.
>
> In keeping with the European style upon which it was based, Forsyth Park was also designed to

magnify the beauty of the city. To this end a magnificent fountain was placed at the north end of the park in 1858.

Why a Fountain?

The Forsyth Park Fountain, is, unarguably, a unique and wondrous work. The fountain is the most photographed object in the city, and that includes the Jim Williams Mansion, and the bench on which Forrest Gump sat while expounding his philosophy on life and lemonade. No one would visit Savannah without spending some time at the park and fountain. But the purpose behind its existence greatly exceeds the simple desire for civic pride.

Again, let's go deeper in a quest to understand, what I believe is the greater significance of the fountain. We must consider the sovereignty and providence of God as involved with the process, and what this fountain would communicate to mankind about His purpose and destiny for Lady Savannah.

The Forsyth Fountain rightly stands in the heart of the Savannah community, with the downtown district lying to the north and a concentrated variety of dwellings on the south, east and west sides. The water of the fountain stems from one source and the outflow is then dispersed in various directions, seemingly arcing toward the four corners of the city.

Why would *water* be the central substance on display in Savannah? It is because it speaks of life! Water is the primary source of refreshment that God created and made available to mankind. As irreverent as it may sound, God did not create Coke or Gatorade. Water is therapeutic to both the inner and outer aspects of our physical being in that it quenches the thirst of our inner body and is a means of cleansing the outer body with its application. Water is a source that sustains life as without it, the human body would die, as would other living creatures that inhabit Earth. Water is an accommodator of life as evidenced by the multitude of sea creatures that inhabit the lakes, rivers, and oceans of the earth.

But how does this relate to God's purpose and destiny for Lady Savannah? You see, it is not by chance that the fountain was placed in the heart of the city, as it is intended to represent and express the One central source of life, that of God. His creativity is to flow out from her citizenry and those drawn to the city in a variety of ways. His life expressed through her gifted people will be refreshing, sustaining, and edifying, to those she encounters. It is worth taking note that Scripture refers to God as "The Fountain of Living Waters." It is the waters of *His life* that are to spring forth from the people, to refresh and revitalize those who encounter Lady Savannah.

As what Lady Savannah has been given by God is in turn freely released for the benefit of others, the life flow will increase, showering even greater prosperity and blessing upon all. However, to the degree that the flow is restricted, will be a corresponding measure of stagnation. Hope will quickly become despair.

Eugene Talmadge Memorial Bridge

This engineering feat of man is a perfect complement to the natural element of the river that it bridges, as both are thoroughfares and support the role that Savannah plays as a major port. The iron and steel structure, completed in March 1991, replaced the earlier Talmadge cantilever truss bridge built in 1953. The present version sits 183 feet above the river, has a main span of eleven-hundred feet, and a total length of 1.9 miles.

The wheels of commerce turn much faster since the building of the original mid-century bridge, and the bigger, better version that followed. But there is another significant aspect of this structure that reaches beyond its role as an accommodator of cars and trucks. The "original truth" is that this bridge exists as a grand gateway through which people would pass as they enter a shining city of refreshment and revitalization. However, the Devil has successfully distorted that fact, leaving its significance shrouded in a fog of controversy.

To understand Eugene Talmadge, is to understand a significant side of Savannah. Talmadge was a local politician who served as the Commissioner of Agriculture and then elected to four terms as Governor of the State of Georgia. His grip on power spanned twenty years, from 1926 to 1946. Talmadge was a firm supporter of State's rights who often thumbed his nose at the attempts by the Federal government to lure Georgia into dependency. He also did much good for the rural farmers of Georgia. However, he is primarily remembered as a strong advocate of white supremacy, and an unswerving, staunch proponent for enactment of the Jim Crow laws that promoted racial segregation and inequality among the former Confederate States in America.

"Jim Crow" was a racist, coined name for a black man. The Jim Crow laws were legislated in the South and founded on the ideology of white supremacy. The South was under the scrutiny and control of the Federal government for its failed coup and the Jim Crow laws were a knee-jerk response to the impositions of Reconstruction. The laws established one set of regulations for whites, and another set for blacks. The economic depression of the late nineteenth century stoked the fears of whites who felt that they may lose their jobs to blacks. Both politicians and the print media fanned these flames by propagating that blacks were a criminal threat to society. The racist sentiment among whites culminated in a Supreme Court decision in 1896 that established the legal *separate but equal* doctrine that would prevail over American society in the south for the next 50 plus years.

It wasn't until May 17, 1954, when the nine Supreme Court Justices announced their unanimous decision in the case, Brown v. Board of Education, that a major change was effected. They held that racial segregation of children in public schools, even in schools of equal quality, hurt minority children. "Separate educational facilities are inherently unequal" was their conclusion. This was a violation of the Constitution's 14th Amendment, and their order put into motion the desegregation of public schools.

For a governor to preside over a state embroiled in the controversy of the equal rights of race, and to staunchly support inequality, it goes without saying that Eugene Talmadge was a divisive force among the rank and file of Georgia, as well as the southeast region of America.

Present-Day Controversy

An article written by Sean Horgan in February 2013 entitled *New Bridge Name on Horizon* and printed in the Savannah Morning News is rather enlightening. Horgan wrote,

> Today, the sail-like, cable-stayed bridge that serves as an iconic backdrop to Savannah and a dramatic low country portal into Georgia is named the Eugene Talmadge Memorial Bridge.
>
> That might not be the case much longer.
>
> The debate over the bridge's name has raged for nearly a quarter-century. It has involved polarizing public figures, political subterfuge, confusion,

simmering undercurrents of race and issues of local rule.

At its essence, the debate concerns the relatively simple task of naming a bridge. This task, however, has been anything but simple.

The debate has included elements of self-determinism, with many Savannahians believing political forces elsewhere in the state imposed the Talmadge name on the bridge without any regard for the preferences of the local citizenry…It has involved the city's grasp of history, with many here making the case that a structure so tied to the international image of the city should bear a name that reflects the city's colonial past.

Finally, for many, the debate has included a redemptive quality entwined in a belief that one of the city's most iconic structures should cease to memorialize the bitter angels of the Jim Crow past that sat squarely on the shoulders of the race-baiting, white supremacist who was Eugene Talmadge.

The article goes on to detail more of the 2013 debate among both elected politicians and the general citizenry of Savannah about why the bridge should be renamed, and suggestions for the new name. The offerings focused, primarily, on honoring James Oglethorpe, while some suggested the more general names of The Savannah Bridge, or the Savannah River Bridge. The hope was that the change could be made quickly and that the issue would be settled, once and for all.

However, this wasn't the case. Confusion marred the process, so city elders tabled the issue and move on to other business.

With the resurgence of racial tension in America over the past several years (fueled during the administration of former President Barack Obama, and the continual stirring of this bubbling cauldron by the nation's mainstream media), there have been rancorous debates throughout America's cities over what is, and what is not acceptable to be displayed in public forums relative to certain historical events. This has included violent protests, centering, primarily, on issues of race equality. Sadly, the result has been the destruction and removal of statues and monuments that speak of what has contributed to the soul of the city. We cannot "sanitize" our past. We can learn from our misdeeds, but nothing is gained when we ignore them.

This prompted the presiding city elders of Savannah in 2018 to renew the discussion of what is to be done with the Talmadge Bridge problem. Then presiding Mayor Eddie De-Loach and the City Council conducted meetings to discuss the issue. However, confusion and controversy continued to dominate the process. The meetings amounted to another trip around the mountain and, once again, nothing was resolved.

Futile Efforts

The idea that changing the name could remedy the problem is devoid of any real substance or power. This is another prime example of how mankind's assessment of an issue is based on what is seen on the surface, the exterior, and not the deeper, underlying cause, invisible to the human eye, and indiscernible by human intellect.

You see, nothing will be resolved by focusing on the *external* elements of the problem. The issue requires a response by the body of leadership and common citizens whose hearts have been enlightened and empowered by Truth. Only then can a society of people become armed and dangerous and confront the unseen, *internal* dark forces that keep their city bound.

Savannah's basic problem, and I'm sure your city's as well, is the people's lack of knowledge that spirit entities bent on their destruction have influenced the human decision-making that has shaped society. What is needed is the enlightenment to understand that the city, by invitation, has been infiltrated by dark powers that hold the populace in their grip and keep the city from realizing her true destiny.

The Connection

It is important to note the relationship between these two major Savannah landmarks. The irony lies in that a gateway bridge, purposed to accommodate the entrance of people into Savannah, a city intended to immerse people in her fountain of living waters, has become a symbol of an entrenched ideology which, at its core, is bent on the suppression and captivity of that life! And we shall see how the bridge represents what still prevails within the confines of her society to this very day.

So, the question begs asking: Why the stalemate? Why the continuing deadlock? I believe it is the inability to recognize the origin of the problem, and what is required to effect change. But before we journey farther into the spirit realm, let's continue to identify aspects of God's intended purpose for Lady Savannah.

Chapter 15

A City of Great Importance

Strategic Placement of Your City

A good storyteller will first tell you a little about where the story will unfold. As we touched on earlier, the geographic location of your city or town in relation to other societies of people, is not a random occurrence. If the city is an object of destiny, then her geographic situation is strategic and has a distinct bearing on her intended purpose.

Let's look again at Oglethorpe's journal entry of February 10, 1733,

> I went myself to view the Savannah River. I fixed upon a healthy situation about ten miles from the sea. The river there forms a half moon, along the South side of which the banks are almost 40 foot high and upon the top a flat which they call a bluff… Ships that draw twelve foot water can ride within ten

yards of the bank. Upon the riverside in the center of this plain, I have laid out the town.

The words, "I went myself," speak of his wisdom to seek out the location for the new colony away from, what I am sure would have been conflicting opinions of both those who had sailed with him, and those who received him upon arrival. Surely, his sensitivity to God's direction and His confirmation of the "chosen place" was much more acute away from the din of human opinion. God's Spirit was directing the path of this man for very specific reasons.

As Oglethorpe surveyed the possible site for the Georgia colony, his intent was to find a section of land that not only possessed elements that would serve as a natural defense from enemy advances, but, just as importantly, would be a natural channel through which goods and supplies, and, especially, people could flow. Oglethorpe knew what was brought into Savannah would influence what would be carried out of Savannah, and would have profound influence on the region, the nation, and the world.

Lady Savannah is foremost known for being a port city. This broad aspect of her identity has both natural and spiritual implications in God's long-term plan. Understanding the concept behind the word "port" helps us to grasp God's intended destiny for Savannah.

Port, the Latin root meaning is to carry, and is closely associated with the word *gate*. Savannah, then, is a port city or a gateway city.

The derived word *import* has a double meaning in that it implies the action (verb) of carrying in or bringing in, as well as something (noun) of great significance, expressed by the word *importance*.

Another derivative of port is the word *export*. This involves the action of carrying or sending out, or to cause the spread of in another part of the world.

The significance of Savannah's development would initially be determined by what was carried in (imported), and the ongoing spread of her influence among others would be a result of what was carried out (exported).

The Business of Savannah

When I first crossed the southern border of South Carolina and entered the state of Georgia, it involved driving over the Savannah River by way of the massive Eugene Talmadge Memorial Bridge, the major northern gateway to the city. At midpoint of the traverse, I immediately understood what Savannah is primarily about: commerce and enterprise.

Covering the land to the immediate west of the bridge, and protruding at various points onto the river, are a network of warehouses, docks and massive cranes that accommodate the continuous parade of giant container ships arriving from or bound for other distant ports.

Over the past two decades, the Savannah port has accommodated ships that usually carry between 4,000 and 5,000 truck-size containers that measure 20' x 8.5' x 8.5', referred to as TEUs (twenty equivalent units). That is a considerable load. However, just a few days prior to the writing of these very words, my wife witnessed history as she stood in one of the shops that line River Street and watched a 10,000 TEU vessel, the Zim Tianjin, as it cruised by other spellbound observers. This is the length of four football fields, 150 feet in width, and if stood on one end (which isn't likely), would reach nearly as high as the Empire State Building.

With a population of about 147,000 people, in 2018, Savannah was ranked as the #4 container port in the United States, trailing only New York, Los Angeles, and Long Beach.

The growth of Savannah as a port city is not a recent phenomenon of the twentieth or twenty-first centuries. In fact, prior to the onset of the Revolutionary War, Savannah was the source of a plentiful flow of exported commodities. Following on the heels of the conflict was Eli Whitney who spear-headed an economic revolution with his invention of the cotton gin. Interestingly, Whitney developed the device while on land presently owned by the Georgia Ports Authority. The cotton gin immediately catapulted Georgia into a top exporter of cotton.

The Maritime Heritage website reflects,

> By the early 1800's Savannah had earned a reputation as "King Cotton Port of the World." In 1794, Savannah with a population of 2,500, exported less than $500,000 worth of goods. Twenty-five years later it was the sixteenth-largest city in the young nation with exports of more than $14 million. In 1855, exports from the Port of Savannah to all foreign destinations totaled more than $20 million, with cotton representing 89 percent of the total. Although Georgia's export activity waned during the five years of the Civil War, production increased shortly after the conflict ended in 1865. By the late 1870's, cotton production in the South had regained its pre-Civil War status and Savannah was the leading cotton exporter once more.

Although there has been a historical pattern of waxing and waning of the commercial prosperity within Savannah; eventually, she always seemed to find her feet. Today, as in stilettos, she stands tall among the world's competitors as a gateway for the inflow and outflow of material goods.

So, in addition to these commodities, what has been produced in Savannah that has been carried out to other parts of the state, nation, and world?

Savannah Influence

From the founding of Savannah, immigrants from various nations and continents poured into the new world through this gateway, eager to discover, develop, and employ their skills and talents in their quest for a better life. Over time, these continuous contributions of her citizens gave expression to the unique features of the city and modeled what other communities strived to become. As this influence rippled out, it became evident that God's intention for Lady Savannah was to be a *trendsetter* and *pacesetter* for the region and the nation.

Countering this plan was the Devil, whose goal was to mark the Lady with his personality so that a greater area of land and populace would be adversely affected. The Devil has always been aware of God's intent for Savannah to have a far-reaching, powerful influence.

William Jay, the brilliant young English architect who arrived in Savannah in 1817 and during the ensuing years built The Owens-Thomas House, the William Scarbrough House, the Alexander Telfair House, and the Bulloch House, was witness to the unrest within the soul of the city. Disillusioned and disenchanted over the changing fortunes of the Lady, he wrote these words, prior to this return to England in 1822,

> Savannah had become a Niobe of cities, a chaos of ruins. Who can trace the void without remembering

her former greatness? She was a rising model; she has fallen as a monument.

However, again, the Lady would prove herself resilient. Despite being under the control and tight watch of a small circle of self-absorbed political and commercial personalities, the soul of Savannah would survive, and continue to exert influence far beyond the grip of her powerbrokers.

An Eccentric Lady

The Conde Nast Traveler Readers' Choice Awards are the longest-running and most prestigious recognition of excellence in the travel industry. In October 2019, Lady Savannah was voted the fourth best "small city" in the country by Conde Nast readers, and has consistently rated among the top 10 over the past decade.

Annually, Savannah plays hostess to approximately fourteen million visitors, drawn to her soil by her purported mystique and charm. The tourist element fuels the engine by which Lady Savannah is sustained financially and continues to shape and influence people and lands far beyond her borders.

Again, we see that Savannah's imports and exports are not limited to commodities but also include people. The ongoing inflow and outflow of these millions that pass through the gateway every year, become touched by the city in one way or another. Her citizens have the opportunity to impact multiple millions each year without ever having to leave their native soil. And those she touches carry back home some mark upon their lives and, inevitably, influence others.

What do these people encounter while moving within the atmosphere that pervades Lady Savannah? Is she fulfilling her intended purpose? What aspects of God's character or nature are on display? And what aspects of the Evil One are perceived?

A city takes on a kind of personality that reflects the sum of its parts; and in this case, the "parts" are its *citizens*. In addition to her apparent class, charm, and elegance, Savannah is well-noted for her unconventionality, or, more plainly put, she's weird. And this bizarre side of the city is clearly reflected by certain home-spun, resident fixtures you will certainly encounter if you spend any significant time among her people. It's as if a schizophrenic side of Savannah is embodied in these characters and betrayed by a kind of carnival side-show peculiarity.

John Berendt recognized several of these personages during his visits and subsequent period of residency in Savannah. In his blockbuster expose', *Midnight in the Garden of Good and Evil*, he attributed this "tilted" aspect of the city to the following:

> For me, Savannah's resistance to change was its saving grace. The city looked inward, sealed off from the noises and distractions of the world at large. It grew inward, too, and in such a way that its people flourished like hothouse plants tended by an indulgent gardener. The ordinary became the extraordinary. Eccentrics thrived. Every nuance and quirk of personality achieved greater brilliance in that lush enclosure than would have been possible anywhere else in the world.

I concur with Berendt's depiction of individual and corporate eccentricity. With the history of Savannah spanning almost three-hundred years, these people come and go, including the recently deceased Lady Chablis, aka The Grand

Empress of Savannah, who had strutted her/his "stuff" at a downtown cabaret since 1988. While most of the unique characters introduced in "The Book" (the locals name for Berendt's *Midnight*) have passed on, they have certainly left an indelible impression, perhaps, a mantle, that has come to rest on still more victims of this cultural dynamic. Over time the names change but the anomalous, bizarre spirit about them seems immutable. Here are a few that I have encountered while a Savannah citizen:

There's Mr. Willie, an instrumentalist whose guitar playing was an integral part of several local bands. There's one catch, however: his guitar was missing strings; all six of them. But even that's debatable. You see, Mr. Willie stood with other band members and played his "axe" with such passion and zeal that his "music" was heard and defined by the stimulated imaginations of all those present. This well-loved Savannah legend died in 2014 at the age of sixty and will be missed.

And Oji Lukata, the black, ageless basket weaver of River Street, and weaver of local folklore, demonstrating his giftedness with hands and tongue to curious tourists from nine in the morning until, sometimes, two or three the next morning.

Then there's The Walking Woman, who of advanced age, continues to defy physical law. She lives on Skidaway Island and can be seen seven days a week, come heavy rain or baking shine, rabidly walking the eight-mile stretch to and from the south side of Savannah.

And then there's Diana. Wow, she's a throwback to the early twentieth century, with the appearance of an aging "flapper", she tickles the ivory o' so sweetly and knows how to belt out a song. Catch her weekends at Vic's on the River.

Lastly, Zulu the Rastafarian. Humanist, truth seeker, servant of mankind, survivor of incessant near-death experiences, a loose liver who believes "we are all alone" in this life, underscoring the need to pursue human relationship.

While Berendt's assessment is accurate, and the contributions of many of the "eccentrics" positive, I see the dynamic at work in the city that produces these characters, as generally destructive. Rather than "an indulgent gardener", as Berendt wrote, I would use the description, an intoxicated gardener. And I would identify the various "gardeners" as the city elders who have greatly influenced what kind of fruit the city has borne over the course of time. You'll see why as you read on.

The Law of Stagnation

Berendt may have accurately concluded that Savannah's isolation and resistance to outside influences have served to preserve and enhance the personality of both city and citizenry. Although she may excel in her eccentricity, a city designed to accommodate an uninterrupted flow of vitality will not thrive in the ways she was intended. In fact, something quite the contrary will take place.

Harold Wilson, former Prime Minister of the United Kingdom said, "He who rejects change is the architect of decay. The only human institution which rejects progress is the cemetery." So true. To grow into one's potential and destiny involves the continual process of *change*. Growth is change. It is forward, upward motion. To resist change is to halt and suspend the process of life, to stagnate. And stagnation is a breeding ground for destructive elements, an introduction to a slow death.

Let's apply the stagnation principle to the city of Savannah. The word *stagnation* comes from the Latin, *stagnatum*, meaning standing water. My contention is that the flow of life and creativity intended to mark Savannah has been stalled and contained, primarily, by certain individuals in positions of authority. In so doing, the Spirit of God has been disallowed from guiding the process that would lead to the prosperity of the city. Instead, criteria have been imposed that only allows for what serves to increase the material wealth and social status of a privileged few. This self-serving, devilish philosophy and activity has been perpetuated in Savannah ever since the tenets of the Oglethorpe Vision were discarded by the powermongers of his day. And what it has bred is not very pretty.

Nothing has *changed* over time. They are the same demonic entities that deceived the first generation of Savannahians that continue to hold the present generation of citizens in their grip. The cast of human characters are different, but not the spirit participants. And, as we have seen, with the life flow having stagnated, the result has been perverted and malformed representations of what could have been the city's highest good.

Also, it is common knowledge that stagnant water is the perfect environment for bacteria and parasites to thrive. An interesting side-note is that the rash of deadly Yellow Fever epidemics that plagued Savannah between 1820 and 1876, were attributed to mosquitoes that bred in still pools of water that had accumulated throughout the city. Perhaps, this was a visible, physical manifestation and representation of an invisible, spiritual malady.

In addition to mosquitoes, there is another insect that thrives where the life process has ceased. The fly.

Lord of the Flies

Among the memorable, dysfunctional characters portrayed in Berendt's book, was one that I found of unique interest. You'll remember him as "the guy with the flies". His name was

Luther. Of interest was Luther's gravitation toward the insect, and the insect toward Luther. He didn't seem to have any objection to them buzzing about, so much so that he secured them to his body with fine lines to assure they would not stray. I don't know about you, but when a fly invades my picnic and performs a touch-and-go on something I'm about to eat, the food finds the garbage can. You never know where the fly was hanging out prior to its encroachment on your lunch.

The ancient Israelites termed the pagan god of their arch enemy, the Philistines, as *Baal Zebub*. The words literally mean Lord of the Fly (although Hebrew uses a singular form where in English a plural would be proper: Lord of the Flies). When Jesus walked the earth, he referred to the Devil with a form of the name, *Beelzebub*, the equivalent of the Hebrew. In effect, both the Hebrew and the Aramaic words mean the same.

Why was the Devil likened to a fly?

A fly is drawn to an environment where the life process in organic matter has ceased. Flies, by nature, exploit the lifeless and thrive in that environment.

Recently, my wife and I took a four-day getaway to a mountain community known as Big Bear Lake. Prior to leaving, we had been periodically visited by three cats who would show-up at random times, usually during the night hours while we slept. True to her maternal instinct, Elizabeth left a plate of canned tuna on our enclosed patio. Upon our return, she eagerly checked the porch, expecting to see a clean plate. I recall her immediate retreat into the house, and the one word that accompanied her scream, "MAGGOTS!" I reluctantly ventured outside and saw not only was the plate swarming with the creepy things and a host of dive-bombing flies, but they were throughout the patio surface and nestled into the carpet that covered most of the floor. For the next three hours, the extermination process included disposing of the carpet and power-washing the patio floor, walls, and furniture.

What had happened was the tuna, saturated in its natural oil, fell victim to the decaying process. After a while, the unrefrigerated tuna attracted, and was inhabited by flies. The infestation included the laying of eggs, that, in turn, became maggots, that, without our intervention, would've become more flies.

God is light and life. When a man or woman rejects the brilliance of His presence, intended to illuminate the soul, he or she is choosing to remain in the darkness of ignorance. When a man or woman rejects the life of God, he or she, is choosing to remain in a state of death. The potential for regeneration of the spirit, and renewal and restoration of the soul is abated, and the individual stays bound in a darkened, dormant state, void of God's life.

Like a fly, the Devil is drawn to the above human conditions. Like a fly, he's drawn to the environment, and thrives where life and change have ceased. This vulnerable condition is a place, "ripe" for him to inhabit.

In practical terms, when any person cuts himself off from constructive personal relationships, involvements and activities, the combination of being *idle* and *alone*, is a breeding ground for the presence and works of darkness. The person who has become inactive, lazy, and lethargic about their personal development, will fall prey to many temptations and potential evils. The adage is true: "Idle hands are the Devil's workshop."

The State of Chaos

Flies speak to another condition that exists when they have found a suitable environment in which to prey: *chaos,* the state of complete disorder and confusion.

Referring back to that decomposing tuna, do flies conduct themselves with any hint of notice or regard of their fellow fly? Do they line up and take turns? I don't think so. It is every bug for itself. The swarming that takes place is like one-thousand panic-stricken passengers on a rapidly sinking ship, trying to board a life raft that will accommodate only ten. Or, perhaps a hockey match where there is no teamwork or designated positions, only individual players trying to score and simultaneously defend the goal. It is disorder and confusion in raw form.

Once again, this aspect of the behavior of the insect applies to the nature and activity of evil.

The following Scripture found in the writing of James (3:15), contrasts the condition of the person void of God's life and subject to the influence of evil, with that of the individual who is the recipient of God's divine wisdom:

> Such "wisdom" does not come down from Heaven but is earthly, unspiritual, demonic. For where you have envy and selfish ambition, there you find disorder and every evil practice. But the wisdom that comes from Heaven is first of all pure; then peace-loving, considerate, submissive, full of mercy and good fruit, impartial and sincere.

This passage identifies what occurs when one embraces and conducts their life solely by the dictates of natural, human understanding, absent of divine wisdom. Because human nature is self-centered at its core, there exists an inherent confusion and a breeding ground for all things evil.

Where there is confusion and chaos, there you will find the presence of the demonic. It is interesting that in the New Testament book of Revelation, Satan is described as an "enormous red dragon" whose "tail swept a third of the stars out of the sky and flung them to the earth." This describes the Devil's attempt to disrupt the order of Heaven while leading the rebellion against the Most High, resulting in the expulsion of 1/3 of the angelic hosts.

In direct contrast is the atmosphere and activity that exists when God is present, where His Spirit has been invited and is free to rule and reign. Where God is, there you will find goodness and mercy. His presence brings a permeating peace, for He *is* peace. The atmosphere of heaven is one of peace, and within that kingdom there is order, cooperation and a presiding authority to maintain justice.

However, this atmosphere of disorder within the ranks of evil does not mean that there does not exist a structured hierarchy. The fact that Satan is referred to as "Lord, of the Flies", implies his position as chief of the demons.

Although there is an apparent authority power structure among demonic forces, their inherent evil nature would indicate a co-existing, continuous state of anarchy and mayhem within their domain. In the same way that the Italian Mafia maintains a pecking order, it still doesn't keep those within the structure from eliminating one another when given the opportunity. The bond exists only because of the mutual, intrinsic drive to "steal, kill and destroy." Harmony and brotherly love do not exist among the ranks of evil, nor among the people that have come under its sinister influence.

This is the goal of the Devil, the enemy of God and mankind. The method of this prince of darkness is to trick and deceive the human into believing his lies, so that the man or woman remains in an isolated, perpetual state of darkness and death.

If an individual is to prosper and blossom with the beauty of God's intended identity and purpose, then the vital flow of

God's life must be accommodated and encouraged. So, it is true of your city and mine. For Lady Savannah to experience all that God has in store, the citizens and city leaders must welcome God's presence and yield to His wisdom. This is just as true now as it was in her initial years of existence.

Chapter 16

A Haunted Lady

The City Built on its Dead

We do not know the source of this coined name for Savannah; however, why she was given the name is not a mystery.

For a city that was originally (and still is) intended to stand strong in the defense of her people as well as other communities, she has often been subdued by her enemies, human and inhuman. The blood of her citizens, and that of domestic and foreign armies, has saturated her soil and has left an indelible stain on her soul.

It is a fact that so many have died in Savannah due to turbulent weather, the ravages of disease, and the violence of war that there has not been sufficient room to accommodate the bodies.

Located within the Historic District is Colonial Park Cemetery, formerly known as the Old Brick Graveyard. The rusted, discolored iron fencing that stretches for a block along Abercorn Street, the west side boundary of the property, betrays a long, difficult history. This ground had served as the main public cemetery from 1750 to 1853. It was the final resting place of many Revolutionary War soldiers as well as victims of the deadly Yellow Fever that periodically plagued the city during the nineteenth century. Over ten-thousand bodies were believed to have been buried in the six acres, but only 557 gravestones and markers have stood the test of time. The cemetery is believed to have originally taken up considerably more area then the six acres, but the urban expansion over the years has encroached the boundaries of the sacred ground. In fact, sometime in the 1960's, while construction was being conducted on Abercorn Street, the workers' began unearthing human remains.

If General Sherman had not relented in his determination to level the city during his March to the Sea, much more of the dead would occupy Savannah soil. I believe that the decision by the Union Army to spare the Lady was a sovereign act of God's mercy on the people, and His means of honoring those who sowed righteous seed over the preceding years. Later, we'll look further into the external evidences of the ebb and flow of spiritual battle that have marked Savannah over time.

The existing cemeteries and graveyards, both in the Historic District, and in more outlying areas of the city, are brimming not only with victims of war and disease, but the dead stemming from weather-related events and devastating fires. There are many controversial aspects of Savannah's history, but the fact that she has played hostess to tragedy and death is not one of them.

Reputedly Haunted

In addition to being rich in American history and the birthplace of many celebrated heroes, heroines, and villains, the city bears other features for which fourteen million tourists make their vacation reservations every year. Probably, the most renowned aspect of her reputation is reflected in her title as The Most Haunted City in America. And for that reason, tourists flock to the city to get a glimpse of the dark side. We shall see that it is not something to boast about.

In her groundbreaking book, *Savannah Spectres*, published in 1984, Margaret Debolt was first to chronicle past events and experiences of people who have occupied or visited, in her words, "antebellum estates, house museums, long-conquered forts, and restored townhomes", and their apparent encounters with the supernatural.

Since Debolt's work, the shelves of the local Barnes and Noble and numerous gift shops throughout Savannah are lined with books that spin the tales of various spook houses within the Historic District, including the Hampton Lillibridge House, The Olde Pink House, the Davenport House, the Kehoe House, the Lucas Theater, the River Street Inn, the Mulberry Inn, and the Pirates House Restaurant. These just scratch the surface.

As you walk through these beautifully restored structures, you find yourself immersed in the aura of what went before. You sense they consist of more than brick and mortar and, perhaps, are endued with aspects of the human souls they sheltered over time. And as you hear or read the stories about their lives, you find that many shared a common experience: tragedy.

Author Mary Allice Kellogg, posed the fundamental question, as well as an answer,

> Are there really ghosts in the South? You bet your sweet magnolia there are! The antebellum South isn't dead – it's merely wandering, rising, hovering and drifting from plantation to plantation, searching for

lost loves and old enemies. And in the process, it's scaring the bejesus out of a lot of normally sensible folk.

Whether you do, or do not believe in ghosts or hauntings, one thing is for certain: something significant has captured the attention of locals, tourists, and the swelling ranks of both amateur and professional ghost-hunters. Let's see if we can identify what has caused such a stir among these masses of humanity.

Ghost Tours

Presently, more than twenty ghost tour companies do business in Savannah. While the majority of start-up businesses find themselves belly-up within two or three years, these ghost tour operations are apparently thriving, with new additions each year. Most of the more popular paranormal-based television shows have visited Savannah and produced specials focused on the local haunts.

Among Savannah's multitude of tourists are visitors from every part of North America, as well as every other continent on Earth. These eager people spend their money in Savannah, often while participating in one of the many ghost tour companies that spin their tales, comprised of a mixture of fiction, embellishment and cold fact. These unsuspecting patrons carry the stories home to share with others…and Savannah is the source from which this tide of information flows.

This can't be Lady Savannah's offering to the world, can it?

These are a few of the more prominent ghost tours in Savannah and excerpts from their marketing brochures and website text.

Blue Orb's Zombies Tour focuses on "the spiritual viewpoints of the large Conjuring (Hoodoo, Voodoo) communities we have in Savannah, Georgia...we wrote the book (literally) on hags, shadow people and conjuring in Savannah."

Savannah Ghost Walks features a Dark Crimes Walk that invites visitors to "Follow Historic Savannah's Grisly Walking Trail of Murder and Mayhem...in the most chilling tour ever conducted in Savannah. Enter a time when Violent Corruption and Dark Crime was the City's Calling Card. Adults Only."

6th Sense Savannah offers to "take you up-close with first-hand encounters of disembodied spirits, Ouija board sessions gone awry, poltergeists in plethora, shadow people." With regard to the Bonaventure Cemetery Tour, they advertise it is "a great point of pride that we became the first company to offer daily cemetery tours in Bonaventure; to share her secrets and serenity with visitors from all over the world!"

Six Feet Under Savannah offers a tour "led by an actual psychic and paranormal sensitive. Learn how to work with paranormal seeking equipment and tune into your inner gifts to attract and sense the supernatural beings around you . . . Learn about the haunts and history of prominent downtown Savannah only to realize that you are surrounded by spirits with every step."

Tara Haunted Tours promises "to keep goosebumps on your arms as you explore dimly-lit streets and hear scary ghost stories of creepy encounters that took place in the very areas you'll be standing." They also promote the Hearse Ghost Tour where "the participants ride in real Hearses that were in service for more than 15 years with actual funeral parlors."

Ghost & Gravestones Frightseeing Tour declares "The evening hours are upon you. Unseen spirits stroll among the living in the streets and squares of Savannah – America's Most Haunted City!" They include "a stop at the site of the Gribble House, the scene of a triple murder in 1909."

Shannon Scott Tours, author, storyteller, and pioneer of many of the city's specialty tours, Scott states the following regarding his guided excursion of Colonial Park Cemetery, "It's full of mass graves . . . the last public executions on this street were in the early twentieth century, 1911, in fact . . . the living wouldn't take them, the dead won't take them, the afterlife won't accept them, they're like an earth-bounder wandering in an in-between world."

I don't doubt that these tour operators have tapped in on something that is real, something that exists and emanates from the spirit world. However, my contention lies in the identification of the *presence* and the *nature* of the source from which this power emanates.

In reading the foregoing marketing texts, one can't help but sense a *boast* that these entities may exist within the city limits, and a degree of *pride* in this being the identity of their city.

It is common opinion that accounts of events that have taken place in Savannah have become exaggerated, and in some cases, completely fabricated for the sake of promoting the ghost tours. James Caskey, in his second book on the subject, *Haunted Savannah: America's Most Spectral City*, took strides to get the trolleys back on track. He relates that in his comprehensive research of the local happenings, he discovered that "Not only was this twisted history more interesting than the stories being made up by unprincipled guides, it had the benefit of being absolutely true!"

Whether these tour operators are genuine seekers of spirit realities, or if their motivation is for financial gain, is inconsequential to me. Either way, I contend that they have encountered something real, but have fallen victim to deception, bred of ignorance.

There is a distinct veil that shrouds the minds of the locals in these ventures because of their involvement in these supposed hauntings. Whether knowingly or unknowingly, their promotion of this foremost feature of the city has only served to increase the influence and control of these spirit entities among the populace. Instead of gaining understanding and enlightenment, they have fallen prey to a demonic strategy that only intensifies the darkness that blankets the city.

Curiosity and Desperation

The various Savannah ghost tours are, primarily, an exploitation of this natural curiosity, as well as a morbid fascination that human beings have with the spirit world. It is an intrigue, that often results in spirit *attachments* to the seeker, and a dependency on occult arts and practices. The idea that an unseen realm may exist, populated by spirit entities, whether benevolent or wicked, is often bait that is too inviting to not bite.

In addition to the curiosity seekers are the gullible and desperate; individuals who are eager to believe a loved one can be contacted following their passing. It may be because of remorse or guilt over something said or done, or the chance to say a final goodbye, that renders the individual vulnerable to the idea that the veil beyond death can be penetrated. To have some nugget of proof that there is a hereafter, that the spirits of the dead are still within reach, is a life ring thrown to people drowning in a sea of regret or sorrow. This is one of the main explanations for why the ghost tour industry thrives.

Now we'll take a closer look at the idea of the paranormal.

Chapter 17

The Paranormal

Science can be defined as the intellectual and practical activity involving the systematic study of the structure and behavior of the physical and natural world through evaluation and experiment.

Earlier, we mentioned that science in practice, does not incorporate the idea of *spirit*. Generally, this is true. However, there is one stark exception when the scientist is inclined to bend the rules. That is in his pursuit to explain the *paranormal*. The word has come to be defined as events or phenomena that are beyond the scope of *normal* scientific understanding.

Traditional science does well in evaluating and explaining the make-up of the physical earth and the process of natural life, but completely rejects the idea of a Maker of the earth who is spirit. If one begins their analysis with the physical and attempts to process the idea of spirit, an exercise of frustration is guaranteed. Paranormalists find themselves in this quandary. But if one begins their journey toward understanding with spirit as the origin from which all things exist, then one has hope for real discovery.

Terence Hines, professor of neurology at Pace University and adjunct professor at the New York Medical College, in his book *Pseudoscience and the Paranormal* wrote,

> The paranormal can best be thought of as a subset of pseudoscience. What sets the paranormal apart from other pseudosciences is a reliance on explanations for alleged phenomena that are well outside the bounds of established science. Thus, paranormal phenomena include extrasensory perception (ESP), telekinesis, ghosts, poltergeists, life after death, reincarnation, faith healing, human auras, and so forth. The explanations for these allied phenomena are phrased in vague terms of 'psychic forces', 'human energy fields', and so on.

And what is pseudoscience? According to Wikipedia.com,

> Pseudoscience is a claim, belief, or practice presented as scientific, but which does not adhere to the scientific method. A field, practice, or body of knowledge can reasonably be called pseudoscientific when it is presented as consistent with the norms of scientific research, but it demonstrably fails to meet these norms.

So, if my understanding is correct, the study of the paranormal is the frustrated and futile attempts by natural or physical scientists to understand and explain certain phenomena that falls "well outside the bounds of established science", using established "scientific method" and "norms."

The lesson to be learned is that the litmus tests of mankind's science are simply inadequate when it comes to evaluating and understanding the supernatural.

Speculation, Opinion, and Theory

Among the ranks of those that seek knowledge of the supernatural are psychics, parapsychologists, spiritists, occultists, and ghost-hunters. There is very little agreement among these devotees as to what actually is taking place. On the contrary, there is no shortage of speculation, opinion, and theory put forth. Alice's pronouncement of Wonderland as "curious and curiouser" seems fitting for these seekers of hidden knowledge.

James Caskey in *Haunted Savannah, America's Most Spectral City*, details two of the more prominent explanations for "hauntings". The first we'll call the Dry Charge Theory. He states,

> Houses can possibly store a 'dry charge' of the energy expended in the structure, much like a battery stores electrical power. This energy could be bound to the property by moments of extreme emotional distress, such as death or great sadness. Caskey gives the example of sound waves: energy is released in audible form, and when the conditions allow, such as an object bouncing the sound waves back toward the point of origin, the energy returns in the form of an echo. He asks, If energy can return in this way several seconds after the actual event, why can't psychic energy return at a later time as well, sometimes years, decades or even centuries after the fact?

Caskey also offers an alternative option that we'll call the Port City Theory. He states,

> Many old port cities have a reputation for being haunted. Seaports (particularly in the American Deep South) like Charleston, Savannah, Wilmington, and

New Orleans have garnered the reputation of having many supernatural occurrences. Perhaps it is tied in with the close proximity to the water – if ghosts are life-force energy that has not faded away, then maybe the tidal ebb and flow has somehow polarized the entire area, preserving the remaining energy and capturing it for a time when conditions are right.

I can't help but notice sprinkled throughout these proposed explanations of paranormal activity, words like "possibly", "could be", "if", "perhaps", "maybe", and "somehow". There may be rare evidences of the existence of something lurking in an unseen world; a generation of electro-magnetic energy, or a vague manifestation of light or sound, but any realistic definition of these occurrences is as aloof as the spirits they seek.

Also, apparently, the contemporary hi-tech approach to paranormal investigation, has yielded no answers. Instead of the traditional, archaic means of tapping into the spirit world such as crystal balls, Ouija boards, séances, tarot cards, and palm reading, a modern brand of investigative and communicative devices have been introduced. They include Electro Magnetic Radiation detectors, Electronic Voice Phenomena recorders, and Ghost Boxes. This paraphernalia appeals to the sophistication and lifestyle of a society of people geared to gadgets. Although the high-tech approach has detected evidences of something lurking within the atmosphere that fills certain houses and graveyards of Savannah, the efforts have resulted in more questions than answers.

The Devil works to sow controversy and uncertainty among hobbyists and professionals that seek to understand the paranormal and the occult. As both these mysterious frontiers involve unexplainable (by science) manifestations of spirit, and supposed secret knowledge of the supernatural, the Devil is right at home weaving his webs in this environment of darkness. Again, the Devil's goal is to bait the curious, to enhance the lure and enticement of the unknown, and exploit a person's inherent drive to understand the nature of spirit.

John the Beloved, in his Gospel, reports on what Jesus said about the disparity of purpose between the Devil and God, "The thief comes only to steal and kill and destroy; I have come that they may have life, and have it to the full" (John 10:10). Jesus didn't mince words when defining Satan and his demons as robbers, murderers, and annihilators. In the estimation of Jesus, the Devil and his hoards target and strategize to obliterate life wherever it may be found.

God is the sole source of life and Creator of all things living. While He desires to prosper and satisfy his creation, the Devil seeks to disrupt and destroy the living. His is a vendetta against the Most High. His way of striking back is to injure those closest to His heart, you and me. If men and women were to truly understand the nature and intent of evil, and that we are the targets of its wrath, we wouldn't be so casual in how we order and conduct our lives.

Only a handful of those who have attempted to explain the *haunted* reputation of Lady Savannah, have tied citywide or regional decision-making and violations by governing political powers or institutional leadership as possibly giving entrance and a measure of control to these dark influences. Despite this insightful observation, there remains a basic lack of understanding as to the following: What is the identity of these malevolent entities? What is their origin? What degree of power do they possess? And with what weaponry are they armed? Unless these questions can be addressed, then all you're left with is speculation, presumption, and controversy; the equivalent of "blind leaders of the blind" (Matt. 15:14 AKJV).

Ghosts, Apparitions, and Specters, Oh My!

In traditional belief and commercial fiction, a ghost is a manifestation of the spirit or soul of a person whose body has died. Sometimes the term *ghost* is used synonymously with any spirit or demon; however, in popular usage the term typically refers to the spirit of a deceased person.

The prevailing explanation of what lies behind the hauntings of Savannah is that they are the manifested activities of the spirits of the departed dead. The *ghost* or *presence* or *apparition*, heard, felt, or seen is a human spirit in *limbo*, a condition of being trapped between this present life and the afterlife, either unable or unwilling to move on due to unresolved issues. A common reason given for the ghost's quandary is that he or she has been the victim of some severe emotional or physical trauma and can't transition until justice or vengeance has been exacted. Until then, the spirit is destined to wander. The idea of evil or that of the demonic is often emphasized, but usually as a backdrop to the ghost's dilemma. The demonic element is vague and undefined, intended to evoke curiosity and to enhance the mood or atmosphere of the tale.

This philosophy originates from the mind of the Evil One. By preying on mankind's ignorance and inability to discern the truth, the Devil has the residents and visitors of towns like Savannah, believing that the various venues, whether houses, hotels, pubs, or a variety of other structures, may be inhabited by spirits of the human dead. This provides these entities with an environment of darkness necessary to breed and exert control over individual lives and whole groups, including a town or city.

This is how the Devil wants it. It is part of his master plan. He is the Father of Lies and Master Deceiver and has been since before the dawn of mankind's appearance on planet Earth. His tactic is to *bait and hook* us so that we choose to believe and follow the deception, thereby becoming trapped and bound in darkness.

The Egregore and the Power of Agreement

It is our consent and will to believe and follow the dictates of evil that keep us imprisoned. Scripture tells us two cannot walk together until there is *agreement*, and this is the intended goal of the demonic. The greater number of people among society that are in willful agreement with demonic lies, will result in a corresponding degree of demonic control over the populace.

Prominent in the field of psychology and occult practices is the term *egregore*. The original word is the Greek ἐγρήγορος, transliterated "watcher". It is first found in the ancient Hebrew manuscript, *Book of Enoch*, attributed to the great grandfather of Noah. These Watchers were believed to be fallen angels that inhabited the earth, described by French author Eliphas Levi as "terrible beings" that "crush us without pity because they are unaware of our existence."

Over time, the word has been "exorcised", and the nature of the egregore tamed by psychologists and occultists. The element of an egregore as a distinct malevolent personality or entity has been watered down and is now said to be something of *human origin* that develops as a result of an intense common desire or belief.

In the so-called art of Magic, the egregore is defined as the following:

> Summation of the physical, emotional, mental and spiritual energies generated by two or more people vibrating together toward the same goal;

being a sub-product of our personal and collective creative process as co-creators of our reality.

Wikipedia provides this explanation:

> An occult concept representing a 'thoughtform' or 'collective group mind', an autonomous *psychic entity* made up of, and influencing the thoughts of a group of people.

Pastor Randy King Richey identifies the true power behind an egregore. His succinct definition is as follows:

> A collective agreement that brings forth the spirit that takes on the role they give it.

Simply put, it is a demonic entity whose presence and influence manifests among a group because they have given themselves over to the nature of the spirit. This spirit power can take control of two or more individuals or any size group of people who are in agreement with the lies of that malevolent spirit entity. Deceived humans are subject to the control of this real spirit power, and mistakenly define it in context of their particular belief system.

The nature of the spirit or egregore *becomes* the *atmosphere* or *personality* that develops among groups independent of any of its members. We see this spirit control manifest among citizens that engage in violent protests. We hear the term "herd mentality" or "mob mentality", a kind of irrational behavior that permeates and controls a group that would not normally be embraced by the individual if separated from the "pack". It is by definition a delusion that becomes the subjective reality of the group and dictates attitude and actions.

A stark example of this dark reality is what has been called the Jonestown Massacre. This tragedy took place in Guyana,

South America, on November 18, 1978, and involved the mass murder-suicide of more than 900 members of the Peoples Temple, a cult that originated on American soil.

This group was founded in 1955 in Indianapolis, Indiana. The founder, Jim Jones, a handsome, charismatic individual, initially, seemed to have the welfare of people at heart. His message was a form of Marxist "liberation theology" that emphasized social concern for the poor and political emancipation for oppressed peoples. Jones dream of a utopian society drew thousands to his "church" who were searching for purpose and something to believe in.

However, as his following grew, so did his control over the people. In 1965, following the relocation of his group to California, Jones grip on the people tightened, as he began using drugs and mind-control techniques as methods of manipulation. By mid-1970, Jones faced charges of financial fraud, physical mistreatment of members, and the abuse of children.

In 1977, under heightened scrutiny by authorities, Jones led hundreds of his group to a remote compound in Guyana.

One year later, Jones gathered the group and oversaw a ritual during which each member drank a "Kool-Aid" kind of beverage laced with cyanide. The result was the deaths of 918 people, more than 300 of them children. It is known that some of the adults were threatened and pressured to participate and would be gunned down if they attempted to escape. It was the largest single-day loss of American lives, second only to the September 11, 2001 terrorist attacks.

This is the trap laid by the Devil. He seeks to draw the ignorant and curious by appealing to the desperate, basic human drives to know and understand who we are and why we exist. He is quick to respond with deceptive explanations that appeal to the group mindset, and when believed, result in destruction for those in agreement with his lies.

It is very natural for men and women to gravitate toward anything that may provide clarity and understanding about the unseen realm, given the fact that the essence of our being is spirit, eternal spirit. The human spirit, although, in effect, dead because of trespasses against God's law and under the judgment of sin, still seeks the One, by and for whom it was created. The simple, but profound reason is best articulated by Saint Augustine, "Thou hast made us for thyself, O Lord, and our heart is restless until it finds its rest in thee."

The Devil and Ignorance

Upon the death of the physical body of Jesus, the angel asked the mourners who had gathered at His empty tomb, "Why seek you the living among the dead" (Luke 24:5 AKJV)? That question still applies today for those who have lost loved-ones or for whatever reason seek to establish contact with one that has passed from this life. We can traipse through the graveyards and antebellum mansions of Savannah seeking contact with disembodied spirits or a glimpse into the "other side", ignorant of the fact that the person sought, like Elvis, has left the building.

Scripture puts it this way: "To be absent from the body is to be present with the Lord" (2 Cor. 5:8 AKJV), and, "the dust returns to the ground it came from, and the spirit returns to God who gave it" (Eccles. 12:7) The spirit remains alive after the death of the physical body but, in cities such as Savannah, is no longer in that spooky house or graveyard!

If it is valid that truth will set us free, then it stands to reason that the lack of it will be like iron shackles to our hearts and minds. The bliss of ignorance has a short shelf-life.

Wisdom from Oz

You probably remember this line from Frank L. Baum's classic, *The Wonderful Wizard of Oz*, "Pay no attention to that man behind the curtain." In the context of the story, these words are spoken by the Wizard when he is exposed as just an ordinary man with no exceptional powers, and not the fiery, supernatural "great and powerful Oz." In a desperate attempt to maintain his ruse, he commands Dorothy, Scarecrow, Tinman, and Cowardly Lion, to ignore what they have seen, and continue believing his lie.

This, in effect, is what the Devil asks of you and me. As evident as it is that evil exists given the atrocities man perpetrates upon man, and upon one's self, we continue to deny the existence of a personal Devil intent on our destruction, and that of our family and friends. We choose to reserve the idea of evil for the mediums of science fiction or fantasy, or the irrelevant practice of religion, and go about our lives with a casual, nonchalant attitude toward the prospect of wickedness.

The idea that people, left to themselves, would be naïve and vulnerable to the presence and threat of evil is understandable. The simple fact is that if a man or woman has not been "reborn" into the kingdom of God, then he or she remains a captive, bound in the darkness of ignorance.

The disciple John declared, "God is light; in Him there is no darkness at all" (1 John 1:5). The nature of God is to *enlighten*. The activity of His Spirit among mankind is to impart knowledge and wisdom, so that people comprehend who they are as a created being and their accountability to their Maker. God clearly reveals to mankind, their purpose and responsibilities while present on Earth and what lies beyond the death of the physical body.

Michael K. Mancha

The Holy Scriptures, as they do in all aspects of physical life on Earth, provide definition and understanding of the spirit world and the activity generated from that realm. God does not want us ignorant of such matters, as ignorance does not excuse us from individual accountability, nor will it ward off the inevitable destructive repercussions.

Chapter 18

Two Kingdoms

Time has witnessed the rise and fall of many nations and empires. However, there are two kingdoms that predate the creation of mankind and remain in existence today. Both are spiritual kingdoms in their essence. One is eternal and unlimited in space, and the other is temporal and operates within the confined boundaries of the Earth and its atmosphere.

Although invisible to man's naked eye, the activities in which these kingdoms engage determine the fate of all individual humans and communities of people that exist in the visible, natural world. Since the creation of human life, all men, women and children that have ever lived upon the earth, have been "citizens" of one of these two kingdoms.

The Bible identifies these kingdoms. One is described as a kingdom of light, and the other as a kingdom of darkness. The word *kingdom* means the *king's domain*; hence, both have kings, or rulers who exercise their authority within that sphere.

The Scriptures also tell us that these two kings are the personification of the fundamental nature of their kingdoms:

one *is* light and the other *dwells* in darkness. More importantly, one promotes life and the other death.

You and I are citizens of one of these two kingdoms. No others exist in which mankind may live. We are either *children of light,* or, *children of darkness.* There is a basic animosity and hostility between the two camps. The clash is manifest daily within all human societies and has been since the dawn of time. The moral attitude and activities of those living in accordance with fallen human nature, and those set free and committed to God, are in a perpetual state of hostility and battle. It is a conflict that originates in the invisible, spirit world, that is manifested in the visible, physical world within and among mankind. Just as physical light and darkness are opposed to one another, so moral light and darkness cannot peacefully coexist.

The Kingdom of Darkness

What is spiritual darkness? Simply, it is the absence of God's presence. The person from whom God must separate Himself because of rebellion and sin is left in darkness, void of the light of His presence.

However, mankind is not alone in the darkness.

When Lucifer rebelled against God and was exiled from Heaven and the light of His presence, the void and darkness of planet Earth became his place of abode; the ideal environment to conduct his evil activities.

The Devil, according to the Apostle Paul, presides over the "rulers of the darkness of this world" (Eph. 6:12 AKJV). This evil kingdom operates within the world system. It is the Devil's domain, his territory subject to his will. He is the author of the values and activities embraced by its unredeemed citizens. The Devil is in control and preys on the rebel nature of his human subjects.

Before a man or woman is delivered from their sin, their habitat is spiritual darkness, their company dark, wicked spirits. There is a compatibility as man's deeds are in conformity with the one who has bound their soul. Man experiences a perverse pleasure when engaging in depraved and immoral acts. But the satisfaction is shallow and short-lived.

It may be difficult to believe that this world is rift with darkness when we see a beautiful sunrise and watch the sky change colors as the curtain is drawn on a new day. But remember, darkness is a condition of spirit, void of the light of God, and proceeds from the unseen, spirit realm. And within that darkness, the Devil is enthroned.

The Kingdom of Light

Paul encourages the believers of the Colossian church of his day to give "thanks to the Father, who has qualified you to share in the inheritance of his holy people in the kingdom of light" (Col. 1:12).

David the Psalmist offers this insight, "For with you is the fountain of life; in your light we see light" (Ps. 36:9).

Life and light are the heart substance of God's domain. And, life and light are inseparable because God *is* both. God doesn't *possess* these qualities, for possession implies that at a point in time, loss may occur. Man *has*, then, eventually, he *has not*. With God, for whom was no beginning, and is without end, that which He *is*, has always been, and will always be. Life and light have always existed, and will forever exist, only because God eternally exists.

Rejection of the Light

The disciple John also wrote in his Gospel,

> And this is the condemnation, that light is come into the world, and men loved darkness rather than light, because their deeds were evil. For everyone that does evil hates the light, neither comes to the light, les his deeds should be reproved (John 3:19, 20 AKJV).

The Son of God's entrance to the darkened earthen realm was a lightning bolt that exposed the condition of fallen men and women. Even so, the individual still held in the bonds of sin, will continue to follow the dictates of their rebel nature. The essence of that nature is easy prey for the evil influences of the Devil. The individual hides out in the darkness avoiding the light that would expose their shameful thoughts and acts. By rejecting God's light, the condemnation, the judgment upon their fallen soul, remains.

Our merciful God will always take the initiative to seek out the man or woman huddled in death's dark corners. There, His invitation is given to receive His light and live. With it comes a measure of understanding, of enlightenment, to the human heart. The choice to step forward into the light or recoil and remain in darkness must be made. This is the will of the individual in operation, and how they choose will ultimately determine whether they will prosper or perish.

The Way into the Kingdom of Light

We have touched on the concept of *agreement* in the context of mysticism and the occult. We must not underestimate its power. The idea is derived from the original Greek word ἐξομολογέω, transliterated in English to *exolomogeo*, which means to fully agree and to acknowledge that agreement openly, hence, to confess or openly declare. In life, we are either in agreement with God, or agreement with the Devil.

This word, exolomogeo, is used repeatedly in the New Testament when individuals were confessing their sins or their belief in Jesus Christ. When we acknowledge what God says about our need for forgiveness and confess our trust in Christ as the means for that forgiveness, then we have entered into agreement with God.

In this act of agreement with God is *repentance*. It is a choice involving a 180 degree turn away from darkness toward the light. The result is an instantaneous regeneration of our human spirit that ushers us into the light of His presence. The shroud of darkness upon our soul is lifted and expelled, as light is on the heels of fleeing darkness. There now begins the process of enlightenment, the gaining of understanding of He who is light. Jesus said, "I am the light of the world. Whoever follows me will never walk in darkness but will have the light of life" (John 8:12).

As we grow in the intimacy of relationship with God, we flourish and prosper, because where God is present, is where fullness of life is found.

Transferring of Kingdom Citizenship

The scripture declares this about those who have received the King of Light:

> You are a chosen people, a royal priesthood, a holy nation, God's special possession, that you may declare the praises of him who called you out of darkness into his wonderful light (I Peter 2:9).

> He has rescued us from the dominion of darkness and brought us into the kingdom of his dear Son (Col 1:13).

The kingdom of darkness has been infiltrated, and its king stripped of his authority. He has been utterly routed. Theoretically, those subject to his rulership have, effectively, been delivered from his rulership. The Devil's tyranny over humans only existed as the condemnation and judgment of sin was in force over the human separated from their Creator. Jesus sacrifice removed the penalty of sin and its power over the wayward human.

However, this dark kingdom is continually populated by the majority of people in existence on this planet.

If this deliverance has been made possible, then why the resistance and refusal from those still in captivity? Why would one choose to wander in darkness, shouldering the excruciating weight of guilt and shame, and the tyranny of hopelessness, while there exists a way of escape? Primarily, the Devil keeps them blinded to the fact that they are lost and in need of rescuing. The other problem is pride, the reluctance of the natural man to bend a knee and humble themselves before their Creator. Ultimately, their confinement is self-imposed.

With God's approach to the human spirit comes a measure of understanding to the human mind. As we have previously discussed, the choice is then ours to receive life or continue in a state of spiritual death.

The apocalyptic Book of Revelation includes this dinner invitation from God,

> Behold, I stand at the door and knock. If anyone hears my voice and opens the door, then I will come into him, and will dine with him, and he with me (Rev. 3:20).

Artist Warner Sallman's rendition of this scripture depicts Christ knocking at the door of a common house. Of interest is that there is no doorknob or handle, nothing by which the door may be opened from the outside. It is apparent that Sallman is conveying the truth that Christ can only gain entrance to one's "house" by the action of the one already inside. This is also true of how the Devil is given entrance to one's life.

Carl Von Clausewitz, in his classic, *On War*, writes, "…war consists of a continuous interaction of opposites." Rightly said. It is *continuous* and involves *opposites*. Simply put, the nature of this spirit-world war is an uninterrupted state of conflict between angelic forces of good and demonic forces of evil. God seeks to shine His light into the hearts of mankind so that they may choose life, while the Devil works to keep men bound in darkness. This continuous struggle also includes our involvement, as the fate of every human life depends on this: Will the individual respond to the invitation of God's Spirit, or choose to remain with the dead in outer darkness?

Arise and Shine!

Isaiah wrote, "Arise, shine, for your light has come…darkness shall cover the earth, and gross darkness the people; but the Lord shall arise on you, and his glory shall be seen on you" (Isa. 60:1, 2 AKJV).

It was Jesus of whom Isaiah wrote seven-hundred years before his arrival on Earth. Paul clarifies that amazing fact in his letter to the Ephesian church, "Awake, and arise you that sleep, and arise from the dead, and Christ shall give you light" (Eph. 5:14 AKJV).

As we welcome the light, we see that deliverance from the power and penalty of our sin has been secured through the substitutionary death of Jesus Christ. His dying in our place, for our sin. Only a fool would choose to remain in the dark, covered and fettered in shame and condemnation.

Jesus, the Light of the World, has come! We can now rise, stand, and carry the light to others who are lost in the dark!

In the extreme opposite is the presence and influence of the dark prince, Satan, and his forces. When a person, or a community of people are in agreement with the deceptions and lies of demons, then darkness advances. The manifestation of evil; the chaotic, blinding influence of demonic presence intensifies.

We will be considering the strategy and methods employed by the Devil in his quest to keep mankind bound. Of greater importance, we will also learn about the weapons that God has provided those who trust in Him, that if utilized diligently, will set the captives free.

Chapter 19

The War in the Spirit World

We spoke of the two spheres of existence: the spirit, supernatural world and the physical, natural world. There are no boundaries separating these realms as each is *a world within a world*. The activities occurring within both, relate to the other and are taking place simultaneously and constantly. The issues contested pertain to life and death. These two realms make up a single arena wherein the destiny of every human soul is determined.

A.W. Tozer writes of the spirit world and warns against the "common fault of pushing the 'other world' into the future. It is not future, but present. It parallels our familiar physical world, and the doors between the two worlds are open."

Within the unseen spirit world, opposing forces are battling for the hearts and minds of Earth's inhabitants: men, women, and children. While the spirit entities can continuously observe the physical world, human beings are oblivious and blinded to the activities within the supernatural realm. Our vision into the invisible world is totally dependent on the working of the Spirit of God so we may understand what is taking place, how it is influencing the physical world around us, and our role in the process.

The Scriptures make it clear that to the natural man, the things of spirit are "foolishness to him, neither can he know them, because they are spiritually discerned" (1 Cor. 2:14 AKJV). However, all men and women are candidates to receive insight and direction should they turn to God and ask and seek. It is crucial that we quiet our hearts and be receptive to what the Spirit is saying, as he is our Counselor and Guide in such matters.

Just the Facts

As we journey forward, we must avoid speculation and focus on what has been revealed by the choosing and wisdom of God. Not everything there is to know has been disclosed; however, enough has been revealed so that we are not ignorant and left at the mercies of our own presumptions.

We can also consider the witness of *human experience*. What God reveals is intended to be lived out so that we grow in our relationship to Him as sons and daughters, and in our partnership with Him in bringing about His purposes here on this planet. Faith was never intended to be isolated from experience and relegated only to the compartment of our mental assent. Faith is active, alive, and brings forth *substance* as we walk it out in our daily lives.

Much of what I put forth in the coming pages will counter natural reason. Therefore, many readers will tend to quickly dismiss the assertions. Others will respond with a degree of receptivity to the thought or concept. I would challenge all readers to exercise contemplation to what is written; to move forward and allow the information to pass from the mind, into the heart. If it is true that your eternal fate depends on your response, then the matter is worthy of your utmost consideration.

Remember, you and I are citizens within one of two kingdoms: the kingdom of those living under deception, darkened in their understanding, and ignorant of the truth, or the kingdom of Light wherein is truth and understanding about the issues of life and death. No others exist.

In our quest to understand the makeup of our beings and the purpose for our existence, we have considered aspects of God and the Devil, good and evil, and touched on the idea of spirit powers and how they impact our lives and our cities. We have waded knee-deep into the troubled pond of spirit activity. We will now tread into deeper waters.

With the help and guidance of the Spirit of God, we will answer the following questions:

Where is the battlefield?

What is taking place in this unseen world?

Who are these spirit entities in contention?

How do they operate, and with what weaponry?

Although the war being waged is not visible to mankind's physical senses, there is a means by which we may detect spirit activity.

First, let's define in greater depth where this conflict is taking place.

The Realm of Battle

The language of the ancient proto-Indo-Europeans is thought to be the origin of all human language. This original language is revelatory with respect to aspects of their culture. Their use of the word *deywoes*, meaning sky beings or sky gods, is evidence of their belief in a deity, or deities, whose thrones were above the earth. This recognition of sky gods continued among the ensuing cultures, including the Greeks (Zeus), the Romans (Jupiter), the Norse (Thor), the Slavs (Perun), the Balts (Perkunas), and the Celtics (Taranis).

Within ancient Hindu Sanskrit texts are detailed accounts of wars fought in the skies between gods. There also exists ample documented evidence that these gods would descend from the sky to the earthbound people.

These various idols were not just products of the ancient's imaginations. Actually, these *sky beings* were demonic entities to which these deceived societies of human beings paid homage. And these various dominant, evil spirits ruled from within planet Earth's atmosphere. Remember, they are not physical creatures, hence, they are not earthbound. They do not walk the earth as we do, but they do inhabit and move within its atmosphere.

Science tells us that Earth's atmosphere is comprised of five layers, each containing various gases and chemicals and degrees of ultra-violet radiation generated by our Sun. The atmospheric layers grow thinner and cooler, the farther from the earth they are. Earth is the only known planet that possesses an atmosphere capable of sustaining life.

The atmosphere can also be referred to as *air* and contains the oxygen that human life is dependent upon, as well as other chemicals that enable other life forms to thrive. This all exists by design.

The layer of atmosphere closest to Earth's surface is the troposphere. It is four to twelve miles thick and contains half of the earth's total atmosphere. It is within this area of our atmosphere, that I believe war between supernatural, spirit forces is taking place. So, why this particular area of the earth's atmosphere? Simply, because it is the physical realm of *our* existence, and human beings are the object for whom the battles are being waged.

The Wind of Spirit

In the book of Hebrews, there is an interesting statement about God,

> He sends His angels like the winds (vs. 1:7).

Why the likeness of angels to winds? Perhaps it is because they are invisible to the natural senses (both are invisible to the eyes of man), or, perhaps it is because they possess great power (depicted when God commands both for a specific purpose), or, it may also be the speed in which they travel (evidenced in the rapid angelic response to Daniel's prayer; Dan. 9:21-23). There is basis for all three elements within the biblical narrative.

There also is evidence derived from the Scriptures that actions by entities within the spirit realm can generate motion in the physical world that is *felt* by people and other living, physical creatures.

There are several references in scripture during which the natural force of wind accompanied activity originating in the spirit realm. The context of these examples implies that wind can be generated by both the actions of the Spirit of God and His angels, as well as demonic entities. Consider the following:

Job was the victim of a whirlwind that demolished his home and claimed the lives of his wife and children (Job 1:19).

Elijah the Prophet was engulfed by a whirlwind that transported him directly from the physical realm, into the invisible realm of the spirit world (2Kings 2:10).

Jonah, who was on a ship, fleeing from the presence of God, was engulfed by a "great wind" and a "violent storm" (Jonah 1:4), sent by God to get his attention.

In John's gospel, Jesus likened the workings and movement of the Spirit of God among mankind to that of the wind (John 3:8).

And following the resurrection of Jesus from the grave, He sent the Holy Spirit to convince human beings about the power of sin and the deliverance from it made available through Christ's sacrifice. The coming of the Spirit is described as follows, "And suddenly there came *a sound from heaven* as of a mighty rushing mighty wind, and it filled the house where they were sitting" (Acts 2:2 AKJV).

Of interest is that, in each of these examples, the wind influencing the circumstances and those present in the physical world, was caused by activity that originated in the invisible, spirit realm!

The Ruler of the Kingdom of the Air

In the Apostle Paul's letter to the Church in Ephesus, he wrote,

> And you were dead in your trespasses and sins, in which you used to live when you followed the ways of this world and of the ruler of the kingdom of the air, the spirit who is now at work in those who are disobedient (Eph. 2:1, 2).

In addition to clearly underscoring the Devil's targeting of mankind and the exploitation of his fallen nature, the above words connect the activities of Satan and his demonic forces, to the sphere of the earth's atmosphere. As "ruler of the kingdom of the air", the Devil is defined as having dominion throughout the physical environment in which mankind lives. This may also explain the existence of severe and destructive weather conditions that often wreak havoc upon mankind and the earth. Surely, God did not create this planet and place human beings upon it to be subject to injury and death by the existing elements of weather. Something must have occurred that changed God's intended order. The Scriptures clearly reveal that the natural balance of creation was affected by the fall of mankind, resulting in what I would call a *tilt* effect.

According to a passage of Scripture in Matthew's gospel, Jesus and His disciples were on a boat when "suddenly a furious storm came up on the lake" (vs. 8:24), that threatened their lives. Jesus exercised His authority over creation and stilled the elements, causing the disciples to declare that "even the winds and waves obey Him" (vs. 8:27). This clearly demonstrates God's influence and control over nature. But does it also imply that demonic entities can influence the natural elements in potentially destructive ways? In this passage, it may have been that Jesus exerted His authority over nature, as well as the Devil who had generated the stormy conditions with the intent to do harm.

Ebb and Flow

If in fact winds can be a gauge of spirit activity of both good and evil, then there will be a recognizable ebb and flow. Like the ocean tide, life on this planet is subject to advances and retreats of constructive and destructive time periods. The cyclical pattern of times of war, followed by seasons of peace, are representative of this truth.

Even the weather patterns, generated by the wind, that move across the surface of our planet are indicative of this ebb and flow. The clear, calm, sunny day eventually gives way to a stormy, hostile atmospheric condition carried by the winds, or, vice versa.

Savannah's Stormy Past

Lady Savannah is no stranger to adverse weather and its deadly repercussions. Hurricanes have been frequent, unwelcomed visitors to the city. Here's a run-down of the headlines:

(August 27, 1881) A major hurricane hits the coast, killing 700 people.

(August 27, 1893) A major hurricane hits the Georgia and South Carolina coasts, killing 1,000 to 2,500 people and leaving 30,000 homeless.

(August 31, 1898,) A Category 3 hurricane hits the Georgia coast, 179 dead in Savannah.

(August 11, 1911) A Category 2 hurricane hits Savannah killing fifty people.

(October 145, 1947) A Category 2 hurricane hits Savannah causing death.

(September 4, 1979) A Category 2 Hurricane hits Savannah, causing massive property damage.

(October 8, 2016) Hurricane Matthew hit the southeast area with 105 mph winds. More than 370,000 homes were without power. Record coastal storm surge flooding left three dead. Hunter Army Airfield measured a rainfall amount of 17.48 inches.

(September 11, 2017) Hurricane Irma skirted Savannah to the west, but still managed to cause a mandatory evacuation of 147,000 people, and sent a new record, five-foot storm surge onto coastal areas.

(September 4, 2019) Hurricane Dorian threatened Savannah, swinging just east of the city, prompting mandatory evacuation and leaving the economy with a 35-million-dollar loss from tourism.

Statistics show that the Savannah area has averaged having experienced either a significant tropical storm or hurricane every 1.93 years.

In addition to the wind-force damage of major storms, the accompanying flood waters are often the potential carriers of serious, deadly diseases, including malaria, cholera, and dengue. As we previously put forth, this threat is posed from stagnant water.

The Guardian.com reported the following in 2010, which is, sadly to say, a common state of circumstances in this region of the world:

> More than 2 million cases of malaria are expected in Pakistan in the coming months in the wake of the country's devastating floods, aid workers have warned. Two months into the crisis, large areas remain submerged in southern Sindh province, creating stagnant pools of standing water that, combined with the heat, are powerful incubators of a disease spread by mosquitoes that breed and hatch in the pools. The malaria threat is part of a wider health emergency, with more than 20 million people affected by the floods struggling to cope as the winter approaches... Last night the UN reported 881,000 cases of diarrhea, 840,000 cases of skin diseases and almost 1m cases of respiratory disorders.

Black Vomit

Relative to Lady Savannah, the cause of considerable suffering and death can be laid at the feet of stagnant rainwaters. In fact, the killer disease, known as Yellow Fever that decimated the city in 1820 and 1854, was carried by mosquitoes that bred in the city's standing waters. The death toll reached 666 and 1040, respectively.

"O COME IS DEATH!! DEATH!! NOTHING BUT DEATH!" the headlines shouted in the October 11, 1854, edition of the Savannah Morning News.

Jacqueline Jones, in her well-researched analysis of the city in the mid-1800's, *Saving Savannah* wrote,

> In early September 1854, Savannah was diseased, dying. At dusk, tar fires kindled on the public squares threw a plume of acrid smoke into the air, an immense black shroud that settled over the desolate, oppressively hot and humid city . . . The usually raucous marketplace was empty, stately homes were abandoned, schools and hotels shuttered. Many people had fled . . . Behind closed doors, the ill, unattended, lay side by side with the dead, and in poorer areas of the city, human corpses mingled with refuse piled in black alleyways. Deprived of supplies from either the surrounding countryside or from arriving ships, the river port risked slow starvation. 'How changed is our beautiful, growing, healthy city, lately full of enterprise, noise, and business,' despaired one of the city's clergymen, exhausted from ministering to the ill. Racked with fever, chills, and convulsions, hundreds of all ages were succumbing to the 'black vomit', more commonly known as yellow fever.

A later epidemic struck in August 1876 and claimed 1066 lives within two weeks. By September, five thousand of the twenty-eight thousand residents had fled the city. It is interesting that history records the local politicians and powerbrokers to have either ignored or minimized the severity of the outbreaks in an effort to protect the image of the city, and, no doubt, their own.

The bottom line is that the prince of the power of the air will manifest dominion and control through the destructive effects of volatile weather, which is often a precursor to plagues of disease that result in greater degrees of human suffering and death. He is the god of this world and he makes his presence known.

Now let's look at what is taking place in the spirit realm.

The Nature of the Fight

Paul Billheimer, pastor and author of several books, writes in his classic, *Destined to Overcome,*

> Evil spirit personalities under the direction of their ruler, the god of this world, swarm the earth in an attempt to foil God's government and control Earth's inhabitants; they are constantly inciting them to rebellion against God, against His purpose, aims and plan. The war that began in Heaven when Satan was expelled merely changed locations and now continues on Earth. All wars, all crime, all violence in the world is incited, is stirred up, by evil spirits operating in the unseen world on the fallen nature of mankind.

For those who deny that a personal devil exists, that evil, supernatural beings are merely products of one's imagination, then how would they explain some of the acts that one human being perpetrates upon another.

We hear or read of a horrific home invasion where the family is tortured and murdered, or the imprisonment and abuse of children by their parents within their home, or of a terror attack on the people of a city, and we ask, "How could a person do such a thing?" We are at a loss to explain what could motivate or drive a person to that kind of violence.

But if we recognize and understand that the personification of all evil and evil acts is moving about planet Earth, preying on the weaknesses of mankind, with myriads of wicked spirits at his command, intent on the destruction of the human race, then we begin to understand how and why these things take place.

Although it is true that the human being born into this world is in a "fallen" state and possesses natural bents and drives that are contrary to the nature of God, the powers of darkness cannot just barge in and take control of that individual. But neither can the Holy Spirit.

The battle in the spirit world is for the right of entry, to occupy, and then to control the man, woman, or child. In order to enter, the *consent* of the individual is required, and consent is given when the person is in *agreement* with what is offered. Agreement is not only mental assent to an idea or an attitude, but action based on what is presented. It is obedience that puts the man or woman under the power of either good or evil. Jesus said we become the slave of the one we choose to obey!

Darkness and light cannot cohabitate. Only one will gain predominance through the willful consent of the individual, by their agreement and conformity with what one or the other represents. Good or evil. Edification or destruction. Life or death. As we emphasized earlier, it is crucial that we learn to choose wisely, so that we give entrance to God's Spirit, and allow for His jurisdiction over our lives.

Before either God's Spirit or demonic entities can enter, occupy, and then control aspects of a person's soul (mind, emotions, or will), a battle takes place in the heavenly realm, the spirit arena, within the very atmosphere that surrounds us, and the very air we breath.

The Power of Sin

Bottom line, our battle, personally and corporately as a race of intelligent, spiritual beings, is against the power of sin intent on our enslavement and destruction.

The power of sin operates in three distinct areas of life: our humanness, the world system, and the supernatural realm of spirit. The esteemed college professor and missionary to Latin America, Dr. Ed Murphy, wrote,

> Sin is personal – it comes from within. Sin is social – it comes from without, and Sin is supernatural – it comes from above.

There exists not a human being, since Adam and Eve walked in the Garden of old, that has not been the target or the victim of the insidious working of sin in these three ways. The tempest of sin is at work in our entire physical and mental makeup, as our members involuntarily bend and incline toward rebellious thoughts and actions contrary to God's will. The draw and lure of the energy of the world's glitter and glamor leaves us spellbound with an insatiable desire to participate and possess. Meanwhile, the source of sin, Satan, along with his demonic minions strategize how to deceive and blind so that we sink deeper into the mire of darkness, and further down the pathway of destruction.

Dr. Murphy puts it in stark terms,

> Behind the wickedness of the flesh and the corruption of the world is the true original source of all

sin, Satan. It is a spirit enemy with whom we battle and war against, as the flesh and the world are the channels through which evil supernaturalism oppresses and seeks to destroy the human race.

Now, let's examine who is in contention in this spirit-world war.

The Combatants

In this spirit war, there exists three groups of participants. They consist of the spirit forces of good, the spirit forces of evil, and mankind. Primarily, it is for this latter group that the war is fought. The fate of individual human beings lay in the balance.

In the previous way we explained that God *is* light and life, so he *is* also good. If God did not exist, goodness could not be found. Good only exists because God exists; He that is good. And because God does not change, He always has been, and always will be good.

The main goal of the angelic forces of Heaven, is to assist the Holy Spirit as He seeks to influence the will of an individual to receive the gift of life offered through the sacrifice of Jesus Christ. Simultaneously, the spirit forces of evil seek to keep the individual bound and in a state of death.

The man or woman is not just an idle spectator in the battle, awaiting the outcome. The person who has yet to receive the offering of Christ is in a perpetual position, through the exercise of their will, of responding to the penetrating light of Truth. One's soul is embattled as either steps toward the light are taken, or, a stubborn refusal persists that keeps them anchored in darkness.

The one who has received Christ as their Deliverer from the power of sin, is also an active participant in this war. Each is commissioned and equipped in a variety of ways to advance the purposes of God and His angels. The believer is in a unique position in that, while seeking to encourage the unbeliever, he or she is not immune from the attacks of evil. He or she continues to be harassed and hindered as the Devil seeks to disable and render the believer ineffective in this fight.

We've touched on the natural bents within our humanness, and the worldliness that appeals to those deeply rooted drives. But because it is these two areas that are targeted for exploitation by Satan and his demonic forces, we understand more about the nature of this dark enemy and how he works to destroy our lives and our cities. The good news is that we are provided with *all* that is necessary to counteract the works and powers of darkness. We are afforded the guarantee of total victory over Satan and his cohorts.

We previously mentioned that Satan and his demons are angels who fell from their favored position in relation to God and His kingdom. The Scriptures tell us that one-third of the total population of Heaven's angels followed Satan in his rebellion against God, and were cast from His presence, into outer darkness.

Simple math informs us that two-thirds of the angels remained in allegiance to God, and still populate Heaven, twice as many holy angels as wicked fallen angels. Those are good odds in any fight. And, as we'll see a bit later, the weaponry available to God's angels, and to men and women who have entrusted their lives to Him, guarantee the outcome of the war in the spirit realm.

God's Angels

God wrote the book on angels. It's called the Bible. In fact, aside from the Scriptures, I know of no other non-Christian, religious text, that identifies the order of the angelic, and details the means by which good can triumph over evil. So, we will yield to Scripture for definition and clarification regarding these somewhat peculiar creatures.

Of the sixty-six books of the Bible, thirty-four refer to angels. Jesus Christ clearly validated their existence as he taught His disciples and the "multitudes" drawn to Him (Matt.8:10; 24:31; 26:53). The angels were created before mankind and the earth were formed. They came into existence as morally pure creatures, with full access to the presence of God.

The aspect of their nature that is often misunderstood is that they are *personal* beings. They possess intellect (Matt. 28:5) and emotions (Luke 15:10), as well as volition (Jude 6).

Angels are spirit beings, and do not possess physical bodies, although they can appear in human form. They possess far greater power and strength than mankind. They are not omnipresent, therefore, can only be present at one place at one time. Angels are eternal, just as you and me.

Angels act as guardians and protectors of God's people (Psalm 91:11,12), they oppose our enemies, and can refresh and strengthen the physical body.

Angels also bring comfort to the believer at the time of physical death.

Allow me a brief personal reflection. I have had experiences wherein I was mercifully spared serious physical injury and was well aware of the presence of angels. The following is my journal entry from 2013, that describes one of the more graphic episodes where I was rescued from a potentially disastrous situation:

> *God kept me from serious injury or death on 1/14/13 at 7:09 p.m. As darkness was falling, I was nearing the end of a 6-hour drive on mostly rural Georgia highways. My attention drifted and I failed*

to see the old pickup truck stopped in my lane of travel. I was doing about 75 mph and was less than 100 feet from the truck when I looked up and saw it. During the ensuing split second of time, I hit the brakes and braced for the impact. Then the miracle. It felt as if the car was now on a track, like a runaway train or an amusement park roller coaster, as it shifted left and then shot straight ahead. Whereas the car should've skidded and slammed into the rear end of the truck, or went sideways and flipped, instead it felt as if the wheels were in a groove from which they could not break free. I flew past the truck, inches from contact, and once past, I again had control of the vehicle. I recall being dizzy from the emotional blitz of the impending crash and then the realization of the escape. This experience has reaffirmed to me, like never before, how fragile life is, and, also, how near God is to those who fear Him. Angels DO encamp about us and God's Spirit lives within us… and that is as near as 'near' gets. God is a VERY present help in the time of trouble; even the troubles we bring upon ourselves. I didn't deserve this kind of attention; but fortunately, this is the unmerited care and love we can expect from God our Father.

In the context of our study of spirit warfare, it is important to know that there is an organized ranking of angels. The Scriptures refer to an "archangel", and to "chief princes", "seraphim", and "cherubim". Although there is much more to be revealed, we do know that angels execute the process of God's government as servants and messengers. They can exert control over nature (Rev. 7:1), nations of the world (2Kings 19:35), and demonic power (Dan. 10:13; 12:1).

The Devil and His Angels

The Old Testament Scriptures refer to Satan in seven of its books, and the New Testament in all twenty-seven books. Jesus clearly acknowledged his existence.

Satan, too, is a personal being, possessing intellect, emotions, and will. The various names assigned to him in the Scriptures give us a vivid portrayal of his personality. In addition to Satan (*adversary*) and the Devil (*slanderer*), he is referred to as Beelzebub (*Lord of the Flies*), Belial (*lawless*), the evil one, the tempter, the prince of this world, the god of this age, the prince of the power of the air, the accuser of the brethren, the serpent, and the dragon.

In the same way that God *is* good, the Devil *is* evil. The Devil has not been corrupted by evil. He *is* evil. It is not something that he possesses and, therefore, can lose, or outgrow. The Devil cannot be rehabilitated. He "gives a face" to evil, as he personifies all that is wicked and immoral.

There was no evil to be found anywhere, at any time in the history of the created universe until the Lucifer rebellion in Heaven, resulting in his banishment from the light and life of God, to the confines of a lifeless ball of dirt. Evil was now present upon the earth, within the physical realm of existence, and within the spirit realm, outside the boundaries of the kingdom of God.

Then mankind came along and became a target for the Devil. People are not inherently evil, either, but can become become evil in attitude and conduct as they give their allegiance to the Evil One. There is hope for the immoral person. He or she can be *delivered*, brought out from the influence and grip of the Devil, but only by the power of God.

Satan

We previously identified his position in Heaven, and the rebellion he led, resulting in his expulsion and exile to the void and dark of planet Earth (Ezekiel 28:12-18; Isaiah 14:12-15; 1 Timothy 3:6).

The Devil's is not a co-equal of God. He is just another created being. So, unlike the Almighty, he is not omnipotent, as he is limited in his power and abilities. Unlike God, he is not omniscient (all knowing) or omnipresent (can be everywhere simultaneously). Like you and I, he can only be one place at one time.

The Scriptures detail Satan's attempt to derail Jesus Christ from accomplishing His mission and purpose while on planet Earth. The Devil employed temptation in his quest to have Jesus disobey God the Father (Matt. 4:1-11; Heb. 4:15). He used other men and women as instruments in his attempts to hinder and obstruct Jesus.

The Devil works to keep humans in a state of unbelief concerning the death and resurrection of Jesus Christ. He blinds their mind to hinder understanding (2 Cor. 4:4), and uses persecution (Rev. 2:10), and false religions (Rev. 2:13) to steer people from knowing the truth.

Satan directs his attention at those that have received the truth. He tempts believers to pride, materialism, immorality, lies, and discouragement. He seeks to cause division among believers by promoting anger, bitterness, jealousy, and unforgiveness (2 Cor. 2:5-11).

Demons

The original Greek word δαιμόνιον, ου, τό, transliterated to the English word *daimonion*, meaning evil spirit. These are angels that were cast out of Heaven because of their rebellion.

They are followers of Satan, evidenced his title in Scripture, *prince of the demons.*

The number of demons is unknown; however, there is reason to believe that their ranks are a great many as they can simultaneously influence the whole of human population throughout the earth.

Demons are also referred to as "unclean spirits" (Matt. 10:1), and possess a wicked, depraved nature. The art of deception has its origin in these beings (Tim. 4:1-3).

Demons are personal beings that possess a high level of intelligence, having once dwelt in the kingdom of God, and having observed the behavior and activities of mankind since his existence. However, their knowledge is limited.

They possess great strength (Acts 19:16), and the ability to appear in the physical world (Rev. 9:7-10).

Demons are committed to keep mankind from a knowledge of Truth, so that God will not receive the honor He is due as Creator and Father.

Their mission on this planet is "only to steal and kill and destroy" life, in whatever form it exists (John 10:10). They are the source of physical disease (Matt. 12:22), mental disorders (Luke 8:27-29), addictions, and suicide (Mark 9:22).

Demons are steadfastly committed and organized in their intent to occupy and control all that takes place on the ground and within the atmosphere of planet Earth (Eph. 6:10-12).

The Basics of Warfare

We must be clear about with whom we battle against in this spirit war. Understanding the nature and tactics of our enemy enables us to equip ourselves with the proper weapons. There are two foundational facts we must know if we are to be effective in our participation in the battle.

Firstly, quoting the Apostle Paul in his writing to the ancient church in Ephesus,

> For our struggle is not against flesh and blood, but against the rulers, against the authorities, against the powers of this dark world and against the spiritual forces of evil in the heavenly realms (Eph. 6:12).

Humans are not the enemy in this fight. Although people may be the vehicles through which demons operate, ultimately, it is the spirit behind the attitudes and actions of the human, that must be confronted. The human is responsible and accountable for their deeds, but the deeper root problem lies in the exploitation of the wayward nature of the individual by the demonic entity.

In his Bible commentary, Charles Ellicott, the distinguished English theologian, rightly observes,

> The struggle is not a struggle with the 'flesh and blood' of wicked men—a struggle which may still admit of some reserve of sympathy—but a truceless war with the spiritual powers of evil themselves.

Our interactions with our fellow man may be seasoned with grace, but we must be ruthless in our dealings with the Devil.

Secondly, Paul stresses in his letter to the Corinthians, "The weapons we fight with are not the weapons of the world" (2 Cor. 10:4).

Since our real enemy isn't human, it is reasonable that the weapons we employ in battle are not human or physical in nature. Our intellect, reasoning, or persuasive speech will not sway demonic power. Neither will brute, physical force, or even a nuclear device for that matter, result in a chink in the armor of our demonic adversary.

Paul finishes his thought to the Corinthians, "On the contrary, they have divine power to demolish strongholds". Paul uses a military term, *strongholds*, which are fortified positions secured by those at war. Our enemy has "dug in" and is encamped in spiritual darkness.

There is one means by which evil will be uprooted and put to flight. It is only with spiritual armament, empowered by the Spirit of God. The weaponry we are given produces profound results in the spirit world that are manifested in the visible, physical world.

Paul now describes the effect of these *supernatural* weapons on the strongholds of our spirit enemy, "We demolish arguments and every pretension that sets itself up against the knowledge of God, and we take captive every thought to make it obedient to Christ" (2 Cor. 10:5).

The Devil is not interested in attacking the spirit of our being. He knows it is already in a darkened, deadened state due to the judgment of sin upon our lives. So, the Devil targets the soul of man, primarily, he seeks to inject his poison into our minds. His intent is to shape our concept of God and, if possible, cause us to reject the existence of an "almighty". If there is no God, then there is no Jesus Christ, and, ultimately no forgiveness and deliverance for the wayward man or woman.

Chapter 20

Evil Strategies

The general goal of our dark enemy is to sow into the minds of people, false ideas concerning the origin and purpose of mankind. These thought processes, or *arguments* as Paul describes them, involve speculations and imaginations of the human mind that are often the fruit of demonic influence. They produce the creeds of false religions, ideologies, and philosophies, wherein the human is presented as an equal with God, or, as part of the whole of god, or, one of a multitude of gods. James, in his New Testament letter, concludes that, "Such 'wisdom' does not come down from Heaven but is earthly, unspiritual, demonic..." (James 3:15). This poison invades the soul of the human who has embraced the Devil's lies.

The *egregore*, as we earlier defined, is a demonic stronghold in which the evil spirit has influenced the thought process of a group and holds them in a vice grip due to their willingness to believe a lie.

Paul also referred to these as *pretensions*, meaning arrogant obstacles. At the root of these beliefs is the sin of pride, which was the basis of Lucifer's expulsion from Heaven, evidenced in his declaration, "I will ascend above the heights of the clouds; I will be like the Most High" (Is. 14:14 AKJV). Even the professed non-religious atheist is bound in pride, as he or she rejects the existence of a Supreme being. However, that individual fails to see that they worship in the church of Humanism, a religion by definition, in that it is a belief system that places *self* on a throne above all else.

If left unchallenged by the power of Truth, these demon-inspired religious and political belief systems will spread and grow like Wisteria vines and strangle the whole of a society within a city or nation. We've seen this in human empires and kingdoms throughout the course of time that hold fast to a mindset that has rejected eternal principles of Truth. The economic poverty, rampant disease, and violence that pervades these societies are deplorable and are evidences of the invisible demonic power that has poisoned the soul of the people and produced the fruit of death in their midst.

Modern mankind needs to heed the ancients who learned, "What has been will be again, what has been done will be done again; there is nothing new under the sun" (Eccl. 1:9).

This entrenched control, Paul's *strongholds*, gained by demonic forces among mankind are targeted by the Spirit of God. It is only with the counteracting power of irrefutable Truth that these lofty, invisible, demonic fortresses within the spirit realm, can be torn down and demolished, and the souls of deceived multitudes freed to consider and embrace the claims of Jesus Christ.

Angel of Light

Satan is an angel, a fallen one, but still, an angel. This means he possesses certain powers that you and I do not; powers that can easily overwhelm any human ignorant of his devices and strategies.

The Scriptures describe those who present themselves as seeking the good of others, while secretly planning to exploit and deceive, as wearing "sheep's clothing, but inwardly they are ferocious wolves" (Matt. 7:15). We are not to be surprised by such deception, for as the Apostle Paul pointed out "Satan himself masquerades as an angel of light" (2 Cor. 11:14), neither dark nor foreboding to our natural senses. The haunted structures of Savannah are the dwelling places of many of these "angels of light".

William Shakespeare's *Hamlet* is called to mind, who, following the murder of his father, is confronted by his father's ghost who bids him to seek revenge. Hamlet ponders the nature of the encounter and questions the true identity of the ghost. He rightfully recognizes that the ghost,

> May be the devil, and the devil hath power to assume a pleasing shape. Yea, and perhaps out of my weakness and melancholy, as he is very potent with such spirits, abuses me to damn me.

Whether the Devil or his father's ghost, the thirst for revenge overtakes Hamlet. What follows is a bloodbath involving the deaths of Polonius, Ophelia, Laertes, and Claudius at his hand. Granted, this is an extreme example, but extreme dangers do await those who encounter evil, but in their ignorance, fail to recognize it as such.

In effect, this is what I propose is taking place in the shadowy corners of Savannah. Malevolent entities, demons to be exact, are at work, presenting themselves as non-threatening personalities, perhaps a loved-one who has passed on, or a deceased historical figure, stimulating curiosity, and inviting and beckoning one to approach. For those who take the bait, it never ends well.

It is not beyond the demonic to employ truth, blended with error, to steer a soul off the right course, and into a conflicted state of heart and mind.

The Devil Has Come Down

The unprecedented rise of manifested hostility and violence among individual human relationships, and societal groups and nations, is stark evidence of an escalation of demonic activity on a global level.

The main reason for this accelerated activity is stated in The Book of Revelation chapter 12, verses 10-12. The writer recognizes the joy of those who have faithfully completed their course on Earth and are now living in the kingdom of Heaven. In verse 12 we read,

> Therefore rejoice, you heavens, and you that dwell in them. But woe to the inhabitants of the earth and of the sea! For the Devil is come down to you having great wrath, because he knows that he has but a short time (AKJV).

The Devil's actions are similar to those of a wounded animal. It is much more prone to attack in the desperate condition that it finds itself. He is like the person who has lost everything in life, and in his despondency, bitterness, and anger, lashes out at others, intent on taking down with him as many as possible.

As time moves forward and the intensity of the conflict heightens, the veil between the physical and spirit realms is thinning. The evidence of either godliness or evil in the lives of individuals, seems to be more manifest. And the attacks on individuals and families is more prevalent than ever before. If more people were educated about the spirit war over their lives, men and women could be equipped to deal with it God's way. Samuel the Old Testament prophet said this about the Spirit of God, "He trains my hands for battle; my arms can bend a bow of bronze" (2Sam. 22:25).

We live in a day where we must choose whom we will serve. No more riding the fence. No one foot in and one foot out. Jesus made it clear that, "No one can serve two masters" (Matt. 6:24), and "He that is not with me, is against me" (Matt. 12:30 AKJV).

Harass and Obstruct

The Devil's quiver contains a diverse collection of arrows. Two favorites of our foe are harassment and obstruction. They work together as a means to an end, as detailed in the following personal accounting.

My wife and I are committed to following the path that God has mapped for our lives. The Scriptures tell us, "You are not your own; for you are bought with a price; therefore, glorify God in your body, and in your spirit, which are God's" (1 Cor. 6:19,20 AKJV).

In our attempts to be faithful, we have moved across the country five times in the past twenty years. In 2016, we moved from Savannah to southern California, and had certain expectations of what would await us in the new area we were settling. We firmly believed the bend in the road would lead to aspects of personal fulfillment promised by God, prior to our exodus from Savannah. However, as I pointed out in a previous chapter, our plans often tickle God's funny bone.

Not only was our preparation in leaving Savannah chockfull of unexpected challenges and roadblocks, the first twelve months of our residency in California ushered in a succession of experiences, listed below, that caused us to question the wisdom of our choice to relocate.

#1 Just after settling into our home, we were in Merced, California, on a business trip. The morning after our arrival, we were awakened by a phone call from the front desk of the motel where we were staying. We were told there was a "problem" with our rental car, parked in the front lot. We responded to the scene and learned that our car was the victim of a high-speed pursuit involving three local police units, and two men in a stolen vehicle. Apparently, after a considerable chase, the stolen vehicle had jumped the front curb of the motel and crashed into the driver's side of our rental. We found it interesting that a pursuit that began many miles from the motel, terminated on our doorstep.

#2 Shortly following the above event, I was working away from our apartment, and Elizabeth was at home, alone. I received a phone call from Elizabeth that another vehicle police chase had terminated with the perpetrator loose and armed on the complex property. She said residents were on lock-down as the police conducted their search. Four hours later, she got the all-clear notice.

#3 Within the first two or three months of our residency, two separate murders took place in the neighborhood that borders our apartment complex. To date, the crimes have not been solved.

#4 About three weeks after moving in, there was a moderate earthquake, the epicenter about twenty miles from our home.

#5 During the twelve months of our residency, our car has been broken into two different times.

#6   For the two-month period, prior to the time of my writing these words, Elizabeth and I have been dealing with "the neighbors from hell" that live in one of the tract houses that border our complex. Our direct, third-floor view of their property has produced evidence that they are involved with a dog fighting operation. The issues remain unresolved.

#7   Four weeks prior to writing these words, our two terrier dogs and I were attacked by a Great Dane that was let off its leash while on the complex property. Bailey had to undergo surgery. Also, I was bit five times while trying to dislodge the one-hundred fifty-pound dog from our eighteen-pounder.

Despite the hassle and time and effort spent in dealing with these things, we knew we were exactly where God wanted us, at the exact time he intended.

We understand that there will be a *cost* exacted when seeking to walk God's intended pathway. Mankind's enemy is an expert at hindering and opposing any advance toward the light of God. If he can't commit his sabotage instantly, he will try to wear us down to the point where we throw in the towel and go home.

Proof of Peace

As one is engaged against the demonic for divine purposes, he or she is promised that, "The peace of God that transcends all understanding, will guard your hearts and minds in Christ Jesus" (Phil. 4:7). When writing to the early church in Rome, Paul adds that "The God of Peace will soon crush Satan under your feet" (Rom. 16:20).

Maintaining peace amidst the battle is proof of one's reliance on the presence of God's Spirit, and the protection of His angels assigned to guard over one's life. It is inward, solid assurance and confidence that we, from now until the time of the eventual demise of all evil, are "more than conquerors through him who loved us" (Rom. 8:37). Those who are in Christ are in control.

Handling with peace, patience and perseverance, everything that the enemy throws at you, is a clear declaration to the Devil and his demons that their doom is sure.

Resistance

The Devil attempts to prevent us from experiencing God's highest for our individual lives, and the corporate lives of our cities. The resistance that he exerts is intended to cause us to retreat, to forfeit ground we've gained. If he can't accomplish this, his resistance will be aimed at keeping us stalled in place and settling for only maintaining our present position. If we're not advancing in the fight, then we're losing the fight.

You see, what the Devil has done is stolen a weapon that God has intended for the use of *His people*. The Scriptures promise us that if we "resist the Devil", then "he will flee" (James 4:7). We must turn the tables and use the dynamic of resistance to our own advantage. There is a prerequisite to this truth, and that is we must first be submitted and obedient to God and His agenda.

The primary fact upon which the human warrior must firmly stand in his or her opposition to evil, is that Jesus has already fought and won the spirit war. The issue of sin's power over mankind has been addressed, and the decree of death has been rescinded through Christ's sacrifice on the cross. The judgment in the eternal court of Heaven has been handed down, as the indictments against mankind, according to Paul's letter to the Colossian church, have been "nailed to the cross"

(Col. 2:14). The victory has been gained and the judgment against the Devil is a life sentence without the possibility of parole. The Devil knows this, and his worst fear is for us to remind him of it. And when we do, he turns, flees, and we have him on the run.

Legal Authority

In the meantime, before this verdict is fully carried out, the Devil is like the man or woman living in a house or on land, of which the owner has secured a legal notice of eviction. The believer is the marshal, bearing the authority of the court to carry out the eviction of the man or woman. The commission of the believer in Christ is to enforce the legal judgment of His victory over the Devil and his minions in this world. We are to expel the trespasser, the usurper, and take possession and occupy that which is rightfully ours. The deed to the earth, once again, bears the names of the sons and daughters of God.

The Christian believer should never neglect their privilege of talking *with* God, spending time communicating with Him through the offering of prayers and expressions of devotion. However, the believer is also *sent* into the fray of human and spirit battle to *exercise authority*. In situations where the demonic oppression of the human is found, our prayers are not *to God*, but are commands directed *at the dark powers* ordering release of the prisoner! In so doing, we introduce the irresistible, life-changing power of God's Spirit into the circumstances.

Mankind has been given the divine privilege of rulership over this planet. As we receive wisdom and direction from God's Spirit, we implement and enforce His will. As we understand the government and order that prevails in God's Heaven, we bring that into existence, here and now, upon this earth. Jesus taught us to pray, "Your kingdom come, Your will be done, on Earth as it is in Heaven" (Matt. 6:10).

Ignorance allows Satan to usurp what humankind is capable of and the potential for Kingdom rule on Earth. Mankind, with the scepter of divine authority once again in hand, can exercise his mandate, or, blindly allow demonic power to usurp his right.

The outcome of Heaven's war with the Devil has been decided. The forces of evil can now take only what is willingly handed to them by men and women. The goal of the Devil and his demons is to keep us ignorant and deceived about what has been secured and made available for us in Christ.

Preparation for Eternity

You may readily ask the question, *Why didn't God strip him of his powers when he was banished to Earth?* The answer is that the Devil's presence among us, with his limited capabilities, is intended for our benefit. The earth, and the authority we possess to enforce God's will, here and now, is a training ground for what will take place after the earth ceases to exist.

According to the Scriptures, the sons and daughters of God will rule and reign with Him for eternity. His domain is infinite. It is boundless and endless, inestimable to the human mind and imagination. The time we have during our brief appearance on planet Earth is our apprenticeship for all that will follow.

The destiny of rulership with God is not just for those who have received Christ's sacrifice for sin, but, potentially, for all human beings created in God's image. In view of this truth, C. S. Lewis poignantly remarked,

> It is a serious thing . . . to remember that the dullest and most uninteresting person you talk to may one day be a creature which, if you saw it now, you would be strongly tempted to worship.

In the Scriptures is a remarkable question that is posed to mankind, "Do you not know that we will judge angels" (1 Cor. 6:3)? Angels, the fallen ones, and those that remain in allegiance to God; angels, who have existed for thousands of years, maybe millions; angels, who reflect God's blinding light, who *thunder* with power, and bolt like *lightning*, yes, man will judge!

Herbert W. Armstrong, the educator and humanitarian, wrote,

> Man, now lower than angels, has a destiny far higher! Neither animal, nor angel, nor any other being except man, was created to be literally begotten by the spiritual reproductive process and then actually be born into the divine GOD FAMILY! Angels were not, and never can be begotten and BORN of God! No angel can ever become a literal member of the divine family of God!

As sons and daughters of the Creator of all things, we exercise the authority bestowed on us as royal family members, through our prayers that are in accordance with God's will and desires for mankind. Our present commands and declarations carry with them authority of the King. They release and empower God's angelic forces to push back the presence and influence of evil spirits preying on men, women, and children, and blaze a pathway for the Spirit of God into their hearts.

Remember, it is only based on what Christ has done for us that qualifies and enables us to enforce His victory, now ours, too, over the powers of darkness.

Supreme Authority

Authority means to *possess the legal right and power*. We all live under authority in one form or another. From the crib to the grave, we must answer to someone. And then, following our physical death, God is there to take an accounting of how we have lived our lives. Regardless of the multitudes who deny it, He is the Creator, we are the creature.

On the top tier of the hierarchy of rulership and authority, "sits" God. In Him is the origin of all life whether visible or invisible. The root of "authority" is the French word *auctor*, or "author", which means a person who *causes* something, or, more broadly defined as *one who originated or gave existence to something*.

For example, I am the author of this book, meaning the writer of this *original work*. Similarly, all human beings are the original work of God, *our Author*, and therefore subject to His authority.

As our Supreme Authority, He is the source and Originator of moral Law, to which we must answer. As the One responsible for our existence, He possesses the legal right and power to enforce His Law and to call us to account.

When people rebel against good authority, whether parental or institutional, they are essentially rebelling against God's authority. They are denying His right to hold them accountable to His Law, the moral principles that are to govern human attitudes and actions. That is the nature of *anarchy*, the unwillingness to recognize and submit to authority. It is the rejection of God's Law and right to dictate and regulate the moral behavior of his creation.

Fathers Who Father

In God's design for humanity, the basic building blocks of any society are the family and the church. One's allegiance should first be to God, then to family, and then to the church.

As Creator, God is Father to all humanity. As such, the entire human race, and every person ever born, would make up His family. However, the greater part of mankind has rejected God as their Father, having turned to their own way. Because of that, He has placed "fathers" among us; into individual family units, and into the various church groups that have come together within society. They are to be representatives of His Fatherhood, exercising compassion and kindness, as well as strength to protect and correct.

The human father, committed foremost to his Maker, is to nurture and care for those divinely placed in the family he has been entrusted. They are to represent God's father heart and tend to both the physical and spiritual needs of each family member.

Then there's the church.

The authority of God is intended to be expressed through the Christian church, those who have been joined to Him and profess a knowledge of the truth. People will derive their concept of God, and, in turn, their view of authority, from the human representation of those that claim to have relationship with Him.

Generally, the church is thought of as a building, not necessarily the group of people that meet inside it. However, according to New Testament teaching, the church is not wood and concrete, but flesh and blood. The church *is* people; the people that have received Christ as their personal Savior and acknowledge Him as the Savior of all humanity. True believers, wherever on planet Earth they are found, makeup the body of Christ, of whom He is the Head. They are sons and daughters of God the Father, His representatives in this world.

Among this body of people, God has also placed "spiritual" fathers, those who come alongside others lacking a representation of God's heart, and usher them along to maturity.

It is how these fathers render their responsibilities that has a great bearing on the course that a society takes. Again, it will directly influence one's concept of authority, and response to authority. Rebellion among people is directly related to the failure of these fathers.

The Evil of Anarchy

When a people group reject God's authority, the foundation of human authority ultimately collapses. It is only when man is in right relationship to God, a place of submission, can he retain his position to rule that which God has placed under him. Any hope for prosperity is nullified.

The Devil knows what rebellion can do. He is the first to have led one. When a society revolts against good authority, a poison enters the bloodstream of the populace that causes a breakdown of the social bonds between the individual and their community. As submission to governing authority erodes, the evil leaven of anarchy spreads within the society. It is a rapid demise as the whole concept of law, the rules that are to govern human behavior, are discarded. And when the rule of law is abandoned, then an arbitrary, indiscriminate exercise of power takes hold. That kind of power is demonic to the core. Chaos reigns and complete destruction is the end result.

So, what happened to Lady Savannah that has prevented her from flourishing? How was she seduced, and how did the enemy gain access to inject his poison? All cities have entry points. Let's identify them.

Chapter 21

The Walls and Gates of a City

The cities of ancient civilizations were characterized by their formidable walls and gates. The walls were defensive fortifications built to protect a city or settlement from outside aggressors. Towers were also built into the walls, usually above the city gates, so that an approaching enemy could be seen, and the gate defended by those stationed on the walls. The walls were typically forty feet high and eight feet wide and could only be crossed by entering one of several city gates, strategically positioned in the walls.

Walls

Twenty-five hundred years ago, the prophet Nehemiah wrote of a city that had been overran by the forces of their enemy. Again, we consider Jerusalem, as her promise and potential, as well as the ebb and flow of her prosperity, is clearly put forth in the Scriptures. Jerusalem serves as a model to all other cities of what can take place, dependent on the response of the people and leaders to God's dealings.

Nehemiah was in exile in Persia, as were his fellow countrymen and women. Nehemiah was the cupbearer to King Artaxerxes. Upon learning of the distress of the few who remained in Jerusalem among the rubble, Nehemiah requested permission from Artaxerxes to return to his homeland to rebuild the city. He knew the personal dangers of such a request; however, God gave him favor with the King who provided Nehemiah with safe passage to his homeland and the material resources to launch the project.

Nehemiah's accounting then details the difficulties he faced as he led the 'remnant' of Israelites in the restoration process. The story emphasizes that in the process, the walls were built *first*, as they represented a defensive fortification against the surrounding peoples who were not eager to see Jerusalem return to her former glory.

The picture that Nehemiah draws for us is that the "walls" protecting a people, the defense of the populace, are only as strong as their commitment to the one capable of ensuring their safety and prosperity as a society. When we seek to honor and serve the Creator of all things, nothing can harm us, as the one bent on our destruction, the Devil, is kept outside the invisible barriers of our lives and communities.

In the ways we have previously discussed, Jerusalem's greatest enemy was not a pagan people committed to their destruction. Resident within them was the real threat. As is true with all communities of people, the Israelites were masters of their own fate. A rejection of divine authority and the law of God resulted in the departure of His presence from among the society of people. The internal corruption had worked its destruction prior to the infiltration of the Persians and the taking of the Jews into captivity. They, simply, walked in and gathered the spoils of a moral war that already had been decided.

These truths were foremost in the heart and mind of Nehemiah, as his primary mission emphasized the people's need to renew their commitment to honor and serve the true and living God. If they refused, the rebuilding of the city would be meaningless.

Gates

In antiquity, the *gate* generally represented authority or power. To "possess the gate" (Gen. 22:17; 24:60) was to possess the city itself. It was an entrance point where control of the people was determined.

The Hypertext Bible Commentary offers the following insights with regard to this term:

> In the Ancient Near East, city gates were neither merely entrances, nor only used for military protection. As a potentially weak point in the defenses, the gates of Israelite walled cities typically had three chambers giving four sets of 'doors' and defended spaces between . . . the chambers were roofed and so available for use as public buildings. It is likely that these chambers served as 'offices' for city administration . . . In the outside gate, market stalls would have been erected, as they are today. The 'gate' was therefore, the marketplace where traders and peasants met with city folk to sell and exchange goods. Inside the gateway too, a space was left without buildings, this served as a communal area for meetings and public justice. Just inside the gate at Dan there is a raised dais that had provision for a canopy to be erected. This would have served for the judge's throne. So, when the Bible talks of the 'gate', it may mean the

'market', the 'law court', the 'public forum' where community business was discussed, or the 'town hall' or administrative center.

So, the term *gates* as it pertains to a city, is a place where those in authority were stationed to oversee the city's affairs or to dispense justice in both civil and criminal matters. The implication includes a meeting place for business trade that would affect the economy of the city. The most fundamental aspects of a city were molded and shaped by those positioned at her gates.

If what took place at a these gates could be influenced and directed by dark spiritual forces, then the city itself would become subject to a degree of control by those entities. Certainly, the way to invade the fabric of the society and take hold of the populace was to secure the agreement (the will and consent) of those in authority who occupied the city gates.

Hence, to research and know the history of a city, specifically, what major events took place, and how civic leaders exerted their authority, is the means to understand what formed and shaped the society at large.

Prime Targets

What are the present-day gates of a city? They are the social institutions, and they are the prime targets of the Devil.

Life on Earth is defined and regulated through hierarchal structures, as it is in the spiritual realm. In human society, everything is governed in one way or another. Marriages, families, schools, churches, labor organizations, community groups, law enforcement, entire cities and nations are all managed and controlled by these groupings of people that have formed within the community for a common purpose. These institutions make up the social order within the city and profoundly influence the attitudes and behavior of its citizens.

If one aspires to gain control of a city, or a nation for that matter, then one will seek to control its institutions. Therefore, the Devil is seeking to rule through these various authority structures. The leaders of these organizations have targets on their backs. The principles they embrace and how they exert their authority and influence will eventually be the issue that serves to undermine or strengthen the society.

Paul urged the early Christians to pray "for kings, and all that are in authority, that we may lead a quiet and peaceable life in all godliness and honesty" (1 Tim. 2:2 AKJV). The city is more readily freed or bound, as the institutional bodies issue policy, regulations, or laws, compatible with the nature of good or evil.

The Seven Societal Institutions

According to author and educator Oliver DeMille, "The seven major societal institutions are family, community, religion, academia, business, media, and government." These are the *gates*, the places where we find authority in operation within the present-day American city. How they function will directly influence the beliefs and behavior of the city's populace.

Let's take quick looks at the intended purpose of each of these institutions in relation to the United States. It is evident that America has prospered as these institutions have executed their responsibilities with integrity. Bear in mind that because the human element of an institution changes over the course of time, the character and nature of a city, and on a larger scale, a nation, is subject to change, as well.

DeMille's summation is concise and to the point. He writes:

Family

"First is family, as it is the foundational institution within any community of people, whether it be a major city or a tiny village.

"The role of the family is to ensure responsible citizens, preserve society, and balance the desires of individual liberty with the demands of community responsibility.

"It is within the family unit that a child develops a sense of individuality and learns how he has been uniquely created to contribute to society. A child learns responsibility and that at times he must forgo his own desires and preferences in order to serve another's interests."

Community

"The original concept of federalism meant that as many decisions as possible were made at the lowest level possible.

"Strong, local self-government was the keystone to the original American system.

"Understanding that power centralizes and expands, the Founders new that the bulk of our political decisions should be made on the community level.

"The role of the community, therefore, is to prevent the centralization of power by keeping responsibility and decision-making close to the people."

Religion

"John Adams wrote that, 'Religion and virtue are the only foundations, not only of republicanism and of all free government, but of social felicity under all government and in all the combinations of human society'.

"George Washington affirmed, 'Whatever may be conceded to the influence of refined education on minds of peculiar structure…reason and experience both forbid us to expect that national morality can prevail in exclusion of religious principle'.

"The role of religion is to remind republican citizens of their duties to and reliance upon God. Virtue is the bedrock of free society, and religion provides a constant reminder of that fact.

"Furthermore, religion serves as a venue where citizens serve God by serving their fellowman; philanthropy is enacted in large part through religion."

Academia

"Academia advances culture through knowledge, helps to prevent socio-economic inequities, breaks through boundaries of human ignorance and fear, helps societies to avoid repeated historical mistakes, and serves as a check on the government by keeping citizens informed of civic affairs.

"As John Adams said, 'Liberty cannot be preserved without a general knowledge among the people…They have a right, an indisputable, unalienable, indefeasible, divine right to that most dreaded and envied kind of knowledge — I mean, of the characters and conducts of their rulers'."

Business

"The role of business is to provide exchange, commerce, and ultimately widespread prosperity. In a free market economy prices tend to decrease through competition and innovation, the ultimate benefactors being end consumers of products and services.

"In a free market economy poverty decreases, the standard of living rises, and people find self-fulfillment as their subsistence needs are met.

"In *The 5,000 Year Leap,* Cleon Skousen wrote that, 'By 1905 the U.S. had become the richest industrial nation in the world. With only five percent of the earth's continental area and merely six percent of the world's population, the American people were producing over half of almost everything — clothes, food, houses, transportation, communications, even luxuries'.

"This occurred because of our free market economy, where business was left free to fulfill its role."

Media

The role of the media is to disseminate information, highlight important current events, and to essentially stand as a witness, an observer of cultural, political, community, and educational events.

"A healthy media provides a check on the government and increases the political astuteness of republican citizens."

Government

"The role of government is to protect unalienable rights. Government is the institutionalization of force, and as such should not do anything that would not be right for an individual to do (such as steal).

"As Thomas Jefferson said, '…a wise and frugal Government, which shall restrain men from injuring one another, shall leave them otherwise free to regulate their own pursuits of industry and improvement, and shall not take from the mouth of labor the bread it has earned'."

An Eighth Institution

Over the course of her relatively brief history, American institutions have been shaped by the personal and political agendas of its leaders, who either succeeded or failed to maintain the ideals of her founders. In recent times, the unprecedented quest for wealth, status, and power have influenced the motives and activities of those positioned in seats of authority. The present path of America mirrors that of Jerusalem, not too far prior to the Persian invasion.

The importance of the various institutions to maintain a balance of influence cannot be overstated. When one or the other exerts an inordinate measure of power over the populace, then a corresponding measure of tyranny will exist.

The existence and influence of an 8th institution is worthy of consideration. *Entertainment.* There can be no doubt that in recent decades, especially, in first world cultures, the popularity and celebrity of sports figures, singers, and actors in stage, television, and motion pictures has provided a "pulpit" from which to expound their ideologies that shape public opinion and lifestyle choice.

Presently, these three institutions are in the Devil's crosshairs: academia, media, and entertainment. These avenues of dissemination of information have the means and opportunity to seduce the general public. As those enlightened by God, we must exercise continual vigilance of these organizations that wield this authority. Our engagement must include protest and an infiltration of the institutions with the light of Truth. We can't sit back, fold our hands, and relinquish these institutions to demonic control.

So, we must ask ourselves: what past decisions of my city's gatekeepers have contributed to her present state of being? Of equal importance is to know what is presently occurring among institutional leadership that could sustain or alter her course?

Chapter 22

Divine Order

Mother Earth

As we have learned, the battle "ground" on which the destiny of human life is being contested is planet Earth, and within the atmosphere that covers it. In our quest for Truth, it would behoove us to dig deeper and take a look at the role the earth plays in this life and death drama. There is an inherent gravitation that draws and connects men and women of flesh and blood to this physical sphere on which we dwell.

Of prime importance is that the Devil no longer has the right to roam the earth and pick and choose whom he will devour. Psalm 115:16 with certainty pronounces, "The highest heavens belong to the Lord, but the earth he has given to mankind." You and I, once again, possess the divine right and authority to preside over what will shape the various societies of human population, and rule the souls of the cities in which we live, light or darkness, life or death.

As we have discussed, all authority originates with God, the Father of all spirit life. Despite people's recognition of "sky gods", He is the Most High, the Maker of all things. Order breaks down, and chaos ensues when humans deny His existence or refuse to submit to His authority, as clearly demonstrated by our forerunners, Adam and Eve.

We also talked of the essence of the soul, and how it must be in submission to the living and enlightened human spirit if it is to prosper. So, there is also the role of the physical body, and the place it has in each of our make-up. The order must be maintained for the plan and intentions of God to be realized for the man or woman, and the society at large.

The human body, the flesh and blood of which it consists, must be subservient to the human soul and spirit that it cloves. Our physical body is a temporal housing for our eternal soul and spirit. I like to call it our Earth-suit. Our body will return to the dust of the earth, following death. Our eternal soul and spirit will return to God, our Maker.

The divine order is that the Spirit of God communes with our human spirit, that informs our soul, that "moves" the body to act in right ways. The body, soul, and spirit must always be in subjection to the Divine. When divine order is violated, then the human and our cities are in dire trouble.

With the temptation and fall of the first man and woman, came an exercise of the human will independent from God, as mankind was now separated from the influence and guidance of God's Spirit. With this occurrence, the creature assumed the place of God, and the human intellect became the fount of all truth. The idea of spirit became foreign, irrelevant, as the gratification of the body and the stimulation of the human physical senses controlled the man or woman.

The Earth, the rotating ball of dirt, also became sacred as it now solely represented the present and future source for sustaining life. It is the *here and now* that became the all-important, all-consuming. Global Warming, environmentalism, preservation of Earth's resources, and protection of endangered species, becomes the focus and activity of those committed to the needs of "Mother Earth" and the various forms of biological life she sustains.

It is interesting that the Hebrew word for *earth*, used in the Genesis account of creation, is *Adamah*, meaning *ground*, and is a feminine form with strong connections with *woman* in theology.

There is nothing wrong with the desire to care for and preserve Earth's natural resources and environment. In and of itself, the pursuit is a good thing. We must remember, the body of man was created from the earth and mankind given the divine directive to tend to the earth. However, when our time and energies are foremost devoted to Mother Earth, and Father God is denied and forgotten, our forests may thrive, and Spotted Owls may be plenteous, but our eternal spirits will remain withered and bound.

A clear example of this inclination to deify the earth is reflected within ancient American Indian cultures. Their religious practice includes a role reversal as they see people belonging to the land, instead of the land belonging to the people. They would attest that all created things, animals, birds, rivers and streams, the mountains, are sacred and worthy of mankind's devotion, while failing to acknowledge the one Creator of all things.

The Organization of Evil and Planet Earth

Satan is the god of this world, not of Earth. Earth is mankind's domain, redeemed man, not the man still wandering and bound in a kingdom of darkness. The world system and its values are a product of fallen mankind's affair with the Devil, an embracing of the demonic lure that appeals to his carnal appetites. The Devil is ruler of that world.

The Scriptures reveal that in usurping mankind's right to rule this planet, there exists a hierarchy of demonic authority over, and upon the earth. The Bible does not go into great detail about this government. I believe this is because God wants us to think and act on the outworking of how we enforce Christ's victory over these evil forces, and not get into the "weeds" of theology. However, we are given a basic understanding of its organization and operation.

It suffices to say that the purpose of these evil entities is to keep as many human beings as possible, bound in darkness. The good news is that the areas over which these demons operate are subject to the penetration of God's light, and the commands of Supreme authority, as His army, consisting of angels and Spirit-empowered human beings, wage war against Satan and his followers.

For entertainment, I'll take in the sensational views of a Stephen King or an H.P. Lovecraft, but when the souls of humans lie in the balance, I go to the Scriptures, aka, The Supernatural According to God. Let's look at what we do know.

The Evil Hierarchy

Since man's fall, Satan has set up his government over the planet. There exists a hierarchy of evil powers with specific assignments. These tasks consist of four distinct functions:

1. Exercising control over land areas
2. Infiltrating human authority structures
3. Opposing Heaven's angelic forces
4. Afflicting individual human beings

In Ephesians 6:12 the Apostle Paul identified the ranking of the spirits of evil that operate within the framework of Satan's governmental administration and execute these tasks. There would likely be a descending order of authority or power in his listing of demonic entities:

For our struggle is not against flesh and blood, but against the **rulers**, against the **authorities**, against the **powers** of this dark world and against the **spiritual forces of evil** in the heavenly realms.

Let's dissect this army of darkness and look at what we are up against. The immediate human reaction to what I'm about to describe is to either feel intimidated or skeptical. It will not benefit any of us for our attention to dwell on the whole of evil government. That contemplation is overwhelming to our finite minds. Our responsibility and accountability is to stay discerning and take action against the evil we encounter in our sphere of human relationships. Our confidence lies in our dependence on God's presence, guidance, and empowerment.

Always keep in mind that we are enforcing the fruit of a victory already won. It is a clean-up operation of a foe who refuses to acknowledge their defeat and must be forced to surrender. We need not be impressed by our enemy, just informed, as we remain in steadfast awe of God.

Among scholars, the range of interpretation is significant with regard to the precise meaning of the original Greek words that identify these evil entities. However, the general nature and operation of each is clear.

Rulers / Principalities

The Greek word ἀρχάς, transliterated into the English alphabet *Archas*, is defined as *Rulers* or *Principalities*, which is the territory or jurisdiction of a prince.

Territory and jurisdiction have to do with authority and control over specific areas of land. Time bears witness to great wars fought between factions of mankind for possession of portions of the earth. People have been subject to great evils by others driven to control land areas.

We see this inherent territorial mentality manifested through tales of the "Old West", when men would stake their claim to pieces of land, work the soil, and with great pride, pass it on to ensuing generations of family. We also see the possessive attitude displayed among ethnic sub-cultures in depressed neighborhoods, where an excessive, rabid watch over their "turf" is evident.

As we discussed, mankind is inherently drawn to possess the land, to exercise his territorial authority. And so is the Devil. He inhabited the earth prior to mankind's arrival. Following God's mandate that mankind rule over the earth, the Devil was intent to steal mankind's legal authority, and maintain his free reign over the planet. He succeeded in that goal and exercised that right…up until Jesus arrived on the scene.

So, according to Paul, the top tier of satanic authority is occupied by evil *rulers* or *princes* whose assignments are to exercise control over specific land areas of the planet. Their activity consists of the oversight of lower level spirit entities.

As his title, "prince of the power of the air" (Eph. 2:2 AKJV) denotes, Satan is one of these princes. However, he is the *prince of princes* among demonic entities, whose jurisdiction is over the whole world, as Jesus referred to him as the "prince of this world" (John 16:11).

Authorities

Next are Authorities. This word in the original Greek tongue is ἐξουσίας, transliterated to the English, *exousia*. It has the combined implication of both supernatural and natural government.

The Apostle Paul is expressing the involvement of demonic spirt forces in influencing and manipulating human structures of authority, such as the institutions we defined earlier.

Powers / Hosts

The Greek word, πνευματικός, ή, όν, transliterated to the English, *pneumatikos*, and speaks of the evil demonic hosts that operate within the atmosphere that surrounds the earth. These *powers*, apparently, do not directly engage human beings, or attempt to influence human authority structures, but are in an invisible, constant battle against God's angelic forces of light. They seek to hinder the advance of Heaven's angels and operate in the atmosphere, also referred to as the *heavenlies*. When Scripture describes Satan as the "prince of the power of the air", it is these *powers* that is being referred to.

Spiritual Forces of Evil

The original Greek word, κοσμοκράτορας, rendered in English as *kosmokratoras*, are the ground-level forces of evil that operate in this world, the practical level of our routine existence. They directly oppose, attack, and afflict individual human beings. They embody specific elements of the nature of evil such as lust, anger, fear, jealousy, bitterness, and hatred, and incite humans to destructive and violent actions, including lying, slander, robbery, assault, rape, murder, and suicide.

Our Basic Strategy

As there exists a descending order of authority in the hierarchy of evil, so there is a corresponding ascending order with regard to the difficulty in taking down these strongholds of evil.

The believer must first deal with the *ground level forces* that seek to immobilize and render him useless in the fight. On a personal level, the believer must be vigilant in "walking" with God on a daily basis, confident in His promises of protection from, and power over the Evil One. With this comes a graduation in the believer's sphere of authority. The man or woman is then prepared to confront the evils that are at work among the larger community of which he or she is a part.

In confronting the higher level of the *powers of the air*, there must be more of a united effort within the ranks of believers. This holds true when dealing with the *authorities*, and, ultimately, the *rulers* and *principalities*. The greater the level of concentrated evil presence and activity, the greater the need for concerted action among God's people.

Demonic forces are weakened and the area of land/territory under demonic control is diminished as the people of God battle His way. Greater power to repossess what the Devil has stolen is the result of agreement about the problem and uniting to do something about it. Greater unity among God's people will result in a greater release of power, and damage to the kingdom of darkness.

The higher up the chain of evil authority that we set our sights, the more preparation and planning is necessary. The Devil will mock the ones that confront him with a token show of strength, devoid of the power of God's Spirit. To seek to undermine the control of the demonic on any level, let alone that of a prince, without considerable individual and corporate sacrifice, will only result in confusion, frustration, and, quite possibly, physical harm.

Engaging in war against the Devil is not an Xbox computer game that may be won or lost comfortably seated on a cushy couch. The individual Christian and the community of believers that challenge evil strongholds will draw the attention of the demon world. Believers that are asleep in the light can do the kingdom of darkness no harm, and the Devil allows them to snore away. It is those that rise up and declare Christ's triumph over the powers of darkness who will experience the fray of conflict, as demonic forces seek to weaken and silence God's man or woman.

The Devil's goal is to divide and conquer God's people, the ones to whom divine authority has been granted in Christ. To that end, he employs ground-level spirits that promote envy, pride, and gossip. To a great degree, he has been successful as these evils are rampant in Christendom. Until God's people get serious, and, together, pick-up and employ their spiritual weapons, the Devil will continue to run roughshod over the people of planet Earth.

But be assured, there is a means by which to confront and dismantle Satan's evil government, regardless of their rank. Those that prevail will be equipped with the full armor of God.

The Armor of God

To those interested in learning what makes the Christian believer unique among the rest of the world's population, I invite them to take a few minutes and read Paul's timeless letter to the church in Ephesus.

Initially, Paul points to the blessings of being a believer in Christ. An amazing, staggering list of all that we now possess as sons and daughters of the Most High. The Spirit of God is emphasized as He who works within the believer and empowers the man or woman in their daily living. Christ's supremacy is then highlighted and culminates with the fact that he is Head over the body of believers, who, in Him, possess authority over all the power of evil and works of darkness.

Paul then issues an acknowledgment that the believer can do all things, that nothing is impossible for the man or woman that is submitted and obedient to the One who has freely given all of these privileges and gifts.

God's people are urged to put away all practice of sin and not give the Devil an opportunity to take advantage. Paul states how we should respond to the grace that we have received from God and emphasizes that unity is the result of actively pursuing goodness and mercy with those within the sphere of our relationships.

Paul then speaks of our deliverance out of darkness, into the light of God. In fact, we are described as "light in the Lord", and our intended effect to "expose darkness", is stated.

Paul wraps up his teaching in Chapter 6 with a list of what we have been provided as *children of light* that guarantees our triumph over the evil we confront:

> Therefore, put on the full armor of God, so that when the day of evil comes, you may be able to stand your ground, and after you have done everything to stand. Stand firm then, with the *belt of truth* buckled around your waist, with the *breastplate of righteousness* in place, and with your *feet fitted with the readiness that comes from the gospel of peace*. In addition to all this, take up the *shield of faith*, with which you can extinguish all the flaming arrows of the evil one. Take the *helmet of salvation* and the *sword of the Spirit*, which is the word of God (Eph. 6:10-17).

It is inferred that as we *go* and infiltrate the places occupied by evil, we are to *stand our ground*, the emphasis on *our ground*, not the enemies, as we repossess our rightful inheritance. In order to stand, our spiritual armor, likened to that of the Roman soldier of that day, must be in place:

1. The *belt* of a Roman soldier was a substantial strap worn about the body. It held the sword and other weapons in place. *Truth* should cleave to us as a belt cleaves to our body. Without truth, the other elements of our armor serve no purpose.

2. The *breastplate* protects the vital organs of the warrior. Without it, the death of the warrior is certain. Christ's *righteousness*, accredited to the believer, gives new life. Without it he or she faces sure, eternal death.

3. The *feet* move the warrior into the fray of battle. Carrying the message of eternal life through Jesus Christ (the *Gospel*), we are prepared to offer the means by which peace with God is secured. From that position, we resist the enemy and stand firm.

4. A *shield* protects the warrior's physical being, whereas the shield of *faith* protects the human soul from the Devil's harassment and accusations. Faith assures us that the "flaming arrows" of the evil one will not find their mark.

5. A *helmet* protects the head of the warrior; the head where the human brain is "housed". The assurance and hope we possess as recipients of eternal *salvation* guards us from discouragement, doubt, and fear, so prevalent in today's world. We know who we are and where we are going.

6. The *sword* is the only offensive weapon in the list. The sword is what delivers the death blow to an enemy.

Our sword, *God's word*, supported by the belt of Truth, cuts deep, right to the core of any issue in life. It brings understanding that the Devil has already suffered defeat at the hands of Christ, and through Him, we have been delivered from the depths of spiritual darkness.

In later chapters we will identify additional means and strategies provided by the Captain of our Salvation (Heb. 2:10) that must be employed as God's people are led forth by His Spirit.

Chapter 23

Evil Presence

In the natural realm, there are two ways that the presence of evil entities is manifested: through the soul of the affected person, and within the atmosphere of the existing physical environment.

Our Souls Emanate Death or Life

We often consider a person for what he or she has done and how their actions have influenced a situation or its outcome. We look at them as the starting and ending points for understanding what occurred. We are overlooking a very crucial step in the process. What was it that influenced them in the first place? What force or power was brought to bear upon their life, upon their mind or emotions, that motivated them to think and act in such a way?

"It's just a bad habit", we often hear. If truth be known, a bad habit is often just an excuse for the presence and influence of bad spirits who have gained a measure of control over the person's life. Not habits such as biting one's fingernails or cracking one's knuckles, but habits of an immoral nature.

Remember, the evil entity is not visible to the human eye, as it is spirit. However, the nature of the demon that has infiltrated the life of an individual, will manifest through their soul. Its presence and nature will be evident to others. The thinking of the mind, the emotions expressed, and the quality of the choices of the man or woman will be in accordance with the *kind* of spirit by which they are gripped.

The God Makers

What is an idol? It is the product of what we consider as supremely worthy of our time and attention, and willingly allow to shape and define our lives.

The Old Testament describes how men and women worshipped *idols* of their own making; that they would hope and trust in an object formed by their hands, that had no ability to move, to speak, or to think a single thought, let alone deliver them from their enemy.

King David made this observation concerning false gods and idols, "Those who make them will be like them, and so will all who trust in them" (Psalm 115:8).

Another psalmist, Asaph, chronicled the words of God, "You thought I was exactly like you" (Ps. 50:21), underscoring mankind's inability to accurately assess His character and nature and to ascribe to Him their own limitations.

We traditionally think of idols as being distorted little characters carved from wood or stone, set before an individual, to which they bow. While this does occur, the greater, more subtle fact is that idols are formed within the mind of a person. We imagine what God should be like and we move through life with that marred concept. Instead of discovering through divine revelation that we are created in God's image, left to ourselves, we involuntarily "create" God in our own image.

So, of primary importance is one's concept of God. We must have *right thinking* about God. Who and/or what does one imagine and think God to be? The answer to that question will dramatically influence the course and activities of one's lifetime. However, left to ourselves, that is not possible. It requires the initiative and intervention of God's Spirit to supernaturally enlighten our thinking concerning God's nature and character.

If a man or woman continually rejects God's advances to impart truth concerning His existence and the nature and purpose of mankind, the Devil will gladly fill the void with his own distorted explanations.

The Apostle Paul makes this clear in his writing to the Roman believers of his day, "They exchanged the truth of God for a lie and worshiped and served created things rather than the Creator" (Rom. 1:25 BSB). He then lists the ways that the presence of evil manifests in and through individuals who have offered their lives to the Devil,

> They have become filled with every kind of wickedness, evil, greed, and depravity. They are full of envy, murder, strife, deceit, and malice. They are gossips, slanderers, God-haters, insolent, arrogant, and boastful. They invent ways of doing evil; they disobey parents; they have no understanding, no fidelity, no love, no mercy. (Rom. 1:29-31).

You and I have observed these extreme evil manifestations in the lives of individuals and whole groups of people. But how often have we attributed them to a spirit source? Or the process by which this evil fruit is born? Once again, it is spirit world activity that dictates what is produced in the physical realm.

The bottom line here is that we become like the one we worship. Our lives will be marked by either the dark nature of evil, or the light and life of God. And because the soul of a city is comprised of the sum of its parts, the citizens, this is also true of the city!

Spirits of Delusion in America

Paul also wrote to the early Christians in Thessalonica of the inevitable end of individuals who in their stubborn refusal to accept the truth become consumed in their deception. In addressing a future time, Paul puts forth,

> (This is) how Satan works. He will use all sorts of displays of power through signs and wonders that serve the lie, all the ways that deceives those who are perishing. They perish because they refused to love the truth and so be saved. For this reason, God sends them a powerful delusion so that they will believe the lie (2 Thess. 2:9-11).

This "delusion" is an evil spirit entity God allows to exert greater influence over the people because of their choice to reject truth. It can encompass the entire population of a city or nation. God will at times manipulate evil to accomplish His purposes!

As I write these words, the United States of America has seen a dramatic rise among her society of blatant opposition to her founding principles and ideals of "liberty and justice for all". Most of these attacks have come from a vocal minority that claim to be inclusive and tolerant of the beliefs and lifestyles of others, but, in actuality, practice a hatred and violence aimed at those who are not in agreement with their narrow goals and methods of achieving them. What they accuse *others* of is, in fact, what *they* are guilty of.

In attempting to further their agenda, these various liberal factions, collectively known as the "radical left", are marked by a distinct lack of common sense or basic rational thinking. In increasing measure, their attacks and accusations have become absurd and bizarre to the point that one would conclude that their mental capabilities are severely compromised. Accompanying this malady of irrational thought are displays of emotional instability expressed by physical hostilities directed at their perceived enemies.

My belief is this conduct and condition is evidence of significant demonic influence gripping these individuals and groups. Theirs is the product of an *agreement* with darkness. When a person refuses God's advances and repeatedly rejects the truth, God will withdraw, leaving that individual subject to greater influence and control by that which they have chosen to embrace, in this case, the spirit of delusion I earlier referenced. These are attacks waged against God and His rule among mankind by the spirit and human inhabitants of the kingdom of darkness.

God-fearing citizens must be vigilant to confront these devilish manifestations with divine authority, and the human being with the light of Truth. Too often we argue politics and economics in an effort to convert their thinking and gain their allegiance to our political views of social issues. Instead we must address their spiritual blindness with that which will deliver them from the hold on their lives and source of their bondage. In the process, some will turn and be freed, while others will scoff at the Truth and remain in darkness.

If left unopposed, this mental and emotional erraticism that we have seen among a segment of the population will intensify and spread like a leaven among the citizenry. As a greater number of people receive what the Devil is offering, it can be expected for the power and personality of the territorial spirit to increase exponentially over a land mass and the human population.

Atmospheric Conditions

The *mood* or *feeling* within the atmosphere of a city is often telltale as to the *kind* of demonic entity that is present. It is also a gauge as to the degree of the demonic hold on people groups within that environment, whether a household, an institution, a city, or even a nation.

In 1990, while working with Youth With A Mission, commonly known as YWAM, I led a team of young adults into what was then the U.S.S.R. This evil empire had run its course and was collapsing from within. We were involved in working with churches in what was the Soviet Republic of Estonia. The people of this land were among the first to rise up and declare their independence against the tyranny of the centralized government in Moscow, that they had suffered under since 1940.

Tallinn: A City of Hope

At the time of our visit, it was a season of great hope mingled with some trepidation for these bold, determined people. Mikhail Gorbachev had seen the writing on the wall and was capitulating to the collective forces of Western powers and rebel republics that were demanding they be loosed from the iron fist of communism. Boris Yeltsin was poised and ready to fill the gap, but with a different vision for the Russian people, and a willingness to allow the various republics to walk a path of their own choosing.

I recall the excitement and the sense of destiny that was in the hearts and minds of the Estonian population. Their spirit of determination and sacrifice was embodied in what came to be called The Singing Revolution, spearheaded by the church leaders in Estonia. It was the outward expression of what was resident within a society of people possessed by great national pride and a willingness to lay it all on the line to live free, regardless of the cost.

The atmosphere of Tallinn, the capital of Estonia, was palatable with this optimism as the people peacefully protested the occupation of their land with voices lifted in songs that proclaimed their unique traditions and identity. This was their choice of weapon and one that the demonic forces behind the communist regime could not contend with.

In direct contrast to this mood and atmosphere that covered the land of Estonia, was what we were to experience in a visit to Moscow.

Moscow: A City of Despair

Near the end of the outreach trip, the team boarded a soviet train in the small, outlying city of Narva, Estonia, that was bound for Moscow. Our plan was to take a low-key tour of the city while taking the spiritual pulse of what prevailed over the society of Muscovites.

As I rode through the night hours and drew closer to the hub of the evil empire that was the U.S.S.R., I wrestled with my natural tendency toward fear and the reality that instead of riding into enemy territory, I could be home, poolside, sipping iced tea. Countering that was the steadfast assurance that, because this team was sent with divine purpose, the One who sent us had our backs.

As the train lurched to a halt in the underground of the city, the team exited into the station, rode several escalators to street level, and then walked into an atmosphere thick with the presence of darkness. Every member of the team was affected, similarly. The buildings all seemed cloaked in gray. It was as if the city was enveloped by a dark, oppressive cloud that was suffocating the people. Their faces were as a blank canvas, void of expression and life. A sense of foreboding, a threatening weight, hung in the atmosphere, like an axe waiting to drop.

During our brief stay, the team prayed frequently asking the Spirit of God for discernment of what spirit powers were in control over the people. As understanding was given, we began conducting pointed presentations of the Gospel message in various art forms, as well as straight-forward preaching, directed against the demonic powers of fear, despair, and the gloom of darkness. Ours was a message of faith, hope, and the joy of deliverance from a bondage far greater than the grip of communism.

As the light of Truth invaded the environment, the evil strongholds were shaken. Many of those present responded with sincere questions, while others made decisions to follow Christ. It is as darkness is expelled that the human heart is enlightened concerning its spiritual condition and need of a Savior.

We were confident that if our physical eyes had been opened to view the activity within the surrounding atmosphere, we would've marveled at the supernatural clash between God's angels and the demonic forces. In awe we would watch as the forces of Light scattered and routed mankind's dark enemies. As His representatives, we had declared Christ's victory, and these devils had no alternative but to flee in terror!

Thus far in our journey, we have focused on spiritual truths that pertain to the individual, and how he or she may be freed to know and walk with their Creator. We have considered the battle that takes place in the spirit realm that has great bearing on an individual's quality and course of life. We have looked at what makes up the soul of a city, and how it is targeted by both the forces of good and those of evil. As we move forward and apply these principles to the city of Savannah, Georgia, continue to contemplate the soul of your own city. I believe God's Spirit will give insight into His plan and strategy to liberate her people.

Chapter 24

Ignorance and Strongholds

As these evil forces execute their assignments among mankind unchallenged, the Devil's grip intensifies within the souls of men and women. The Scriptures call these *strongholds*, and they can infiltrate the soul of one person or a whole city, if ignored and left to spin their evil webs.

The hold and control of demonic power over a land mass or city is a formidable force and not easily dealt with. The roots of an evil stronghold are entrenched. They reach deep and strangle the soul life of the society of people. If there is a lack of understanding as to the nature of the power and how the entity gained control, nothing will ever change. In fact, darkness and destruction will intensify.

This state of ignorance frustrates those with good desires and intentions for their town as, inevitably, they hit an impenetrable, immoveable wall that won't fall because the core issue isn't being properly addressed.

We made mention earlier of William Jay, the designer of Savannah's finest buildings, and his departing declaration of the city as a "Niobe of cities, a chaos of ruins." Jay's was a grave pronouncement of divine judgment. In Greek mythology, Niobe is the wife of King Amphion of Thebes who bore seven sons and seven daughters. Because of her arrogance and pride, she drew the wrath of the divine twins Apollo and Artemis who slew all fourteen children.

John Milton Harney

Another youthful resident, physician, and publisher was John M. Harney who voiced his frustration to the extent that he pronounced a curse on the city, unaware that, perhaps, the Lady was already.

Harney was born in Delaware, March 9, 1789. He studied medicine and settled in Kentucky. After the death of his wife in childbirth, he took work with the New York Enquirer. He then travelled to Europe, accepted a naval appointment, and spent several years in South America. Upon his return, he settled in Savannah and edited a paper, *The Savannah Georgian*. Embittered by what he perceived as a lack of support from the local business leaders and community, he sold it in 1820 to businessman I. K. Tefft, and Harry James Finn, an actor instrumental in opening the Savannah Theater. Harney became a Catholic, joined the Dominicans, then beginning their mission in Kentucky. He moved there with his wife and young daughter, and later died at Somerset, Kentucky, at the age of thirty-six.

In his last issue of *The Savannah Georgian*, Harney published a long, rambling poem, for which he is mostly remembered. It began:

Farewell, oh, Savanah, forever farewell,
Thou hotbed of rogues, thou threshold of hell.
Where Satan has fixed his headquarters on Earth,

And outlaws integrity, wisdom and worth.
Where villainy thrives, and honesty begs,
Where folly is purse-proud, and wisdom in rags.
Where man is worth nothing, except in one sense,
Which they always compute in pounds, shillings, and pence.

After listing indictments against the church, the wealthy, merchants, doctors, lawyers, and loose women, Harney ended his tirade with this proclamation:

Now to finish my curses upon your ill city,
And express in few words all the sum of my ditty,
I leave you, Savannah, a curse that is far
The worst of all curses – to remain as you are!

Harney may have gotten the last word, as not much has changed in Savannah since his departure.

In addition to Jay and Harney, the preacher and founder of the Methodist Christian denomination, John Wesley also encountered this rooted juggernaut of opposition. In what sounds like a tone of resentment, this was his diary entry following his departure from Savannah: "I shook off the dust of my feet, and left Georgia, after having preached the gospel there…not as I ought, but as I was able, one year and nearly nine months."

What did Jay and Harney experience and perceive that would drive them to use such extreme expressions as "chaos of ruins" and "thou threshold of hell" in describing Savannah? And, what did Wesley encounter that restricted his influence and precipitated his hasty departure from the region?

The Roots of Savannah Strongholds

Let's turn back the calendar pages a few hundred years prior to Oglethorpe's arrival and see what was taking place among the people who occupied the southeast territory of North America. What human events and acts of human will took place that either promoted the presence of God, or demonic presence in the region? What was Oglethorpe and his band of adventurers stepping into when they set foot on Savannah ground?

History informs us that violence and hostility, involving the enslavement and slaying of human beings between the indigenous tribal groups, had already marked the Americas, prior to the advent of European exploration. However, with the first wave of European infiltration of North, Central, and South America, came an unprecedented escalation in violence, and the introduction of a variety of deadly diseases.

It was the primal desire to acquire and control greater land areas, and the resultant acquisition of greater wealth and power that brought Europeans to the American shores. And their intent was often expressed with raw force and violence.

Violence and Carnage

The historical record tells us of the war waged by Hernan Cortes and the Spanish Conquistadors against the Aztec Empire in 1519, and the subsequent routing of the vast Inca Empire, further south by Francisco Pizarro and his smaller army of Spaniards. While Cortes motive, in part, was to establish a trade route through the Americas to China, Pizarro was singularly interested in possessing the gold and silver of the Incas. Aside from the intent, the infiltration of the Spanish through these regions was advanced by the merciless slaughter of the indigenous people.

Following those conquests, came a steady flow of Conquistadors that mobilized through Central and South America via the existing infrastructure. Their continuous enslavement of thousands of the indigenous population provided the needed support to wage the ongoing massacre of the more formidable tribes in these territories. Over the course of time the population of the American Indians was dramatically reduced through these evils of war.

The entrance and intents of the likes of Cortes and Pizarro, and the means they employed to subdue the native Americans, perpetuated and intensified the practice that had been in place during previous generations of human existence in that part of the world. These new faces were not an issue in the minds of the demonic, but an opportunity to dramatically increase the rate of human destruction and death in the territories.

At about the same time Cortes was ravaging the Aztecs, further north, and to the east, another Spaniard was encountering the natives of that region. In 1539, Hernando DeSoto and his small army of Conquistadors, landed in what is now Tampa, Florida, and trod north, eventually covering ground in Georgia, South Carolina, North Carolina, Tennessee, and Alabama. During his four-year swing through this southeast region of North America, DeSoto left a bloody trail, as he put to death hostile American natives, enslaved others, and employed the means of kidnapping women and children to use as leverage to secure necessary supplies. He is credited with setting the stage for future hostilities between the various territory chiefdoms and the European colonists that would follow on his heels. DeSoto would not make it home as he died of a semi-tropical fever, near the banks of the Mississippi River, in present-day Louisiana.

The effects of war and violence on the indigenous peoples of the Americas, was indeed dreadful and tragic. But that death toll among the native Americans is nothing to be compared with another manifestation of evil presence that spread among these unfortunate people.

Disease

With the arrival of European colonists in the Americas, came the introduction of guns to the indigenous tribal groups. This, alone, caused a significant escalation in the death rate among the native Americans. However, the colonists brought to their land, something far more devastating: a variety of deadly diseases, including smallpox, measles, influenza, and bubonic plague from which the native populations lacked immunity.

In what is now present-day Mexico, provides a startling example of the devastation. When Hernan Cortes and his army conquered that region in 1519, there were upwards of twenty-five million native people living in the area. However, one-hundred years later, that was not the case. Following the arrival of the first Spaniards, the smallpox epidemic of 1519 to 1520 ended the lives of between 6 and 8 million people. But it was the two epidemics of 1545 and 1576, that spread like wildfire among the defenseless population, taking at least 16 million lives!

It is believed that in the areas most affected, more than 90% of the population had perished, far surpassing the Black Death plague that had decimated one-third of the people in Europe and Asia between 1347 and 1351.

In the southeast region of North America, of what is now the state of Georgia, the predominant Muskogee (Creek) population has been estimated at two hundred thousand before the arrival of the Europeans on the continent. Following the excursions of DeSoto and his Conquistadors, about 90% of the native Americans of that region had died, leaving a population of about twenty thousand people. Records reflect that subsequent European colonists came across empty villages and assumed the area to have always been lightly populated by the indigenous people.

Then Along Came James

With the Devil's hold firmly over the land area, James Oglethorpe would work to evict the demonic presence, and then fill the ensuing spiritual void with the presence of God. Remember, the tenets of the Oglethorpe Vison were based on the restoration of human dignity, and a variety of benevolent means to that end. Oglethorpe would be the first to sit in the gate of the infant society. Others would follow. What would be given entry?

Let's recall the words of Professor Edwin Jackson concerning Oglethorpe:

> With respect to Georgia's Indians, he had an enlightened policy, always respecting their customs, language, and needs. Land cessions were always agreed to by treaty according to proper Indian custom. Also, Oglethorpe actively sought to protect the Indians from unscrupulous white traders.

Oglethorpe's attitudes and actions were in stark moral contrast to what had prevailed in that region for, literally, centuries of time. He would not attempt to take the land by physical force. Oglethorpe knew that to arrive on the scene waving swords and firing muskets would only end in more bloodshed. Oglethorpe's hostility would be directed at the hidden spirit enemies, and not at the visible physical ones. The foundation of Savannah would be laid peacefully, with both parties agreeing to the terms. In fact, the relationship between Oglethorpe and the Chief of the indigenous Creeks, Tomochichi, would eventually culminate with the Chief accompanying Oglethorpe to London, where he was introduced to the "royals" of that day. Goodwill clearly marked the relationship between these two men.

This didn't sit well with the demonic spirit powers of the region. Oglethorpe's declaration that personal gain would come from one's own blood, sweat, and tears, and not that of others, was a pronouncement that got their full attention. The Oglethorpe Vision was a serious threat to the Devil, and the ground that he had presided over since the creation of the planet. What would be the Evil One's response to this new kid on the block?

Specifically, what was Oglethorpe up against? Is it possible to identify the various demonic entities that bind mankind? Is it even necessary to do so? We have already underscored the need for each of us to possess discernment and knowledge if we are to effectively resist and scatter these demonic forces. So, let's plumb deeper into this spirit realm for answers.

Chapter 25

Lady Savannah and Greed

In the existing societal systems of this natural world, *money* is a constant necessity. Whether gained through labor or family inheritance or sheer luck, we all require this practical substance to meet our human needs and sustain life. Money is the fuel of secular society's engine.

The world system's monetary currency comes in a variety of forms, the dollar, euro, yen, franc, pound, peso, etc. There are another 160 official national currencies we could add to this list. Regardless of the name, they all represent the means to conduct transactions that allow you and I to *have* or *possess* something we need or desire.

These acquired possessions come in various material forms, such as clothes, cars, houses, land, etc., or immaterial forms like societal influence and status. Money has the effect of helping us to feel better about our stature in life and influences the opinions of others about us. It affords us a measure of security, independence, and peace of mind.

Money is a *neutral* substance. Money can enable the possessor to accomplish wonderful things in life, or it can be used to harm or destroy. The matter, really, is not about the *value* of the money, but the value you and I place on money. It is an issue of the individual's perspective and attitude concerning money, as that is what will influence our motivations and our actions as we go about the business of acquiring it.

For the Love of Money

This truth is expressed by the Apostle Paul in his letter to his protégé, Timothy. He wrote: "The love of money is the root of all evil" (1 Tim. 6:10 AKJV). The *love* of it, not money, itself. Quite a statement, and one worthy of the attention of all people, as how we view the acquisition and use of money can either make or break us.

The way we can develop right attitude and balance with respect to the green stuff is this: the more we come to know the character of our God, and His unfailing, eternal commitment to each of us, body, soul, and spirit, the less we will feel the need to devote ourselves to acquiring money and the things it affords us. Recognizing that God as our faithful Provider frees us to hold money loosely, to give liberally to others, confident that He will resupply.

What drives our quest to *possess* is our separation from Him, and the fear that we are on our own and anything may befall us. In the absence of faith, is fear. This distrust of God is exploited by dark forces that prey on our insecurities and deceive us into believing that possessing the things of this world will be the answer to our problems.

The love of money that Paul wrote of is a fatal heart condition, a consuming lust that sees the possession of money, and its benefits, as all-important, and all-powerful. You've heard the description, "the almighty buck". That's an applicable summation of how money is viewed, as, in the eyes of the secular man or woman, there is nothing that can't be acquired or accomplished if you have enough of it. But therein lies the snare. If one embraces that attitude, then they can never have enough. The desire is insatiable, a thirst that can't be satisfied. It is an unending, tyrannical loop of being possessed by the need to possess.

The Root of All Evil

Pride is the basic element of our renegade human nature. Inherent in pride is a drive to be in control, to be self-sufficient, and to rise above all others in one's own estimation. However, inner rest and contentment is never attained through one's own efforts. What is gained outwardly, will never address the inward needs of the man or woman. Christ asked, "For what will it profit a man if he shall gain the whole world, and lose his own soul?" (Matt. 16:26 AKJV). It is through receiving the salvation of our souls in Christ whereby our panicky search for what is truly valuable, ceases.

Lucifer's original sin was the exercise of inordinate pride, a desire to usurp God's authority, to gain supreme control and assume the place of the Most High. Hence, it is not by chance or coincidence that the lure of pride prompted the act of rebellion that precipitated the fall of the first man and first woman. So, too, it is at the root of rebellion in the hearts of today's man and woman. It is inherent at birth and drives us throughout the course of our lifetimes.

When left unchecked, this unrestrained human pride draws and gives sway to the evil influences of Greed. The evil principality of Greed can be likened to an octopus that reaches and ensnares the self-obsessed human with its tentacles of lower level wicked spirits.

The ancient Roman historian and politician, Crispus Sallust wrote, "Greed . . . as if dipped in evil poisons, it weakens the body and the manly soul. It is always without limit, insatiable, and it is diminished neither by excess or deficit."

Greed is the ultimate outworking of the pride of man. Pride breeds a "love" for anything that will empower the natural man or woman to attain its elusive goals. It breeds moral insensitivity, a corruption of personal conscience, and the justifying of the actions taken to acquire regardless of the injury inflicted on others or to one's own soul. And in the worldly mindset, *money* paves the pathway that ascends to the pinnacle of pride. In this quest, all is fair game and any method, regardless how foul, is in play.

Eph. 4:18,19 describes those that persist in their resistance and rejection of God's mercy and grace,

> They are darkened in their understanding and separated from the life of God because of the ignorance that is in them due to the hardening of their hearts. Having lost all sensitivity, they have given themselves over to sensuality so as to indulge in every kind of impurity, and they are full of greed.

This is the moral dilemma in which Savannah, and, most likely, your city, as well, is facing. Where humans exist, usually, so does greed.

The Savannah Prince

For at least two-hundred and fifty years prior to the arrival of Oglethorpe in the Americas, a spirit of death reigned over the land as the human population was decimated on an astronomical level, far beyond the ability of the natural mind to comprehend. The soil of the land had been saturated with the blood of tens of millions of human beings who had met their untimely end at the hands of another or fell victim to disease. The control and activities of Satan and his forces, intent on the destruction of human life, were clearly manifest throughout the American territories.

What marked these French, Dutch, Spanish, and English explorers and colonists, that infiltrated and settled in the Americas? Clearly evident was their intent to conquer and control land areas, their quest to possess the earthly treasures of silver and gold, and their pursuit for personal glory. Manipulating the actions of these human puppets was the invisible hand of the ruthless demonic spirit of Greed. This is the territorial prince that Oglethorpe encountered upon his arrival and is the one that bears down upon today's man or woman who calls Savannah "home".

As we move forward in this study, keep in mind that the battle for the individual person, as well as the corporate body of the city, is being contested in the invisible realm, between the forces of good and the forces of evil. Should the human element contending for the prosperity of their city ever lose "sight" of the invisible struggle, and fight in their own strength or wisdom, then darkness will prevail, and God's plan will not be realized.

So, how did the Devil and his demonic followers respond to this threat to their territorial control? The satanic strategy was to stop Oglethorpe and his like-minded allies in their tracks before any momentum was gained. Satan would bring his power to bear on those who threatened to infiltrate this territory of his kingdom.

The Accuser

As we look at the time period during which Savannah was founded, a demonic pattern of opposition is clearly evident. The personalities that were committed to nurturing a community comprised of responsible and benevolent citizens, among other tenets in accordance with God's moral law, came under considerable notice of spirit forces opposed to God and his city plan.

Many who started the race well would fail to persevere when the going got rough. Others would succumb to the fiery darts of slander and accusation. After all, the word Devil in the original Greek means *accuser* or *slanderer*. John the Revelator rightly labels the Devil, "The accuser of our brothers and sisters" (Rev. 12:10).

Early Targets

Therefore, Oglethorpe was the object of suspicion and subjected to accusation. Allegations were even leveled from the religious element of the colony, in the person of Charles Wesley, the brother of John Wesley, founder of Methodism. Charles had accused Oglethorpe of carrying on an adulterous affair, simultaneously, with two married women. Charles, eventually, recanted these charges.

In February 1743, while Oglethorpe was engaged in repelling northward advances by the Spanish in San Augustin, Lt. Col. William Cooke lodged impeachment charges against him, alleging that Oglethorpe made his regiment pay him for their provisions. This, along with 18 other serious charges, required his presence before a board of General Officers in England. This resulted in Oglethorpe's departure from the colony, and on July 23, 1743, he sailed from Georgia and would never again return.

The court martial proceedings commenced on June 4, 1744. Thaddeus Mason Harris writes,

> It continued two days in session; when, after a strict scrutiny into the complaint, article by article of the 19 specific charges, the board were of the opinion that "the whole and every article thereof was groundless, false, and malicious." On the presentation of the report to his Majesty he was pleased to order that the said Lieutenant Colonel Cook should be dismissed the service. This indictment by one who had been treated with great kindness, and who owed his preferment to Lieutenant Colonel to the particular favor of the General, was not only ungrateful, but insidious and base.

It is interesting that five years later, in 1750, slavery would be legalized in Georgia by the Trustees who governed the Georgia colony. The repeal of the ban on African slavery marked the beginning of Savannah's involvement in the Atlantic slave trade.

John Wesley also came under attack. He was accused of taking advantage of "infatuated" women, manipulating and confusing them with a blend of religion and carnal passion. With a court date set to deal with the impending issues, Wesley defied the order. He fled Savannah feeling unproductive and the object of unfounded accusation and persecution at the hands of Savannah's social elite. His final diary entry on December 2, 1737, was to the point,

> Being now only a prisoner at large, in a place where…every day would give fresh opportunity to procure evidence of words I never said, and actions I never did . . . I shook off the dust of my feet, and

left Georgia, after having preached the gospel there . . . not as I ought, but as I was able, one year and nearly nine months.

Wesley's experience underscores the frustration of coming up against a demonic stronghold and emphasizes the bondage that blinds the citizenry and their denial of God's truth.

The Moravians who were committed to non-violence and would not take up weapons, were subject to discrimination, accusation and rejection by the planters of the region as they made efforts to evangelize the African slaves. Apparently, by 1740, the Moravians had all departed, having settled in Pennsylvania where there was less tension.

George Whitefield, the preacher instrumental in the Great Awakening of the 1730's and 1740's, and founder of the orphan house, Bethesda, came under considerable accusation and slander from both his 'brothers in the Lord' in England and others within the American colonies. He, too, was occasionally hindered from his efforts to promote righteousness among the masses and had to answer in writing and in person to charges leveled against him.

Andrew Bryan, who we identified earlier as the former slave and first native African-American pastor, was the object of intense persecution and accusation.

Born into slavery on a plantation near Charleston, South Carolina, Bryan moved to Brampton Plantation, on the outskirts of Savannah. It was there that Bryan awakened spiritually and was raised up a leader among the slave population at Brampton. What followed was a mighty move of God's Spirit that saw hundreds of those in bondage converted and committed to a new Master.

Although Bryan and the other followers were granted permission to meet and worship on Yamacraw land owned by local Edward Davis, other powerbrokers feared that the gatherings were the seeds of an organized rebellion to follow. Bryan and members of his congregation were then subject to harassment, ridicule, and accusation, as well as whippings and beatings, followed by Bryan's imprisonment. However, local white sympathizers, who thought religion positively affected the slaves, helped secure his release.

Bryan is quoted as having said while staring down his accusers, "I rejoice not only to be whipped, but would freely suffer death for the cause of Christ."

The common denominator with each of these individuals is that their time in Savannah was short-circuited by certain individuals and groups that used their power and influence to obstruct the good they were promoting among society. Regardless of the Devil's all-out attempts to abort their efforts, much fruit has been borne within Savannah, and beyond her borders as a result of their sacrifice.

A Defining Moment

In the Scriptures, there are many examples of how the actions of just one individual dramatically influenced an entire people group and ushered them into divine destiny. With mankind, the possibilities are limited. However, with God, all things are possible. The man or woman that brings God into the equation, always has the advantage. A short list would include Noah, Abraham, Joseph, Moses, David, Daniel, Isaiah, Naomi, Ruth, and Mary. The ultimate example of this is Jesus Christ, one man who reversed the course and destiny of all mankind.

Would the settlers and planters of Savannah move forward with the Oglethorpe Vision and make inroads against the evil territorial hold over the land area? Or, would they succumb to the enemy's wiles, and allow the demonic grip over the region to continue unabated? This showdown would significantly influence the course not only of Savannah, but of all the colonies, and a nation soon to be born!

If it is true that what counts is how you finish the race, and not how you start, then Oglethorpe succeeded with much honor. However, the continuing prosperity of a city involves a *relay race*, where the baton is successively passed from one, to another, and then to another, and so on.

Let's now look at what took place as Oglethorpe completed his leg, and others took over. Did they run with his vision, or run from it?

Shadow Boxing

If the demonic forces that influence or occupy the life of a human being, or any societal institution, are to be effectively dealt with, then the one confronting evil must carry the authority of God into battle. Without it, the fighter is only "shadow boxing", merely beating the air. Oglethorpe brought divine authority with him while laying the groundwork for Lady Savannah. The question is, how would others approach the ongoing work of developing the small colony into the more complex functions of a city?

The channels through which the Devil operates to discredit and disable those with the good of society at heart, are often the ruling human authorities; the civil institutions of which we earlier wrote. Remember, it is the operation of the *exousia*, the demonic *authorities*, that seek to influence and manipulate to their advantage, the various institutional bodies of human societal authority.

Seldom do human authorities within cities connect their own deeds and those of the citizens, with the influence of dark forces that impress, suggest, and manipulate. Savannah's elite fell prey to seducing, manipulative spirits that exploited their misguided human passions. In yielding to satisfy their carnal desires, they turned blind eyes to their trespasses, and justified their actions to soothe the guilt of conscience.

Customized Bait

The Devil customizes his bait according to the culture and appetites of his victims. In first world nations, demonic presence is camouflaged to appeal to sophistication and intellectualism, whereas in ancient societies or isolated people groups, the Devil has no need to conceal the satanic nature of his dominance.

Ancient pagan people were clearly aware of demons and the supernatural but knew of no way of escape. They would appease evil spirits out of fear. On the other hand, the means of deliverance has been clearly revealed to contemporary man, but he denies the existence of the supernatural and demonic, and, therefore, remains bound.

Power, control, privilege, wealth, and social status are the basic longings of the natural man. This is the bait that evil authorities and powers at work in the spirit realm dangled, and the human authorities of Savannah swallowed.

These are strong indictments of past and present Savannah leadership. But as we dig up the roots of her founding, we'll find that choices made by those positioned in her gates paved a path of entrance for sinister spirits that have resulted in the so-called haunting of the city.

Chapter 26

Enterprise Perverted

The innovation, invention, and fulfilled vision flowing from the people of Savannah mentioned in earlier chapters, can be summed up in one word: *Enterprise*. The word means initiative, originality, boldness, and creativity. This dynamic flow is a release of divine foresight, perceived by the human spirit, and made tangible through human ingenuity.

The title for Savannah as a City of Enterprise, used often over the years by many, aptly captures her character and personality. Clear physical evidence of this fact stands front and center to anyone trolling the highways and byways of the city.

Savannah has also been called The Cradle of Georgia's Commercial History, identifying the Lady as where abundant industry was birthed and nurtured, and in the ensuing years multiplied well beyond her borders.

Early Enterprise

Among the lesser intentions of Oglethorpe for the founding of Georgia was the production of silk. The objective was to eliminate their dependence on their rival, France, for this upper crust status symbol. When the caterpillar failed to produce, rice became the focus in the 1750's and was how many great fortunes were to be made along coastal Georgia. In fact, the commercial prospects of rice production were the main motivators that would be the undoing of Oglethorpe's and the other trustee's anti-slavery law.

Rice production continued as Georgia's primary cash-cow for one-hundred years when the Civil War, post-emancipation labor problems, a series of weather-related disasters, and, probably more so, international competition, cut the legs out from under the industry. But Georgia was also the largest producer of cotton at that time, thanks to Eli Whitney and his revolutionary cotton gin. King Cotton would reign supreme for decades to come.

We learned earlier that because Savannah would be the recipient of the fountain flow of God's generosity and benevolent compassion, her responsibility would be to impart the same spirit of benevolence to those she would encounter.

With the departure of Oglethorpe from Savannah in 1743, the door of opportunity flung wide open for others to exert greater influence in the shaping and direction of the colony. This key time would determine if Savannah would march forward into God's destiny or take a wrong turn and allow the demonic stronghold of the region to reign unchallenged. Sadly, the human authorities of the city took the latter course.

Oligarchy Rule in Savannah

In Savannah, regardless of how successful in business or active in the community, one is shut out from the privileges of position that for generations have been under the strict control of a few individuals and families, some that date back to the early days of the colony. It is certainly not *what* one knows that gives entrance to the circle of elite in Savannah, but rather *who* one knows, and what one has to offer.

Oglethorpe, and those that sailed with him on the Anne, had been subject to monarchy rule in England. Many of the colonists that followed, came from societies that were under the tyranny of despots. As the formative years of the colony unfurled, a handful of individuals would come to wield the scepter of governmental and economic control. What surfaced was a form of Oligarchy rule.

The word *oligarchy* is derived from the Greek, ὀλιγαρχία (*oligarkhía*) and ὀλίγος (*olígos*), meaning few, and ἄρχω (*arkho*), meaning to rule or to command. It is a power structure in which the authority effectively rests with a small number of people. These people might be distinguished by royalty, wealth, family ties, education, corporate, religious or military control. Such states are often controlled by a few prominent families who typically pass their influence from one generation to the next. Nothing has changed, as the course of the city is still directed by relatively few individuals. Although they may not possess governmental titles, they are still puppet masters pulling the strings of those in formal positions of authority.

Jacqueline Jones in *Saving Savannah* says of the mid-nineteenth century society:

> Interlocking networks of wealthy Protestant families dominated low country politics and economics, yet those few families shared power with anyone rich enough to exploit enslaved workers and could afford the French bonnets, silk umbrellas, and leather-bound books sold at the city's exclusive shops.

Jones adds,

> Savannah possessed only one class, the very wealthy... Though they represented only 1 percent or so of the city's population, Savannah's bankers, planters, railroad officials, physicians, attorneys, merchants, and cotton factors controlled the local government – but only as long as they could maintain the support of the white laborers who were their constituents holding public office remained the purview of relatively few men, a tight-knit directorate of merchants, bankers, planters, physicians, and lawyers. From 1850 to 1860, of the 143 slots for mayor and twelve alderman each year, only 136 different men ran for office. Drawn mostly from the 13 percent of adult whites who owned slaves, three-fourths of the candidates identified themselves as Democrats.

The worship of enterprise to serve the insatiable appetite for personal power and control, has in the past, and continues today, to rule the attitudes and actions of, not only those in seats of authority, but many every-day citizens who live in the atmosphere dominated by these *powers of the air*.

Factor's Walk

In addition to the Forsyth Fountain and the Talmadge Bridge, there are three other physical structures that "shout" of spirit activity that has shaped Lady Savannah. These enduring symbols are situated in the heart of the downtown area of the Historic District known as Factor's Walk.

You can find Factor's Walk sandwiched between Bay Street to the south, and River Street to the north. Factor's Walk is in proximity to the majority of downtown tourist attractions, and within walking distance from many hotels.

The historical marker at Factor's Walk reads, "The first commercial house below the bluff opened in 1744." As we noted earlier, the turn of the nineteenth century saw Savannah as a major producer of cotton and one of the nation's most vital ports.

M'Culloch's Universal Gazetteer of 1840 offers insight to the challenge of having to conduct business in a city built atop a 40-foot bluff,

> Savannah is at present the centre of commerce for a large extent of (the) country... The warehouses are numerous, generally lining the wharves... most of them three or four stories high. The business is generally done in an upper story, entered from the top of the bluff, while the lower stores serve to receive the merchandise directly from the ships.

The offices and warehouses, situated on the various levels of the structure were connected by a maze of walkways and bridges, something reminiscent of the child's metal toy *Erector* sets of the early 1900's. Inside these offices and warehouses is where the *factors* worked. These were the men who factored the amount and worth of the cotton that was produced.

The Old City Exchange

Within Factors Walk is a building that played an integral part in the development of the cotton enterprise of Savannah. It is known as the Old City Exchange (not to be confused with the Cotton Exchange).

Author Jacqueline Jones, writes,

Savannah's commercial spirit remained stubbornly resistant to traditional southern hierarchies that were meant to enforce, and reinforce, caste lines between white and black, free and slave . . . For the most part, city elites tried to accommodate themselves to the disreputable behavior of immigrants and other poor whites, and to keep those men within the white-supremacist fold. The formal site of this accommodation was the Exchange, a building on the bay built in 1799 and home to various municipal offices.

These are the *gates* that we defined earlier. These city elites, i.e., the wealthy planters, the factors, and other industry leaders, would convene at the Exchange to preside over the judicial process of certain criminal acts and trim the fines and sentences to retain the political support of the lower class.

Perhaps Jones, was closer to the truth than she realized as she continues with a physical description of the Old Exchange:

Fittingly, the structure resembled a church, with a portico, steeple, and bell tower, signifying a place where city officials worshipped the spirit of enterprise.

Of interest is that the actual bell that sat on the pinnacle of the Old City Exchange now sits on the ground within a replica of the tower, directly in front of Savannah's City Hall where today's powerbrokers wield their scepters of authority. And, yes, today's City Hall, built in 1905, *does* sit on the same site of the Old City Exchange.

Evidently, the corruption that became rooted within the upper echelon of society and industry following the departure of Oglethorpe, continued unabated into the mid-nineteenth century.

The Cotton Exchange and Gryphon Fountain

The heart of Factor's Walk was the Cotton Exchange, built in 1887 by architect William Gibbons Preston. It has been an enduring symbol of the importance of the cotton industry to the city of Savannah. The building on Bay Street was occupied by cotton factors (merchants) until about 1947. The Savannah Chamber of Commerce moved into the building in 1954. They were displaced in 1976 when the structure was purchased by the Freemasons. Presently it serves as Solomon's Masonic Lodge, A. and F.M.

Directly in front of the Cotton Exchange building is Gryphon Fountain, depicted on the cover of this book. It is surrounded by iron fencing inscribed with profiles of renowned statesman and poets. The original terra cotta Gryphon Fountain, built in 1889, also by Preston, was destroyed in 2008 when a car driven by a Savannah resident, Donna Haddock, jumped the curb on Bay Street, barreled through the iron fencing, obliterated the Gryphon statue, and came to an abrupt stop on the front steps of the Cotton Exchange. A public outcry prompted local government to commission reconstruction efforts that took ten months and entailed forming a new mold. The new concrete replica of the Gryphon was rededicated in December 2009. In a moment we'll see that it may have been wise to leave it in pieces.

Understanding the significance of the Cotton Exchange and the Gryphon Fountain is of prime importance in unearthing how the Devil has undermined Savannah's destiny.

The gryphon is a mythological creature prevalent in Greek lore and depicted in ancient Egyptian and Persian art. It is presented as having the head of an eagle and the body of a lion. Preston's "take" on the gryphon was fashioning it with the head and body of a lion, and the wings of an eagle.

Greek myths were not just moralistic tales in which the characters were viewed as fictitious. The common man or woman was devoted to these "deities" and trusted them for their protection and provision. Although wholesome morals could be promoted within the story and represented by the character, the myths were the means by which the worship of false gods was established among the Greeks. Were these ancient deities merely products of their imaginations, or, could they have been demonic territorial princes, as the Scriptures indicate? And do they still exist but by other names ascribed to them by mankind? Either way, we should be careful in how we present these "innocent" stories in our homes and in our schools.

To the ancients, the Gryphon represented divine wisdom and power. Its image was also emblazoned on the shields of the warriors, intended to embolden them in battle and strike fear among their enemies.

It is revelatory that in mythology, the Gryphon was said to have transported Apollo from the sun, to the earth. Associated with that thought is that the lion and the eagle are the two most dominant creatures of the air and land. This is a clear expression of the Devil's claim to have supremacy over and upon the earth, and all who dwell on it.

Now, watch this: the Gryphon was the guardian of the gold and treasures of Emperors and Kings of that period of history. Hence, it is a fitting choice and symbol to have been planted directly in front of the Cotton Exchange, which, suitably, was originally called King Cotton's Palace. Again, cotton was the commodity that put Savannah on the map and was the lucrative industry from which the city elders, specifically the planters and merchants, derived their influence and power. Cotton was their treasure and nothing or no one in Heaven or Earth was held in higher esteem.

Clearly evident here is the principle reiterated in this writing: that which is established in the spirit world, will shape and determine what manifests in the physical realm. I believe that the Gryphon Fountain was fashioned and installed in front of the Cotton Exchange as a tribute to the entity that was the source of the wealth and power of Savannah's elite. Whether the past city elders and factors did this knowingly or unwittingly, the very existence of the Gryphon testifies of the demonic control under which these humans functioned.

These gatekeepers may have facetiously given the title King Cotton to the source of their material prosperity, but that was simply their name for the physical manifestation of the real master of their enslavement, the evil principality of Greed! This ruling prince that established its stronghold during the murderous plundering of the indigenous native Americans, was the same false god that the politicians and factors of the eighteenth and nineteenth centuries bowed before and remains the object of devotion of today's predominant city leaders and merchants. The representative image of this evil entity still stands front and center before the gates of Savannah, admired by citizens and tourists, alike. And all the time, the Devil has lurked in spirit darkness, snickering and mocking the foolishness and gullibility of mankind.

The fashioning of the gryphon as a fountain is also significant. It is very much like the Devil to *counterfeit* that which God has produced or established, in this case, the Forsyth Park Fountain. However, the stark contrast is inescapable. Whereas the flow generated by the Forsyth Park Fountain, showered in every direction, symbolizes Savannah's purpose to refresh and revitalize all people, the Gryphon Fountain represents a singular flow of ill-gotten gain for a select few.

The Devil competes with the Almighty for the devotion of humankind and is under the delusion that what he offers is more desirable.

Freemasons

I mentioned earlier the Cotton Exchange building is presently owned by Freemasons and functions as Solomon's Lodge, A. and F.M., the oldest Masonic organization in Georgia, founded in 1734. Evidently, the presence of Freemasonry arrived along with Oglethorpe, whose voyage was partially funded by English masons. However, there is no clear evidence that Oglethorpe, himself, was a member of the order.

Freemasonry was founded in 1717 in England and quickly spread throughout the British Empire. It is a fraternity that claims a worldwide following of 6 million men, of which 2 million are U.S. citizens. They deny being either a Christian or religious organization.

The fraternity is *esoteric* in nature. The word is derived from the Greek, *esoterikos*, meaning, *within*. It implies knowledge or ideas understood by the specially initiated, and not communicated, or intelligible to the general body of followers. It carries elements of mysteries and secrets.

The mason advances through the organization by completing three phases: the *Entered Apprentice* degree, the *Fellow Craft* degree, and finally the degree of *Master Mason*. The further and deeper one is immersed in the initiation process, the more secretive and protected is the knowledge.

The relationship between freemasonry and myths, rituals, and symbols is fundamental. Rituals and symbols are very important within religious practice as those who believe in them use them in their worship to invoke their god.

Grandmaster Jean Louis de Biasi in his book, *Secrets and Practices of Freemasons*, touches on the origin of the masons. He credits the "birth of ancient Egyptian and Greek mysteries to the discovery of the essential role of this initiated brotherhood (Freemasonry) in the world today."

Grandmaster de Biasi adds, "Ritual processes are the *visible manifestations of the invisible world* as understood by the ancient adepts of these traditions." These ancient mysteries include elements of astrology, sorcery, and alchemy, and other dark arts.

Many tenets of Freemasonry are based on the significance they ascribe to the construction and builders of King Solomon's Temple in the mid-tenth century BC. Various legends and traditions pertaining to Solomon's temple rituals and observances are at the core of Freemasons dogma. According to de Biasi,

> A temple is a sacred and symbolic place used to raise the inner and unconscious level of the mind to a high spiritual level. The power of the symbols connected together create a real impact on us and something happens . . . it is going through the gates of an invisible world.

Let's again visit the concept of *agreement* and the *egregore* it produces in the context of psychological and occult practices. Author Gaetan Delaforge writes, "The symbols, rituals and meetings of a group, when repeated over time, develop an egregore or group mind which binds the members together." Delaforge details how this "group mind" will retain influence and control indefinitely, as it is empowered through the continued assent of committed people. He adds, "The egregore will continue to grow in strength and can last for centuries" and has "an effectiveness greater than the mere sum of its individual members."

Since the 1734 founding of Solomon's Lodge in Savannah, many formidable political and business leaders have been members of the fraternity. Beginning in 1976, when the Freemasons purchased the Cotton Exchange, the building has functioned as their temple. The relationship between present day lodge members and the foregoing cotton factors is not important. What is significant is the perpetuation, past and present, of demonic influence over the property and the occupants, and, in turn, the populace.

It is compelling that the factors installed the Gryphon Fountain (an Egyptian and Greek idol), and Freemasonry doctrine is derived from ancient Egyptian and Greek "mysteries" (worship of false gods). My belief is both groups have been subject to the same demonic stronghold, perpetuated for generations of time. I also see the physical location of the Cotton Exchange as the former and current *power base* of the territorial prince of Greed!

If the agreement among Savannah's city elite, that has given the Devil a stranglehold within society, continues unchallenged and unbroken, then there will be a perpetuation of the group mindset and activities of those who presently occupy that atmosphere and environment.

Present-Day Factors

For several years during our residency in Savannah, my wife, Elizabeth, worked for a married couple that owned three retail shops in the Factor's Walk area. She would rotate between the shops, assisting and advising customers who were, primarily, tourists. The couple she worked for were long-time residents of Savannah, and part of the core group of business proprietors that also packed some political punch, because of their contributions to the local economy.

It was clear that the orbit of the lives of this couple revolved around their businesses. They ate, slept, and breathed for the operation and success of their shops. This consuming drive was evident in their dealings with their employees and customers. Every policy and action was crafted to squeeze the most out of their worker, for a minimum amount of pay, with the expectation that the worker would pressure and manipulate the patron into parting with the maximum amount of their money. Any attempt by a worker to point this out to the owners would only add to their frustration as the constructive criticism would be scoffed at and brushed aside.

The inability to hear or see anything other than what they believed would further their agenda and result in greater financial gain, was a "brand" on their lives. It clearly identified the object of their devotion. It was the spirit of Greed on full display. These are present-day factors who walk the same corridors and occupy the same rooms of the buildings. The nature of the merchandise has changed, but the spirit influence that dictates their attitudes and actions, has not.

Chapter 27

The Enslaved

The Oglethorpe Vision included three prohibitions that were not to be debated or questioned. These laws were enacted in 1734 and were the only formal laws that governed the actions of the settlers. They were:

1. There would be no importation and use of rum and brandies. Ale, beer and wine were permitted.
2. A statute requiring compliance with the law for maintaining peace with the Indians.
3. There would be no importation and use of black slaves or Negroes.

However, it didn't take long for the colonists to realize that Savannah was not entirely the paradise for which they hoped. They found the composition of the coastal soil unconducive to crop production, and the brutal heat and humidity of the summer season, two formidable challenges. The murmuring and complaining among the ranks began immediately.

These first Savannah settlers were not without supporters, both locally and abroad, who believed their personal fortunes hinged on whether the colony failed or succeeded. The answer to the problem was simple: the importation of slaves. Like children they cried out, "After all, South Carolina is doing it!"

But Oglethorpe was adamantly opposed. He wrote:

> If we allow slaves, we act against the very principles by which we associated together, which was to relieve the distressed. Whereas now we should occasion the misery of thousands in Africa . . . and bring into perpetual slavery the poor people who now live free there?

A less humanitarian viewpoint was expressed by the Trustees, as a whole. They believed slavery would create an idle upper class, citing "they destroy all industry among the white inhabitants", and would create a potential for violent uprisings.

The wealthy Virginia tobacco planter, William Byrd II, put it bluntly when offering his perspective on the influence of slaves on the English settlers. He said, "They blow up the pride & ruin the industry, who seeking a rank of poor creatures below them, detest work for fear it should make them look like slaves."

Profit Possibilities

Peter Coclanis of the University of North Carolina writes,

> The Trustee's original plan – which included a prohibition against slavery – soon fell by the wayside. Many Georgians were aware of the profit possibilities associated with the commercial production of rice on slave plantations in South Carolina, and they realized

that under a similar institutional framework coastal Georgia had the potential to offer similar opportunities. At the same time – perhaps even earlier – many ambitious South Carolina rice planters came to the same realization and mounted an aggressive campaign to make Georgia safe for rice and slavery, if not for democracy. By mid-century proslavery Georgians and South Carolinians carried the day. In 1750 the ban on slavery in Georgia was repealed, and with the royal takeover of the colony in 1752, conditions finally became favorable for the establishment in Georgia as a plantation colony based on rice and slaves.

Coclanis strikes at the heart of those motivated to legalize slavery: *profit possibilities*. Within the next one-hundred years, the number of prominent coastal rice planters mushroomed to about five-hundred fifty. Annually, twenty-five million pounds of rice was being produced, and by 1860, approximately fifty million pounds would continue to line the pockets of the planters with something more than rice.

Two of the most influential coastal planters were brothers James and Thomas Potter. James Potter, alone, owned between four-hundred and five-hundred slaves and 1,253 acres of rice within the low-country Rice Kingdom, as it was aptly named. They had stiff local competition in the form of the father and son duo, Charles and Louis Manigault.

During this same time period, Savannah was exporting four-hundred thousand bales of cotton, annually, and serving as the center of Georgia's domestic slave trade.

Jacqueline Jones points out,

> Savannah was entering a period of explosive growth that was highly unusual compared to other

southern cities at the same time. Between 1850 and 1860, the city's population grew by 50%, to 22,292 residents, driven by the completion of three railroad lines that linked the port to the state's interior and diverted trainloads of upcountry cotton away from its archrival, Charleston.

As production increased, so did the work force consisting of slaves imported primarily from Sierra Leone. The need for increased importation of humans in bondage was heightened by the steady death toll among the Africans due to rampant disease and overwork.

Jones continues,

> For the rice swamps spawned gastrointestinal and respiratory diseases that regularly killed horrific numbers of black men, women, and children. Toiling in standing water during the spring planting season and drinking water polluted by ocean tides and nearby rivers, rice slaves paid for the fabulous wealth of their masters and mistresses with their lives.

The existence of the female plantation slave was a living nightmare. Because of the regular death toll, her burden included repopulating the stable of slaves. This would include being subject to rape by her master or forced to have intercourse with a male slave.

The Weeping Time

On March 3, 2018, on a small plot of land two miles west of Savannah, Mayor Otis Johnson gathered with a solemn group of people to commemorate an event that took place about 150 years earlier. The mayor offered a brief speech, after which the ground was consecrated with the placement of a historical marker. Today, it is the only visible remembrance of a dark occasion that many would like to forget. The marker reads:

> One of the largest sales of enslaved persons in U.S. history took place on March 2-3, 1859, at the Ten Broeck Race Course, ¼ mile southwest of here. To satisfy his creditors, Pierce M. Butler sold 436 men, women, and children from his Butler Island and Hampton plantations near Darien, Georgia. The breakup of the families and the loss of home became part of African-American heritage remembered as "the weeping time." The event was reported extensively in the northern press and reaction to the sale deepened the nation's growing sectional divide in the years immediately preceding the Civil War.

Kristopher Monroe in his July 2014 article in *The Atlantic*, explains,

> The Weeping Time acquired its name colloquially, by the slaves and their descendants, because of reports that the sky opened up and poured down rain for the full two days of the auction. It was said that the heavens were weeping for the inhumanity that was being committed. After what was said and done, 436 human beings would be sold, and their tears flowed with those of Heaven's.

As the event was widely publicized throughout the American colonies, potential buyers and spectators converged on Savannah to participate in the "great auction sale". One of those present was the *New York Tribune* journalist, Mortimer

Thomson. With a country on the brink of a national break over the issue of slavery, Thomson was to report on the auction. His was an undercover assignment so he utilized the pseudonym Q. K. Philander Doesticks, for anonymity. It should be mentioned that Horace Greeley, editor of the New York Tribune, was an avid opponent of slavery.

Thomson's ensuing front-page story, entitled, "Great Auction Sale of Slaves at Savannah, Georgia", immediately went viral, domestically and internationally. The powerbrokers of the South were incensed by what they viewed was northern abolitionist propaganda. The local Savannah paper, the *Republican*, denounced Thomson as a "somewhat notorious person...a hiring libeler", and the article as "a tissue of misrepresentation and falsehood." It was evident that the Savannah elite would protect their interests whatever the cost.

Thomson pulled no punches in his recounting, describing the assembly of buyers as,

> A rough breed, slangy, profane, bearish . . . pulling their mouths open to see their teeth, pinching their limbs to find how muscular they were, walking them up and down to detect any signs of lameness, making them stoop and bend in different ways that they might be certain there was no concealed rupture or wound.

Thomson details the resignation of the men and women to their fate,

> On the faces of all was an expression of heavy grief; some appeared to be resigned to the hard stroke of Fortune that had torn them from their homes, and were sadly trying to make the best of it; some sat brooding moodily over their sorrows, their chins

resting on their hands, their eyes staring vacantly, and their bodies rocking to and fro, with a restless motion that was never stilled.

The two-day sale netted $303,850. The highest price paid for one family, a mother and her five grown children, was $6,180. The highest price for one individual was $1,750. The lowest price for any one slave was $250.

Soon after the last slave was sold, the rain stopped. The record reflects that Pierce Butler made an appearance, and as if to compensate for the human misery, gave each slave a freshly minted one-dollar coin. The once-again wealthy Pierce Butler, following a vacation in southern Europe, then returned home to Philadelphia.

Local Perspective

The following is an excerpt from another *New York Tribune* newspaper article of February 13, 1865, pertaining to a meeting between twenty African-American Christian leaders from Savannah, and Union Military Authorities.

Chosen by the group to respond to the government's twelve questions was Garrison Frazier, described as,

> Aged 67 years, born in Granville County, N.C. Slave until eight years ago, when he bought himself and wife, paying $1,000 in gold and silver. Is an ordained minister in the Baptist Church, but, his health failing, has now charge of no congregation. Has been in the ministry 35 years.

Frazier's perspective on the concept of slavery and the mission of General Sherman is instructive. It reads as follows:

Minutes of an interview between the colored ministers and church officers at Savannah with the Secretary of War and Major General Sherman.

Headquarters of Maj. Gen. Sherman, City of Savannah, GA, Jan.12, 1865 – 8 P.M.

On the evening of Thursday, the 12th day of January 1865, the following persons of African descent met by appointment to hold an interview with Edwin M. Stanton, Secretary of War, and Major-Gen. Sherman, to have a conference upon matters relating to the freedmen of the State of Georgia, to-wit:

Second–State what you understand by Slavery and the freedom that was to be given by the President's proclamation.

Answer–Slavery is, receiving by irresistible power the work of another man, and not by his consent. The freedom, as I understand it, promised by the proclamation, is taking us from under the yoke of bondage, and placing us where we could reap the fruit of our own labor, take care of ourselves and assist the Government in maintaining our freedom.

In the absence of Gen. Sherman, the following question was asked:

State what is the feeling of the colored people in regard to Gen. Sherman; and how far do they regard his sentiments and actions as friendly to their rights and interests, or otherwise?

Answer: We looked upon Gen. Sherman prior to his arrival as a man in the Providence of God specially set apart to accomplish this work, and we unanimously feel inexpressible gratitude to him, looking upon him as a man that should be honored for the faithful performance of his duty. Some of us called upon him immediately upon his arrival, and it is probable he would not meet the Secretary with more courtesy than he met us. His conduct and deportment toward us characterized him as a friend and a gentleman. We have confidence in Gen. Sherman and think that what concerns us could not be under better hands. This is our opinion now from the short acquaintance and interest we have had.

All Are Slaves

The word means *servant*. We are all designed to serve. The capacity lies dormant in our fallen human nature, but springs to life upon regeneration of our spirits, seeking an object to attend to.

Servanthood is the one pure expression of sacrificial love. Real love, true love, is expressed in the giving of oneself for another. To willingly serve God and to serve others is the highest moral position a human can assume. Secular society is dominated by a *class mentality* wherein a person's worth is assessed by the degree of social power and influence they possess. The Scriptures attest to something quite the contrary.

Jesus made it clear that "The greatest among you shall be your servant" (Matt. 23:11). And Jesus does not ask us to live in a way that He didn't while on this earth. Displaying the true meaning of servanthood, he set aside his divinity to take on the limitations and weaknesses of flesh and bone. And His was the ultimate service as it culminated in choosing to die so we might live.

Philippians 2:6,7 tells us,

> Who, being in very nature God, did not consider equality with God something to be used to his own advantage; rather, he made himself nothing by taking the very nature of a servant, being made in human likeness.

The next verse completes the thought,

> And being found in appearance as a man, he humbled himself by becoming obedient to death – even death on a cross.

The Devil perverts the ideal of servanthood. His version of a servant is one who is the property of another and required to do whatever is demanded of them. He seeks to rob the human of their dignity and the liberty to choose the path they will walk in life.

The demonic also works to deceive the human into believing that they will be empowered by controlling other human lives. But true satisfaction will not be found in having mastery over another, just a perverse, short-lived brand of pleasure.

Spiritual bondage is at the core of those who labor under the tyranny of evil. The relationship between the Devil and his slave is dominated by fear, and fear has torment. The outworking of this slavery is visible in many forms in our physical world and societal relationships. It is a by-product of that which exists in the spirit realm, made manifest in the physical world and its system.

The truth is that the planters of Savannah that bought and enslaved other men and women, were themselves slaves, bound in tyranny, and subjected to the will of the Devil. In fact, the type of bondage that gripped the planters was far worse than that of those they enslaved. One was an eternal state of being, the other temporal.

As inherently evil as slavery is, it is not at the root of what has caused Savannah's fall. The installing of slavery among the society was a means to an end. The insatiable desire for power, control, wealth, and prestige, has marked those positioned at her gates. They have been culpable in allowing entrance and a perpetuation of this evil entity that exerts potent control over the city and has polluted her soul. It is named *Greed*. It is spirit in origin, it is demonic in nature, and it is still at work today!

Slaves of Righteousness

The Scriptures also teach that those that have acknowledged Jesus Christ as Deliverer and Savior, are, in fact, servants or slaves. When freed from the bondage of evil, we become "slaves to righteousness" (Rom. 6:18) who have been "bought with a price" (1 Cor. 6:20 AKJV), paid by Jesus on the cross.

Jesus said,

> Come to me, all you who are weary and burdened, and I will give you rest. Take my yoke upon you and learn from me, for I am gentle and humble in heart, and you will find rest for your souls (Matt. 11:28, 29).

A *yoke* is a wooden cross-piece that enclosed the heads of two oxen or horses that forced them to walk together. So how can one be bound with a yoke and still find "rest"? Jesus was saying that our souls would find the rest they seek if we would willingly submit to walking in relationship with Him. The process would be challenging and trying, but accompanied by an overruling inner strength and peace, found by no other means.

Recently, my wife and I were at a crowded, noisy restaurant, occupied mostly by adult couples and adult groups. We noticed a young couple seated at a nearby table, tending to an infant who lay in a baby carrier. The trio stood in contrast to the social interaction that surrounded them. It was clear that their eating out was a rare escape from the repetitive routine of carrying for a wee one, 24-hours a day. I found it interesting that, still, they chose to bring their baby with them. I watched as they went through the process of pacifying and feeding the baby, which was almost a non-stop effort during their relatively short meal.

I thought of how the demands and requirements of successfully meeting the needs of that baby were at the expense of the personal resources; finances, time, and the emotional, mental, and physical energy of these two humans. They could choose not to give of themselves, to daily sacrifice, literally, their lives, knowing that the commitment would require additional weeks, months, and years, of the same demands. But it was abundantly clear that these two had made their choice. They may have been exhausted, but it wasn't the prevalent impression they conveyed.

This young couple went about their duties, seemingly on autopilot, with a synchronicity to their joint efforts. Their interaction was sprinkled with periodic smiles, chuckles and endearing words for their little one. It was also clear that the internal satisfaction they experienced overshadowed the external, practical demands of parenthood.

I was reminded of the well-worn Scripture, ignored by so many, "For God so loved the world that he gave his only begotten son." God's love was proven by His act of giving, by *who* He gave. The sacrifice of the Father is unfathomable to the human mind. And His son, Jesus, demonstrated his love by obediently giving Himself, sacrificing His life, so that others might live.

This young couple yoked to one another, choosing to walk the walk of Jesus, led by his Spirit, were upheld and carried through the practical difficulties they faced, head-on, empowered by love.

Love precedes sacrifice and love empowers service. One will not falter while giving if motivated by love. One isn't mindful of sacrifice as love supersedes the sense of any loss incurred.

The ancient letter to the Hebrew believers includes these words, "For the joy set before him (Jesus) he endured the cross…" (Heb. 12:2). Personal joy is inextricably linked to personal sacrifice.

As we give expression to God's Spirit through the giving of ourselves sacrificially on behalf of others, we discover His joy resident in our own human spirit. That joy permeates our souls and we are lifted above the difficulty of any outward circumstance. There is a peace that passes human understanding. It is the by-product of choosing to love, regardless of the cost it may require.

In the same way that we exist in one of two kingdoms, we all serve one of two masters. One is evil, the other is pure and holy. It is impossible to serve both. The difference between the two is that Christ's "burden" is "easy and light", whereas the Devil's burden torments the body, soul, and spirit of the human being. I found choosing the one I would serve a simple choice. You also have a choice. Who will you serve?

Chapter 28

Preservation of Our Cities

God is good and kind and abounding in mercy. Despite their disobedience, God perseveres and strives with men and women seeking to bring them to a knowledge and acceptance of the truth. God will delay turning us over to the destructive nature of our own vices and the repercussions of our acts, as His desire is for us to turn away from the darkness and take steps toward the light.

God's mercy upon a nation is usually expressed through individuals and organizations He raises up to protect and preserve a society of people. However, God's patience has limits. It is also true that if a society repeatedly ignores God's offerings of mercy and continues to sow seeds of destruction, He will withdraw His presence. His power of restraint against the tide of evil will be removed and the people will be subjected to the consequences of their actions. Hosea the Prophet summed this up when he wrote, "For they have sown the wind and shall reap the whirlwind" (Hosea 8:7 AKJV).

Ghost Towns

The immediate image that comes to mind is a dusty road lined on both sides by colorless wood buildings, and the constant low pitch howl of a wind propelling tumbleweeds and filtering through the empty corridors of the weathered structures. The classic mid-nineteenth century, old west ghost town.

We've coined the name *ghost towns* for those failed societies and communities of the past that once supported life, but now lie abandoned and desolate on Earth's landscape. The reasons for the abandonment are varied, including economic collapse, natural disasters, war, political disruption, and anarchy.

Bodie, California is a classic example. Founded in 1859 during the Gold Rush by prospector W.S. Bodey, in its heyday was a boomtown of 10,000 people. However, prosperity was short-lived as the majority of mines were picked dry in the early 1900's. By 1940, the death knell had sounded, and the town was completely shut down, leaving more than one-hundred deserted buildings. Today it is a historical landmark in a state of *arrested decay*. The buildings still contain many of the furnishings and utensils left behind. The deterrent from the visitor's attempt to make off with an artifact is the belief that the absconder will be cursed.

A village, town, or city is founded on the ideal the human population would increase as the community prospers. Bodie's demise simply proved that the desire to get rich quickly is not an enduring foundation on which to build the life of a city.

So, what happened in these towns that doomed their souls and left the hopes and dreams of the people lost and forgotten? Can a town be cursed? Is Savannah cursed?

We touched earlier on the corruptive nature of evil presence, and the insatiable appetite of the Devil to "steal, kill and destroy." It is demonic forces at work in the heart of the human by which this influence of evil takes root, spreads and intensifies, and, eventually, can consume the entire city and her soul. The pleasures of sin are but for a season as its destructive nature will inevitably bring about internal collapse and total external ruin.

Remember Jay Harney's pronouncement of a curse on Savannah? For many, there exists a sense that Lady Savannah plays hostess to an ongoing wrestling match between good and evil. It is a common thought among those familiar with her history, that she is attempting to wrest herself from the grip of a sinister influence.

Over the years, Lady Savannah has often flirted with disaster. There has been a clear, reoccurring pattern for this fickle woman to experience growth and prosperity, and then dangerous decline. As the city has entertained folly on various societal levels, she has teetered on the cusp of extinction but has rebounded and survived the threat.

Through it all, it is clearly evident that Lady Savannah has been the object of God's grace and mercy to counteract the process and push back the tide of darkness by His divine presence and power. As unworthy as Savannah has been at times, God has, and will still show-up on her behalf.

St. Patrick and Lady Savannah

Lady Savannah boasts the 3rd largest St. Patrick's Day parade in the United States. The original intention for celebration and what now marks the festivities is noteworthy.

Thirteen Irish Protestants formed the Hibernian Society in Savannah on St. Patrick's Day in 1812. Their purpose, stated in the Society's constitution, was clear and straightforward and in line with the Oglethorpe Vision:

The maintenance of filial attachment for the Mother Country; the aid of distressed Irishmen and their descendants; relief of indigent widows and orphans of Irishmen and their descendants; the cultivation of good fellowship and the practice of charity.

A year later, the society conducted a humble procession through the heart of the town, prefaced with a simple public announcement in the *Georgia Gazette*, "Parade today, 9 o'clock."

In 1824 the first parade was opened to the general public. The growth and participation were characterized by the Gazette, as follows: "ST. PATRICK'S DAY on Wednesday was celebrated by the Hibernian Society of this city with usual spirit."

One year later, the Georgia Governor, George Troup, joined the festivities, as did Mayor W.C. Daniell and other local and state politicians. Following the procession through the city streets, this upper crust of society and government gathered at the City Hotel where they lavishly celebrated with music, feasting and toasting into the early morning hours.

Over the years, with the exception of 1830, 1862, 1864, 1913, 1918, and 1921, the parade has continued on Saint Patrick's Day in Savannah. The gathering has evolved, or, perhaps, more accurately, dissolved, from a benevolent, charitable event, into a massive, drunken display where people use the holiday as a justification to party shamelessly.

Elizabeth and I have attended the parade twice during our residency in Savannah. On both occasions, attendance exceeded one-hundred thousand people, the majority of whom could not locate Ireland on a map, and thought St. Patrick was a leprechaun. Unless one can view the proceedings from a house or other private property, one will feel insecure and vulnerable, unless, of course, you're also heavily intoxicated. In that condition you won't feel anything.

Irish born Monsignor Daniel J. Bourke served for 63 years in the Diocese of Savannah in the capacities of assistant pastor, comptroller, and then rector of the magnificent Cathedral of Saint John the Baptist. In 1997, at the age of eighty-seven, Bourke took the entire three-mile stroll of the parade route as the Grand Marshall. He commented,

> The parade committee has no control over the hundreds of thousands of people coming to town to join the party and most of them aren't Irish. To them, Saint Patrick's Day is a pagan's good time.

Over the past twenty years, the crowds of attendees have continued to mushroom, and their licentious activities have intensified. This conduct, energized from the spirit world of the demonic, eats at the fabric of a society. The infestation doesn't take a vacation but spreads like a cancer until the weakened foundation of the society crumbles, leaving the city in a pile of moral rubble.

A Lesson from the Boll Weevil

An interesting side note is at the height of the reign of King Cotton over Savannah, and the accompanying material prosperity of the factors, a little insect showed up in 1920, having migrated north from south of the border. The Boll Weevil. Whether the pest was sent by God to slow the march of the greedy, or it was the inevitable end of the corruptive process of evil presence, the weevils laid waste to the cotton industry.

God's Last Word

The Scriptures contain examples of God sparing a city and prolonging life among the people, if there would be found the presence of righteousness. I'm convinced that when Lady Savannah has been ravaged by sin, and on the verge of extinction, God has been gracious and spared her. Contributing to her survival has been the conduct of good men and women who, over the years have sought to please God and committed their talents and tangible resources in service to their fellow citizen.

In the first book of the Old Testament canon, is the accounting of Abraham bargaining with God on behalf of Sodom, one of the five "cities of the plain" in the land of Canaan. God is withdrawing His protection over the city due to their wickedness, so Abraham asks God if He would "sweep away the righteous with the wicked?" He then asks God to spare the city if fifty righteous people could be found among the population, to which God says he would. Abraham continues his appeal with forty-five, then forty, thirty, twenty and, finally, ten people, to which God agrees to withdraw His wrath should ten "righteous" be found. However, not even one righteous person was found in Sodom. Prior to its destruction, we are told that two angels of God led Abraham's nephew, Lot, and his wife and two daughters, from the city to safety. However, it wasn't because they were pleasing to God, it was for the sake of Abraham, a faithful man whose desire was to obey God, whatever the cost.

God honors such sacrifice and in His sovereignty over creation restrains the destructive forces of evil from consuming a city. To men and women like Oglethorpe, George Whitefield, Andrew Bryan, Mary Telfair, John Wesley, Juliette Gordon Low, and Clarence Thomas, the people of Savannah owe a debt of gratitude. God whispered His promise of compassion and destiny for the people of Savannah. They believed Him and contended for the prosperity of their city.

God's last word is always one of mercy and restoration, the Devil's, terror and destruction. God desires to bestow abundant life, whereas the Devil desires to deliver a death blow! God is committed to His agenda and so is the Devil.

Movements of God

In addition to the more obvious works of God in Savannah, those being the religious bodies previously identified, there exists more subtle products of God's grace, but no less significant.

The following are such displays of God's mercy, conceived by His Spirit and manifested in the physical world.

The Historic Savannah Foundation

The historic preservation movement in Savannah was initiated by a group of alarmed citizens in the 1950s. During the two previous decades, they had witnessed the demolition of many buildings with historical significance that were being replaced with parking lots. The group consisted of seven women who banned together in a commitment to defy the wrecking balls and preserve the heritage and unique beauty of these threatened structures within the Historic District. They were aptly named the Historic Savannah Foundation, and their first effort involved saving the Davenport House.

In November 1966, Savannah's downtown received the designation as a National Historic Landmark District, a direct result of the work of the Historic Savannah Foundation.

Savannah College of Art & Design

Earlier, we spoke of the Savannah College of Art & Design, commonly referred to as SCAD. In addition to contributing to positive growth and change within the city, I believe God has raised up this organization as a channel through which His grace and mercy has been demonstrated and continues to flow.

Since 2010, SCAD has offered several degreed programs promoting the preservation of history. Native Savannahian and sitting Supreme Court Justice, Clarence Thomas, was present for the January 29, 2015, opening of the newly restored Clarence Thomas Center for Historic Preservation. Constructed in 1908, the structure later functioned as a Catholic monastery in which Thomas served as an altar boy and received his elementary school education from the convent nuns.

Since their founding, SCAD has been instrumental in saving and restoring several additional structures that continue to occupy ground in the city's Historic District.

Savannah Landmark Rehabilitation Project

The SLRP was founded in 1975 by Leopold Adler. Adler's stated purpose for this program was "the preservation of historic housing without the displacement of existing residents." The neighborhood he targeted was the Victorian District consisting of houses built in the late 1890's and early 1900's, located just south of the Historic District.

Adler saw the displacement of many low income and minority citizens due to the meteoric rise in property values stemming from the revitalization of the Historic District between 1965 and 1977. He believed the eventual renovation of the houses in the Victorian District would further displace the African-American families that had occupied the neighborhood for over thirty years, families instrumental in the early development of Savannah.

Adler's solicitation of both private and public funding resulted in the renovation of two-hundred sixty dilapidated housing units for low-income families.

Apparently, the SLRP program was criticized by some preservationists as a move toward socialism, since it addressed the issue of social equity.

Whether or not you agree with the purpose of the SLRP, the efforts of the organization resulted in the preservation of numerous historically significant structures within Savannah and sustained the households of many of the less fortunate.

If not for the efforts of the HSF, SCAD, and the SLRP, much of the history of the city would be available only in photos and on the printed page.

The Jim Williams Myth

As previously mentioned, it was John Berendt's *Midnight in the Garden of Good and Evil*, that introduced myself and my wife to Lady Savannah. We weren't alone in our beguilement. Since the 1994 release of his blockbuster, tens of millions have been drawn to the city with a desire to experience what Berendt reported as commonplace, but we found difficult to believe.

Central to Berendt's accounting of Savannah is the person of James Arthur Williams, played impeccably by actor Kevin Spacey in Clint Eastwood's big screen rendition of "The Book". Jim Williams was the epitome of the southern gentleman, overflowing with charisma and charm, and possessing a passion for antiques and the restoration of historic buildings.

But in the early 1950's, Williams was an outsider. Finding his way into the inner circle of Savannah's high society wouldn't be a glass ceiling easy to break. He found that the families with the "old money" saw no historical significance, or profit to be made, in renovating the city's archaic, crumbling houses. So, being a thinking, crafty man, he found another means to get their attention and his hand into their pocketbooks.

In her book *After Midnight in the Garden of Good and Evil*, the late Marilyn Bardsley states,

> Jim learned quickly that a number of wealthy and influential gay and bisexual men were locked into the married life that Savannah society required its upper crust to embrace. Some of these men were at the top of important financial institutions and businesses that would ultimately determine whether or not there would be funding in the future to restore historic Savannah.

Williams was well-aware of that fact. His strategy focused on providing something that was unattainable to those who could not risk that their private vices become public knowledge.

Bardsley continues,

> As a very cultured, handsome man with enormous charisma and persuasive abilities, developing sexual relationships with influential gay men was not difficult for him. Jim represented a 'safe' relationship for men whose married life and reputation demanded for utmost discretion. Opportunist that he was, Jim found a way to serve the needs of his friends. Unfortunately, the service Jim provided . . . was immoral and very illegal.

Williams' strategy involved the local Greyhound bus station, that still operates today from the same location on the western border of the Historic District. There, he approached and lured young male runaways as they arrived in town, usually in need of food and a place to lay their heads.

Bardsley writes of the account provided her by the daughter of the Burger King bus stop Manager,

Seeing Jim month after month checking out the boys in their mid-teens and often leaving the station with them disgusted her. She assumed that he befriended the boys for his own pleasure, and that was partly true. Jim loved sex with young men and boys. Later, when he was much more successful, Jim didn't have to hang around the bus station looking for young talent for himself or his friends. All he had to do was to go out into the squares around Bull Street and persuade some of the teenagers to come home with him. He got to know which ones he could trust.

Williams operation of what in effect was a male prostitution ring, gained him acceptance into the upper level of Savannah's oligarchy. With that came the network that eventually gained him the wealth and status he sought.

In 1955, at the age of twenty-four years, Williams purchased and restored his first three houses located at 541, 543, and 545 Congress Street. Fourteen years later, following his ascension to the top rung of the social ladder, Williams crème de la crème achievement was the restoration of the Mercer Mansion, now named the Mercer-Williams House and Museum, originally constructed in 1868 for Confederate General Hugh Mercer, and situated in Monterey Square. Williams purchased the property in 1969, worked his restoration magic, moved in, lived there and died there.

Another of Williams' claims to fame is that he is recorded as the only person in Georgia to ever be tried four times for the same crime. In 1981 he was arrested for the shooting death of local Danny Hansford, a younger man with whom he had a sexual relationship. Williams pled self-defense. After his fourth trial in Augusta in 1989, Williams was acquitted and freed. Six months later, he dropped dead in his Savannah home at the age of fifty-nine years, apparently, in the same room of the house where he alleged Hansford had threatened to kill him, and where he shot Hansford.

Prior to his purchase and residency in the Mercer house, Williams had saved another property from the wrecking ball. The three-story house built by Hampton Lillibridge in 1799 was in dire need of a little tender loving care when Williams purchased the place in 1963. He immediately had it moved to its present location at 507 E. St. Julian Street. Credible events that took place during the move, restoration of the structure, and while Williams resided within the house, are right out of a Hollywood ghost story. Included was the commissioning by Williams of an Episcopalian priest to perform a ritual exorcism to rid the house of its unseen, unwelcomed guests. Subsequently, during a couple's residency, they had a paranormal team from Duke University conduct a study that resulted in their "expert" declaration of the Hampton Lillibridge House as the most haunted building they have ever encountered. Today, you'll find the property at the top of the list of stops on most of the Savannah ghost tours.

It is interesting that with the release of Berendt's book in 1994 following Williams death, the personage of Jim Williams has contributed to the economic growth of Savannah much more than during the years he was alive. The book sold millions, then came the tourists, and with that, tourist dollars.

The significance of the fact that Berendt's book was focused around the investigation and trial of Williams, an accused and probable murderer, that trafficked underage males for sex, cannot be overlooked. And a rampant murder rate continues unabated to this day.

Some credit Williams with the intellect of a genius, others see him as a spiritualist who dabbled in the occult and relied on the counsel of a local voodoo princess, and there are those that focus solely on his involvement in saving over fifty houses in Savannah and coastal areas of Georgia and South Carolina.

Whereas Williams worked and exercised his gifts in ways that would make the "dirty face" of Savannah more attractive to citizens and visitors, his most significant contribution served to intensify the moral darkness of the Lady's heart. There is no doubt that his dogged commitment to the city resulted in the enhancement of Savannah's outward beauty. However, behind the closed doors of the mansions he saved, he was contributing to the deterioration of her inner moral fabric.

Chapter 29

Legacy of Corruption

The Devil's goal for any city is *subjugation*. The word means dominance and control. In the spiritual context we apply the word, subjugation is the outworking of moral corruption.

We have detailed that demonic presence cemented its dominance and control in North America by way of the misdeeds of the early European colonists and their mistreatment of the indigenous peoples. We have also identified the choices made by those who ruled over Savannah in her infant stage and how those decisions resulted in perpetuation of the dark spirit power that obstructed and continues to thwart God's planned destiny for the city.

Let's now present a timeline that identifies the more significant perpetrators and nature of their acts, that culminates in the day that we live. We'll see that this entrenched demonic presence has continued unabated, without any significant challenge to its dominance and control over the city.

The First 100 Years

During the late 1700's and up until the onset of the Civil War in 1861, the years were marked by the iron grip of plantation owners such as the brothers James and Thomas Potter, the father and son duo of Charles and Louis Manigault, and Pierce Butler of The Weeping Time. These powermongers perpetuated the evils of slavery in Savannah, and throughout the southeast region of the young American Republic.

The moral turbulence of government politics in Savannah was accurately depicted during the Congressional election of 1791, that was to determine representation for five Georgia counties, including Chatham County. The contestants were incumbent General James Jackson, and challenger General "Mad Anthony" Wayne, both Revolutionary War heroes. The culprits were Henry Osborne, a Superior Court judge, and Thomas Gibbons, a local politician and future Savannah mayor. Osborne and Gibbons worked behind the scenes and engaged in voter intimidation and manipulation that resulted in the election of Wayne. The ensuing political drama saw the involvement of the Governor of Georgia and the United States Congress, that culminated with the voiding of the election, the removal of Wayne from office, and the impeachment of Judge Osborne.

The Second 100 Years

In 1858, Savannah businessman Charles Lamar, along with three associates, purchased The Wanderer, a luxury yacht that they converted into a slave trade ship. In defiance of the 1818 Federal legislation that outlawed the slave trade in the United States, Lamar completed a successful run in which seven-hundred fifty males from the "dark continent" were delivered and sold. That same year, another run was attempted but the ship was seized, and Lamar charged with violation of the federal statute. After much political wrangling, the case was closed in 1860 with no convictions having been secured. The Wanderer was then publicly auctioned in Savannah and secured by, you guessed it, Charles Lamar.

During the late 1890's and midway through the 1900's, Bossism, the system of political control centering about a single powerful figure, established its stranglehold in Savannah and much of Georgia. Instrumental in sparking this societal malady was the Law Firm of Osborne and Lawrence, founded in 1890 by principals W. W. Osborne (yes, son of the impeached Judge) and Alexander Lawrence. They found that developing a political power base in Savannah wasn't difficult in post-Civil War Savannah.

According to Malcolm Maclean, former Savannah mayor (1960-66), "Voter turnout was low, and the establishment got people jobs with the city or county government, and the political machine began to manage the ballot boxes during elections." Election rigging found a home with Lady Savannah.

This political stronghold, with its roots in the demonic, was fortified by the presence of John Bouhan (1881 to 1971), whose law firm of Bouhan and Atkinson had merged with Osborne and Lawrence in 1931.

Tom Coffey, reporter and editor of the Savannah Morning News, commented,

> Bouhan didn't control every official, but he manipulated enough to have his influence felt whenever needed. His political machine gained control of city hall, the county commission, and Chatham

County's state delegates. Mayor Macleand added, Not since occupation (General Sherman's troops) had the city witnessed such subjugation.

Early to mid-twentieth century Savannah was also infiltrated by a variety of dark vices such as gambling, bootlegging, and prostitution. Where was the church establishment in all of this? Apparently, many religious leaders either turned a blind eye or were paid off, rather than take a stand against the political juggernaut that operated within the city.

Neither was the local understaffed police department a force that Bouhan need worry about as his "machine" controlled the hiring and placement of the undertrained and underpaid rank and file officers, a problem that is woefully evident in today's Savannah police force.

Bouhan was also instrumental in collaborating with Georgia governor and white supremacist, Eugene Talmadge, in the building of the massive bridge that connected Georgia with South Carolina. Apparently, the arrangement was a sweet deal, financially, for Bouhan.

The Recent Years

We looked at the deteriorated physical condition in which Lady Savannah found herself moving into the mid-twentieth century, and how the emergence and efforts of the women of the Historic Savannah Foundation staved off further crumbling of the city. This external destruction, primarily, was the result and manifestation of a severe internal moral decline personified by the likes of Talmadge and Bouhan, the predominant gatekeepers of the state, county, and city.

A cosmetic facelift of Lady Savannah has been steadily in progress during the second half of the twentieth century, through the various preservation efforts of both public and private sectors. Again, this ebb and flow of the visible economic aspect of the city is reflective of the invisible spirit conflict contending for the soul of the city. We'll now see how the forces of darkness reasserted their stranglehold on the Lady in the latter part of the century.

Crack and the Jivens Gang

Mayor Edna Jackson (2012 to 2016) spoke for the people when stating, "This is all over the city. I'm concerned to pick up the paper to see another young person shot or killed. I don't want to see it get back to where it was in the days of the Jivens gang."

In the 1980's and 90's, the trafficking of crack cocaine is credited with the destruction of an entire generation of youth in Savannah. The driving force behind this societal evil was a young man named Ricky Jivens.

Jivens launched his drug-dealing activities while in high school, selling marijuana. From there, he graduated to dealing crack cocaine. At the age of twenty years, he is said to have owned several houses, expensive cars, and had a personal chauffeur. His followers were recruited from the local youth, and they would do his bidding, no questions asked.

The rite of initiation into the gang was to commit a murder. The Drug Enforcement Administration in Savannah estimates that Jivens was responsible for as many as twenty homicides of the fifty-nine total homicides committed in 1991, the highest number the city has ever experienced.

In the 1980's, crack cocaine was first smuggled into Miami from the Caribbean. It quickly made its way into the larger marketplaces of New York City and Los Angeles. Although not nearly rivaling the population of NYC or LA, the third stop was Savannah, apparently, because of her proximity to Atlanta, and location to the Interstate 95. Ricky Jivens established a source of supply and it wasn't long before he controlled 70% of the crack dissemination in Savannah.

The rampant criminal activity that gripped Savannah related to the crack epidemic, affected the whole city. It is believed to have caused the "white flight" of the late 1980's and early 1990's. The city's entire population entering that period of time was about 130,000 people. During the epidemic, the white population of Savannah decreased by 13,338, while the black population increased by 4,492 people, resulting in a majority of African-American citizens.

A dramatic escalation of crime and murder rates occurred within all the states and cities gripped by the trafficking of crack. Black youth were those most ravaged by the invasion. High school graduation rates plummeted by about fifty-seven percent, and job employability dropped dramatically, as well, whereas the rate of fathering children, jumped.

With a touch of sarcasm, The *New Futures Initiatives* reported,

> Kids born to these middle school and high school kids who were caught up in crack's deadly grip are now today's 18 to 24-year-olds. The same ones that have you worried today, no matter what a Conde Nast magazine says about Savannah as a tourist hot spot.

Corruption in High Places

Isaiah, the Old Testament prophet, said this about the overall state of Jerusalem in his day, "The whole head is sick, and the whole heart faint" (Isa. 1:5 AKJV).

The head represents the intellect, the heart represents morality. When the head and heart of a human being is sick and weak, the survival of both the body and soul are in serious jeopardy.

When the thoughts and actions of those positioned in seats of authority are given over to the devices of their own intellect and skewed moral code, the inevitable result, as we considered in our review of societal institutions, is a malady that infiltrates the soul of a city or nation. This sickness, mental and moral, makes for a hotbed of demonic activity.

It would only be partly true to say that the present-day city officials of Savannah minimize the problem of local governmental crime and corruption in order to protect the city's image. The greater reality is that in protecting the Lady's image, a healthy revenue from the flow of tourism is maintained, which has a direct effect on their ability to garner the votes necessary to maintain their positions of power and control. Same problem, same agenda, different faces.

The following is a brief accounting of the more serious trespasses and scandals involving city officials that have come to light during just the last 10 years. And it is likely that several of these authoritarians had aided and abetted the Jivens Gang and the flow of crack into the city.

Mayor Otis and the City Manager Debacle

In April 2011, former Mayor Otis Johnson and the Savannah City Council were investigated by the State of Georgia Attorney General's office for holding three closed-door meetings in November and December 2010 and January 2011, while engaged in their search for a City Manager. As a result, Mayor Johnson and his band of merry Aldermen, were found to have "violated the letter and spirit" of the Open Meetings law. State

Attorney General Sam Olens subsequently visited Savannah to conduct mandatory training for the city officials.

Rochelle Small-Toney was the individual that came out of those illegal meetings as the City Manager hired by Mayor Johnson and the council in March 2011, with an annual $200,000-plus salary. Small-Toney was the first African-American female to fill that position, and Mayor Johnson, a self-described "militant" for civil rights, was criticized as having based his choice on race, rather than experience and skill. This opinion was fueled as it came to light that Small-Toney had a past scrape with the law and had been fired from a similar city position, before coming to Savannah.

This was followed by a series of heated local protests that included a hastily organized, special public meeting at the Savannah Civic Center, presided over by the Mayor and his council, during which citizens were encouraged to vent their frustrations.

In December 2011, Mayor Johnson was replaced by Mayor Edna Jackson. Within a year of her election, she led the charge for the removal of Small-Toney based on allegations of negligence, violation of policy, and mismanagement of staff. In September 2012, Small-Toney resigned after holding the City Manager position for a mere eighteen months.

Tony Thomas

This embattled five-term City Alderman's contributions to Savannah society have been the subject of controversy. Over the last several years, his actions have come under increased scrutiny.

In February 2016, an ethics complaint was filed against Thomas by two female constituents relative to his treatment of women on social media. Later in the year, the Georgia Bureau of Investigation released their eighty-two-page report regarding sexual misconduct claims against Thomas, filed by several different men who were minors at the time of the alleged misconduct. The grand jury that heard the claims decided against forwarding the complaint to a criminal grand jury because the statute of limitations had expired on all cases. Apparently, fourteen of the eighteen jurors felt the claims had merit and suggested a pattern of predatory behavior. At the March 2017 St. Patrick's Day Parade, Thomas was seen drunk and berating a parade float operator and then passed out at a local hotel, for which he later issued a public apology.

In May 2017, a vote to censure Thomas was conducted among the other city council members relative to his treatment of a local female journalist. The vote was unanimous to censure; however, the action was described as "toothless and watered down to the point of meaningless", in the estimation of Jim Morekis of *Connect Savannah*.

More from Morekis,

> Thomas – sitting in his usual Council chair and acting if he, not the Mayor, were running the meeting – went down the line attempting to expose everyone else's dirty laundry, at a meeting which was supposed to be about his dirty laundry.

Despite the unethical and, quite possibly, criminal actions of this conflicted human being, for some strange reason Thomas served several consecutive terms. He was finally ousted in the City Council elections of 2019.

Michael Berkow

In November 2006, following a year when crime statistics across the board soared to new heights, Michael Berkow was installed as Chief of the Savannah - Chatham Metropolitan

Police Department (SCMPD). He was fresh, new blood, recruited from his former position as Deputy Chief of the Los Angeles Police Department. After just less than three years as Savannah's Chief, he abruptly resigned amidst accusations of sexual misconduct while he served in Los Angeles. Those charges were never to be substantiated but were sufficient to drive him prematurely from the city, shades of John Wesley.

Willie Lovett

On the heels of Berkow's resignation, Willie Clinton Lovett, a veteran of more than thirty years of service with the Savannah Police Department, was promoted to Chief of Police of the SCMPD in 2010. However, in September 2013, he, too, abruptly resigned.

It would be just a little more than one year later that Lovett was the subject of a press release from the U.S. Attorney's Office of the Department of Justice. The first paragraph read:

> Former Savannah-Chatham Metropolitan Police Chief Willie Clinton Lovett, 66, was convicted last week by a federal jury on charges of extortion, participating in an illegal gambling operation, conspiring to obstruct the enforcement of state criminal laws, and providing false statements to federal agents. United States District Court Judge William T. Moore, Jr. presided over Lovett's 5-day jury trial.

The Savannah 11

The ongoing moral corruption of Savannah's governmental and political leadership has given entrance and control to dark, sinister powers. We just looked at the more recent events attesting to that fact. We know that the strategy of the Devil is to maintain his cover for as long as possible. However, evil cannot avoid tipping its hand, as the nature of wickedness is to wax worse and worse. Eventually, demonic presence becomes evident even to those skeptical of its existence.

In his October 2015 article entitled, *The Mother of All Law Suits*, Jim Morekis details litigation aimed at bringing some long-term human players in this local drama to account. His description of the case filing is as follows:

> A massive racketeering civil lawsuit against some of the biggest names in recent Savannah political history: Former City Manager Michael Brown. Former County Manager Russ Abolt. Former County Commission Chairman Pete Liakakis. Former Interim Police Chief Julie Tolbert. Former Police Chief Willie Lovett sardonically described in the complaint as 'a citizen of Georgia who is temporarily residing in a federal prison in West Virginia'.
>
> Because of the remarkable scope of the lawsuit—four plaintiffs, 15 defendants, and a narrative going back to the mid-'90s—it has potential to be the Rosetta Stone, the Holy Grail, linking the days of the Ricky Jivens crime syndicate and today's Willie Lovett-era police corruption.
>
> Allegations in the suit include purported rank and file corruption within the department, as well as the collusion between Savannah's CNT (Counter Narcotics Team) and IA (Internal Affairs) in covering up activities as well as direct involvement in the protecting of drug dealers and drug dissemination throughout the city.

As of the time of this writing, the case continues to move through the court system. And given the history of Savannah's institutional failings, there is no guarantee that justice will prevail.

Murder in Savannah

Oglethorpe's dream of nurturing a citizenry that would place the needs of others above their own has been far from realized. The deliberate taking of a life is the opposite of one laying down their life for another. This has become part of the legacy of darkness for which Lady Savannah is known. It is a continuation of the human activity, prompted by demonic influence, that was occurring for hundreds of years prior to the arrival of Oglethorpe.

In May 2016, CNN reported that in 2015, fifty-three homicides were perpetrated in Savannah, "the city's most violent year in a quarter-century", a 66% increase from 2014, and "the bloodiest year since 1991" when Jivens and his boys terrorized the city.

More "grave" statistics show that the Savannah 2015 murder rate among U.S. cities with a population over two-hundred thousand, placed her at #10 with 22.4 killings per one-hundred thousand residents.

2016 wasn't an encouragement as fifty homicides were tallied during the year, and a 1% increase in violent crime.

In 2017, the total homicides dropped to 34, and violent crime also ticked downward. However, the year also produced a rise in the number of aggravated assaults using guns and a hefty 22% increase in aggravated assaults without the use of a gun.

In 2018, 31 homicides were perpetrated in metro Savannah. However, by July 20, 2019, violent crime, which includes robberies, rapes, aggravated assaults and homicides, was up 32% from 2018.

Community Efforts

The downward trend in homicides has been credited to the formation of groups like *CrimeStoppers*, which is a call-in tip line, *CHAOS* (Change Helping Agents of Savannah) launched by several local mothers, and city government initiatives such as *End Gun Violence*.

CrimeStoppers allows residents to call in anonymous phone tips about crimes committed or potential criminal acts, with the incentive of a possible monetary reward.

CHAOS efforts to combat the rash of homicides includes conducting monthly "Die-Ins" and rallies throughout Savannah, in an attempt to heighten awareness and encourage activism among the citizenry.

End Gun Violence has a more direct approach. They host "Call-Ins", a forum where members of local law enforcement bring in violent offenders on parole and issue stern warnings to "clean up or we're coming after you."

The community efforts to abate the wave of crime and corruption within Savannah, and, I would assume, similar efforts in your city, are admirable. The desire and the goals are good and just. However, the sum total of these projects and works amount to nothing more than damage control. The root issue, the spirit nature of the problems, must be acknowledged and dealt with. Remember, our fight is not against flesh and blood, but against formidable spirit powers that blind people to their need for a Savior, who alone can deliver them from the ills of fallen human nature. Nothing will be accomplished until we first acknowledge the reality of the spirit world and the ongoing conflict, therein.

Haunted Savannah: Abodes of Evil

The haunted element of Lady Savannah is widely recognized, and, I'm sad to say, celebrated. Her wheels of commerce are oiled by marketing her as the Most Haunted City in America. Considerable money is made, and influence gained by locals via the tourists that flock to these various venues, including mansions, restaurants, pubs, shops and warehouses, as the local media boasts of the presence of evil spirits and ghosts that are waiting to be encountered.

As I have proposed, these hauntings are a direct result of city gatekeepers; those in positions of civic, business and political leadership, who have chosen despite the grave moral repercussions for the people of Savannah. As man's spirit enemy has gained entrance, the poison of malice has infected the soul of Lady Savannah. This inner malady at work in the darkness of man's heart, has been the source of outbreaks of hostility and violence, including murder.

These evil beings populate the atmosphere, wander the streets, and occupy many dwellings and structures of the city. It is revealing that the stories behind many of the Savannah haunts, detailed in the various books on the subject, involve past residents who fell prey to these kinds of vices and met their tragic end. As much as the Devil would like to conceal his culpability, the nature of these acts betray his presence. Even still, his mastery of disguise and deceit have sufficiently kept the masses confused and enticed.

It is evident that on a human level, there has been considerable efforts to stem the flow of criminal activity in both the private and public sectors of Savannah. However, nothing has changed. The public outcry and activism have produced no lasting results. The dirty face of the Lady has been prettied-up, but her heart is on life support. The advance and retreat of the tide of wickedness continues without any significant evidence of sustained victory within the spirit world where, ultimately, these issues are decided.

So, what action can we take to confront and expel this wickedness that preys on the souls of men, women, and children, and restrains Savannah, and your city, as well, from fulfilling her divine destiny?

For the vast number of towns and cities of our land where a standard of righteousness has not been raised, there is a way to effect their liberation. The proverb simply says, "Trust in the LORD with all your heart, and lean not on your own understanding; in all your ways submit to Him, and He will make your paths straight" (Prov. 3:5, 6). This includes the pathway of deliverance and release for your city!

As men, women, and whole families become committed to their God and burdened by conditions within their community, citywide spiritual warfare should be planned and carried out. The starting point is to expose and confront the ground level workings of wicked spirits, preying on the weakness and ignorance of mankind. As we move from victory to victory in the battle, the stronghold over the land and people will weaken. In increasing measure, the weight will be lifted from the city's soul and a prevailing peace will settle over the society of people.

Let's look more closely at the means to this end.

Chapter 30

Vision and Compassion

Before we explore the more practical activities of our engagement in spiritual warfare, it is essential that a degree of enlightenment of our minds, and sensitivity of our hearts be cultivated. We must be prepared by the Spirit of God to "walk as Jesus walked" (1 John 2:6) while he was among us, clothed in flesh.

Vision for Your City

Too often, people base their opinion of where they live, or where they want to live, on external economic and social aspects such as the crime rate, cost of housing, schools, recreational facilities, and others. Not that there's anything wrong with that. But our lives can be much more meaningful if we consider how our time and energy can be directed in assisting our fellow citizens in realizing their potential, and, ultimately, the potential of our cities.

Since initiating this book project, I have intently focused on listening to what is said about Savannah by others living in the city. There is a keen public awareness that the city is subject to frequent criminal activity and there exists considerable corruption in the political institutions of both the city and Chatham County. Despair and disgust are often expressed through the vehicle of social media. The frustration of the law-abiding segment of the population is energetically vented, and the issues heatedly discussed. The fact that problems exist is clear; however, understanding of the underlying roots is not, nor is the pathway by which to resolve the issues.

Again, I solicited input on Facebook, as follows:

I need your feedback to help with the completion of a project. Those who have lived, or now live in Savannah, know of the unique and wonderful aspects of the city, but also of her failings and needs. In a sentence or two, please state what you envision Savannah would be like if her full potential for good was realized.

Three days after the posting, there were still no responses. The lesson learned is this: People are long on opinion but short on vision when it comes to their cities. Opinion is an assessment manufactured by the mind and emotions, whereas vision is born of the spirit.

Solomon, in sage-mode said, "Where there is no vision, the people perish" (Prov. 29:18 AKJV).

Another translation of the same verse says it this way, "Where there is no revelation, the people cast off restraint." Interesting. This tells us that without God in our midst, disclosing His will and plan for our individual lives and corporate city life, society becomes ungovernable. Eventually, confusion, disorder, and rebellion take over. The end result is the destruction of the society. This is true of our individual lives, our marriages, our families, our cities, our nation, and the world. We must be in touch with God and directed by His Spirit if we are to survive and prosper.

Jesus likened himself to a vine, and you and I to the branches of that vine. He was emphasizing that the prospering of our individual lives and corporate city life is dependent on receiving the life-flow of God working in and through us as we remain *connected* through our devotion to Him and His purposes.

So, this being the case, you and I must ask ourselves: Do I possess vision, a revelation from God of His desires and plan for my life, and that of my city?

We all want the best for the city in which we dwell; a reduction in crime, and integrous religious, business, and political leadership. But hoping that will come to pass and bantering with our fellow citizens about the cities shortcomings, will not get it done. It is only when we draw near to the Architect that we gain understanding, direction, and glimpse the possibilities and potential for ourselves and others. Revelation, if vigilantly pursued will instill vision necessary to transform our communities.

Compassion for Your City

Before God will reveal to us His plans for our cities, our hearts must be tenderized. The actions we take must be conducted not only with understanding, but also the right heart attitude.

I recall mine and Elizabeth's visit with a wealthy couple who were considering selling their home and relocating. They mentioned a few different cities and why they were attracted to each one. The husband then identified the one thing that the city would have to possess for them to consider moving there. Good restaurants. I couldn't resist challenging him about that priority; however, he just couldn't understand my point. I came to the conclusion that his condition was a severe case of being led by the stomach and not the heart.

A paraphrased version of President John Kennedy's declaration would have been apropos, "Ask not what your city can do for you, but what you can do for your city."

The Scriptures are clear that it was those who sought the good for their city that God used to effect change. Jeremiah was known as "the weeping prophet" because of his love for Jerusalem and display of grief over her condition. We mentioned earlier of Nehemiah's burden and heart for Jerusalem, and the risks he took in seeking her good. And, Jesus wept over the hard-heartedness of Jerusalem's people. In our hearts, do we condemn our cities? Or do we contend for their release into destiny?

Consider Jonah, who, in eighth century BC, was summoned by God to go to Nineveh, the capital of Israel's sworn evil enemy, Assyria. His mission was to announce the Ninevites destruction should they not turn from their sin. He understood God's plan, but not God's heart.

Jonah's initial response was to condemn Nineveh for her evil conduct and to justify why they should be wiped from face of the Earth. So, he fled by ship to avoid God's call. We all know of the ensuing storm, of Jonah being tossed overboard when his shipmates discovered his disobedience, and then him being swallowed by the "great fish" where he had a little alone time with God. Jonah sought God's mercy, was upchucked onto dry land, and headed straight to Nineveh.

Out of fear for His own life, and not compassion for the people, Jonah announced their impending doom and the remedy. The people turned from their evil ways and in response, God poured out His mercy. The story ends with Jonah outside the city gates, resentful and disgruntled over Nineveh's survival.

Now, here's the object lesson: God provides Jonah with a shade plant to shield him from the desert heat. He also sends a worm to devour the plant, to which Jonah responds with sadness over the fate of the plant. God then draws near and whispers to Jonah's heart,

> You have been concerned about the plant, though you did not tend it or make it grow. It sprang up overnight and died overnight. And should I not have concern for the great city of Nineveh, in which there are more than a hundred and twenty thousand people who cannot tell their right hand from their left – and also many animals?" (Jonah 4:10,11).

So, the question to us is, will we grieve more for the lack of good restaurants in our community, or will our sorrow stem from the impending doom of those fellow citizens bound in darkness?

It is noteworthy that God referred to Nineveh as "the great city." God always sees the potential of a human being and that of a city. He believes the potential will be realized and His dealings are to that end.

However, history records how Nineveh, the city the prophet described as "the city of blood, full of lies, full of plunder" (Nahum 3:1), returned to her evil ways and was destroyed by the Babylonians in 612 BC.

We do not know what became of Jonah. What we do know is that if we view those living in the kingdom of darkness through the eyes of God, what we will see are powerless souls in need of rescuing from the torment of ignorance. When left to ourselves, that's all we see.

Pray for your city. That is the only way of developing a compassionate heart for her people. It is in running to God, not from Him whereby we envision the potential destiny of each individual and the community, as well as the role we are to play in the process.

Vision and compassion are inseparably linked. True compassion for your city will give birth to a vital vision for your city. Within that vision will be the pathway to fulfillment.

Chapter 31

Freeing the Captive City

The Creator has always communicated directly with His human creation. His voice was heard audibly by men and women during the approximate 4,000 years of time, from the creation of Adam and Eve to the entrance of the Son of God upon the Earth. Jesus was then visible as he spoke directly to the people of his day. Today, God continues to speak within the hearts of people and through His the written word recorded by those of past generations. However He speaks, we should pay close attention.

You Must be Born Again

Jesus didn't want His message misconstrued. To limit controversy, He laid out what it would take to inherit eternal life in one uncompromising sentence:

> Very truly I tell you, no one can see the kingdom of God unless they are born again (John 3:3).

Therefore, one must be joined to His family through a personal rebirth of spirit wherein one "has crossed over from death to life" (John 5:24), wherein "The old has gone, the new is here" (2 Cor. 5:17), and wherein we now "live and move and have our being" (Acts 17:28 AKJV) in God, Himself.

The basic prerequisite of the warrior of God is that he or she must first be His redeemed and ransomed son or daughter. Don't misunderstand me, God considers all human beings as sons and daughters; some are lost, some are found. The prodigal son was no less a son of the father who grieved over his waywardness.

From the point in time when Adam and Eve disobeyed God, up until the death, burial, and resurrection of Jesus, God's offspring were far away from the Father's house, separated from his life and prohibited from enjoying the immense family benefits. Because of the dividing wall that sin imposed, the Father could not approach his offspring, neither could they venture into the light of His presence. Whether or not we derive the benefits and wonders of restored relationship with our Father, is now decided by the individual man or woman. Until the person receives God's provision for the forgiveness of their personal sin, he or she is locked out, barred from entrance to the kingdom.

Jesus took care of that problem, revealing Himself as the Way to restored fellowship with the Father, and full inheritance of the indescribable wealth of the kingdom freely provided His redeemed sons and daughters.

Seven centuries prior to Christ's appearance on Earth, Isaiah wrote these words,

> Surely, he took up our pain and our suffering, yet we considered him punished by God, stricken by him, and afflicted. But he was pierced for our transgressions, bruised for our iniquities, the punishment that brought us peace was on him, and by his wounds

we are healed. We all, like sheep, have gone astray, each have turned to our own way, and the Lord has laid on him the iniquity of us all (Isa. 53:4-6).

Being God, he willingly left the perfection of Heaven and came to Earth. Clothed in human flesh, he walked among us, and became our humble servant. Without any trespass of God's divine law, he willingly accepted the punishment for our rebellion and died the cruelest of deaths of that day, so that we might be transported from a dungeon of darkness, into the light of the kingdom. We receive His life because he took our death.

The problem that plagued the human race has been dealt with. The sin issue, the blight on the spirit of mankind that condemned him to an eternity of separation from the Father has been rendered powerless, null and void. Through this rebirth, our spirit and soul life are instantaneously transferred into the presence of God and granted entrance to His kingdom. We are then citizens of a divine spiritual government that reigns within those that have welcomed the King into their hearts! It is God's intent that the invisible aspects of His kingdom would be manifested upon this earth through our obedience to His will. And it is only through Kingdom people that Kingdom rule will be established in our cities upon the earth.

Let's look at several statements made by Jesus about his Kingdom that directly relate to you and me and our time on this earth. We need to see that this kingdom and the authority of that domain, is not something that only pertains to a future time but is as relevant now as it will be then.

The Kingdom Within You

When asked by one of the experts of Jewish law when the kingdom of God would come, Jesus replied,

> The kingdom of God comes not with observation. Neither shall they say, see here! or, see there! for, behold, the kingdom of God is within you (Luke 17:20, 21 AKJV).

What did Jesus mean? He was revealing to mankind that His kingdom is not like those that exist in the natural world, that it would not be physical in nature or found in any geographical setting on the earth. He was saying that this invisible kingdom would exist only in the hearts of those that were born into the kingdom and revealed through the lives of those kingdom citizens. He was saying that the proof of the kingdom's existence in the lives of men and women would be through their expression of a new nature; an ability to overcome the bents of the fallen human nature, and power to subdue the presence of evil in the world. The kingdom would be evident in the love demonstrated and the joy and peace possessed by its citizens.

The Keys to Death and the Grave

Jesus conquest of death was evidenced in his rising from the dead. The tomb into which his lifeless body was placed, was powerless to hold Him. In the Book of Revelation, the risen King declares,

> I am the Living One; I was dead, and now look, I am alive for ever and ever! And I hold the keys to death and Hades (the grave)! (Rev. 1:18)

Because of that fact, we are promised,

> If the Spirit of him who raised Jesus from the dead is living in you, he who raised Christ from the dead will also give life to your mortal bodies because of His Spirit who lives in you (Rom. 8:11).

So, it is by the Spirit of God coming and living within the believer that will enable us to pass from death into fullness of life beyond the grave!

The keys to death and the grave, secured and held by Jesus, are symbolic of His total right and authority over that which previously ruled mankind. Whereas the Devil once presided over the physical death of all men and women, and was the keeper of the dead, as those who have experienced a rebirth of spirit through Christ, we can now declare with confidence and joy, "O' death, where is your sting, O' grave, where is your victory?" (1 Cor. 15:55 AKJV).

We have become sharers in the victory of Christ over death, as our sin, that required our death, has been dealt with. The life of the Holy Spirit, living within the believer, is our guarantee of life now, and beyond the grave!

The Keys of the Kingdom

Jesus again referred to these *keys* while on Earth when speaking to His followers. He said,

> I will give you the keys of the kingdom of Heaven (Matt. 16:19 NIV).

It is clear that those to whom these keys were to be given, would use them during their lifetime on Earth, as present-day kingdom citizens. Interesting; living on Earth, but citizens of a kingdom "not of this world" (John 18:36), as Jesus also made clear. So, if we are already kingdom citizens, then these keys aren't to give *us* access into the kingdom. We are *already inside*. The keys are given us so that we can unlock the doors that keep others out, allowing them entrance, as well.

These keys represent *kingdom authority*, the ultimate authority that exists in Heaven and on Earth. Remember, Christ's sacrifice returned to mankind the authority to rule over life on planet Earth. It is our responsibility to use them. The fate of our family members and the citizens of our communities will be determined by our action or inaction. The means by which they may gain entrance to the Kingdom rests in our hands.

As the redeemed of God come together in one united force, the life and power of the Spirit will be released into the societies in which we live. The result will be that Kingdom people will walk among a fallen race, in possession of the keys by which the captives might pass from death into fullness of life!

Not only do these keys open the way into the kingdom of God, they are also the means by which the destiny of your city and mine will be unlocked and set free. Our message is good news for mankind, and bad news for the Devil!

Basis of Kingdom Authority

Our possession of this authority is delegated to us by God, our Father. The basis of the authority rests solely on the finished work of His Son, Jesus Christ, as the Conqueror of death, the grave, the power of sin, and the power of the Evil One. He is the King of kings whose throne is "far above all rule and authority, power and dominion, and every name that is invoked, not only in the present age, but also in the one to come" (Eph. 1:21). The foundation of kingdom authority is threefold, as follows:

The Blood of Christ

The Scriptures are emphatic on this point, that "without the shedding of blood, there is no forgiveness" (Heb. 9:22). The forgiveness for our individual sins and those of all mankind for all time, was provided for when Jesus died on the cross. We were provided a pathway to eternal life through the spilling of His blood to the point of death. Without that, we have no entrance to the kingdom, and, therefore, no kingdom authority.

The Name of Jesus

Paul wrote to the early church in Philippi about the Father's response to what Jesus accomplished through completing his mission on Earth:

> God exalted Him to the highest place and gave Him the name that is above every name, that at the name of Jesus every knee will bow, in Heaven and on Earth and under the earth, and every tongue acknowledge that Jesus Christ is Lord, to the glory of God the Father (Phil. 2:9-11).

In secular business, when one is hired by a company or corporation, they are now authorized to represent that entity by their words and actions. One carries with them all the resources possessed by that entity, including the influence and power of reputation and material wealth.

When police officers discharge their duties, they do so with the full authority of the agency or department they represent. They possess the right to demand accountability to the laws he or she is commissioned to enforce. If an officer commands you or me to "stop in the name of the law", then we must do so or face the consequences.

In the person of Jesus Christ is the authority of the kingdom of God. As His sons and daughters, we are commissioned to go forth in His name. As we do, we go in possession of all the resources and full authority of God and Heaven behind our words and our actions.

When we confront the powers of darkness, we are armed with a power of attorney to act on God's behalf, with legal entitlement to employ all the assets of Heaven in the process. It is signed in blood and bears the name of Jesus, the name to which "every knee will bow, and every tongue confess" that He is Lord!

The Power of the Holy Spirit

Following his resurrection from the dead, Jesus appeared to his disciples and told them that the Holy Spirit would come and begin a new work upon the earth. Whereas the Spirit of God had only moved *among* mankind in the past, He would now abide *within* the man or woman, creating, transforming and empowering the whole of their being: body, soul, and spirit.

Jesus said,

> I will pray the Father, and he shall give you another Comforter, that he may abide with you forever; Even the Spirit of truth; whom the world cannot receive, because it sees him not, neither knows him: but you know him; for he dwells with you, and shall be in you (John 14: 16, 17 AKJV).

Jesus made sure that His people would be well provided for. God the Son would temporarily leave their side; however, God the Spirit would come to take His place. Such is the love of the Father.

The word *comforter* comes from the Greek word *parakletos*, and also implies the role of helper and strengthener. It is comprised of two common words, *para*, meaning alongside of, and *kaleo*, which means to call. Together they make up one word, literally meaning, someone called alongside another.

The promise is that the Spirit of God would not only walk alongside the man or woman but would take up residency *within* the believer. And not just during our time on Earth, but forever! This indwelling, the most intimate means of relationship with His children for which the Father longed for thousands of years, was now made possible through Christ's obedience.

The coming of the Son of God to Earth, would be meaningless if not followed by the coming of the Holy Spirit. It is by receiving the Spirit into our beings that we are regenerated and transferred out of the cursed bloodline of Adam, into the living seed of Christ. The Scriptures call this the "new creation". The result is we are now enabled to overcome the bents of our previous fallen state of being. The promise is rock solid, "Therefore, if anyone is in Christ, he is a new creation; old things have passed away; behold, all things have become new" (2 Cor. 5:14-17).

The frustration of attempting and failing to live in accordance with God's law is done away with. The commandments of God once carved on stone, are now inherent to the new heart supernaturally implanted within men and women, hearts inclined toward pleasing God and doing His will. New hearts with new attitudes, ruled by a new nature!

Six-hundred years before the birth of Christ, the Old Testament prophet Ezekiel foretold of this indwelling of God's Spirit and the radical change He would produce,

> I will give you a new heart and put a new spirit in you; I will remove from you your heart of stone

and give you a heart of flesh. And I will put My Spirit in you and move you to follow my decrees and be careful to keep my laws (Eze. 36:25-27).

In addition to a new nature, Jesus added that in cooperation with the Holy Spirit, His followers would now possess the ability to alter the realities of the physical world. He clearly stated the manifestation of this power would occur as His followers infiltrated the societies of their day.

The power of which Jesus spoke was not worldly power, but heavenly. Everything had changed with the coming of the Holy Spirit. The heavenly had invaded the earthly. Human beings now controlled their destiny. Kingdom power would be manifested in the display of the miraculous; deliverance from death to life, relief from oppression of the demonic, healing of the afflictions of mind and body, and fortitude to deliver the message of Truth in the face of both spirit and human opposition. The same Spirit power that brought the universe into existence would now mark the lives of kingdom people!

We are not alone as we face-off against the powers of darkness. We have nothing to fear. In fact, it is the Devil who trembles and flees when confronted by those redeemed by the blood of Jesus, standing in the authority of His name, and backed by the omnipotent Holy Spirit.

The Outworking of Kingdom Authority

At the end of Matthew's gospel, he records the final words that Jesus spoke to his disciples before returning to his Father in Heaven,

> All authority in Heaven and on Earth has been given to me. Go therefore and make disciples of all nations, baptizing them in the name of the Father

and the Son and of the Holy Spirit, and teaching them to obey everything that I have commanded you (Matt. 28:19, 20).

Bear in mind, those that truly followed Christ during his ministry on Earth were no slouches. When Jesus issued the above marching orders, they went forth and dramatically influenced the societies to which they were sent. Wherever they walked, people's lives were radically changed, just as their own lives had been while with Jesus. The proof that we can also have this effect within our own cities is in knowing what the Spirit of God did through past generations of ordinary men and women, who became extraordinary as they obeyed the words of their King.

Jesus also said that the works we would do, collectively, while walking in obedience to his will would be "even greater" (John 14:12) than the works he did while on Earth! And what were the nature of his works? Everything Jesus did was to relieve people from the toll of sin and the attacks of the Devil upon their lives. His purpose was not only to heal a disease or physical disfigurement, or meet an emotional need, or provide a meal for a multitude. His aim was to vanquish the source of their suffering: sin and the Devil. His foremost purpose was to engage in spirit battle with a spirit enemy, and, therefore, so is ours.

Jesus said, "The words that I speak to you, they are spirit, and they are life" (John 6:63 AKJV). It is what He spoke and taught, that we, today, must take to our fellow man. Words of Truth. Truth that frees. Nothing else will do.

Jesus made it clear to His listeners that the words He spoke were the words He had received from the Father. He further clarified that the Holy Spirit would now come and "Teach you all things and will remind you of everything I have said to you" (John 14:26). So, that which we speak and do originate from the Father.

This is the basis of our confidence as we contend for our cities. We are not under pressure to figure out how to confront the powers of darkness among society. We are not left to employ some unproven means, unsure whether or not it will be effective. We are promised that if we receive our Father's directions through the guidance of the Holy Spirit, then irresistible kingdom power will be released to vanquish the powers of darkness and free the Devil's captives. That is what we have received, and that is what we give to others.

It is vitally important that we identify what it was that Jesus received from the Father and exercised among the people of His day. What was it that he taught and passed along to His followers? Those principles and truths are the "keys of the kingdom of heaven" of which He spoke. What are these *keys* that unlock such power and potential?

There are seven.

Chapter 32

The Seven Keys of the Kingdom

Like Jesus often did, we have reserved the best for last. As we near the closing of this writing, you will be handed the keys. Whether or not the soul of your city prospers is directly dependent on what you do with them.

There are seven keys that if employed by God's people, will forge a battering ram to obliterate the gates of Hell, and free the souls of our cities.

- Worship
- Prayer
- Unity
- Anointing
- Intercession
- Good News
- Filling the Void

KEY 1: Worship

This is where we start if we are to exert kingdom authority in our cities.

Jesus defined the essence of worship this way,

> The true worshipers will worship the Father in spirit and truth; for they are the kind of worshippers the Father seeks (John 4:23).

You and I are designed to worship. We do so involuntarily, instinctively. We all direct our individual worship on some *one* or some *thing*.

At the center of worship is the idea of *worth*. To whom or what we believe is most worthy of our time and attention will define the object of our worship. Where our treasure is, there, too, will be our hearts. And whomever or whatever we treasure will be revealed by our words and actions.

Jesus made it clear that "true worshippers" will have the Father as their focus. As His creation, the sustaining of our lives is solely dependent upon Him. In fact, worship exists to be directed to our Father, for he alone is worthy. All else is false worship of false gods.

True worship also proceeds from our spirit that is in communion with God. From that sacred place flows a river of life capable of restoring our soul and revitalizing our flesh and bone.

As we worship Him, we grow in our understanding of His nature and character. As we glimpse God's heart of love, our own hearts of stone become tenderized and sensitized. We discover that love is not an emotional display of weakness, but springs from our innermost being, our very spirits, the breathe of God that is the essence of who we are, for God *is* love.

There is a time when we join with others in worship, and that should not be neglected. However, worship is foremost a personal expression, an interaction between an individual and their God. It is when we withdraw from the din of human activity and quiet ourselves in His presence that the most precious discoveries are made, about God and about ourselves.

It is in hiding away with God that revelation takes place. Remember, "In His light, we see light." It is during our alone times with God, in awe of our Father, that human pitfalls are exposed, and we become confident in His wisdom and strength.

It is from a place of worship that we will be sent. Others will know when we have been in God's presence. We can't feign love or holiness. They are foreign to the physical capacities of man, but native to the spirit of man.

Shortly after I moved from California to Savannah, I went from being self-employed to working for another company within the same industry. I had operated my own business for over 20 years and found it psychologically and emotionally challenging to shift gears. I'm sure it entailed some smitten ego. My new job entailed considerable time on the road, often leaving home at 3:00 or 4:00 in the morning and then driving several hours, usually on back, rural highways, to the work site. This change also took some adjusting. However, it didn't take long to discover the silver lining. My routine had been altered for a very concise and valuable purpose.

During these still, early morning hours on the long, lonely highways, I became acutely aware that I wasn't alone, that God was present, my unseen passenger. Much of this three-year season of time was filled with listening for His voice and bearing my heart before Him. I came to understand and receive more of the love of God. The real change was not in my practical routine, but in me.

This was the case with Joseph, Moses, David, Paul, and our supreme example, Jesus. Each was led by God's Spirit into a season of retreat, free from the distractions of the world's sights and sounds, to a place of solitude where the intimacy of relationship with their Father could be nurtured. From that place of worship, each was thrust into the arena of spirit warfare where the hearts, minds, and destinies of people, and whole societies, were at stake. Adoration must precede activity.

We are empowered to love when we have personally experienced God's love. We love because we are loved. It is from that sure foundation we approach our communities, burdened by the plight of our cities, and seek to see them liberated.

KEY 2: Prayer

Jesus said,

> When you pray, enter into your closet, and when you have shut your door, pray to your Father which is in secret; and your Father which sees in secret shall reward you openly (Matt. 6:6).

Worship and prayer are "sister" activities in that they are intimately related. They are both directed to one divine source from which all that exists proceeds. Worship is an expression of prayer, as prayer expresses our devotion to the one true God.

Before we pray before men, we must pray in "secret", before God. We must beware of self-promotion and guard against it. The reward of which Jesus speaks is an open display of His presence, the release of His Spirit through the believer, confirming the message delivered by the believer.

We should avoid adopting a view on prayer that sees the practice as a time during which we talk *at* God. We can fall into the trap of approaching God, presenting our laundry list of wants and needs, and then going our way. Although

Scripture encourages us to bring our needs to our concerned, caring Father, we are not to dwell on what we lack. To the contrary, we should see God as already well-aware of our circumstances and live with a prevailing expectation of Him to move in those areas of our life.

Jesus confirmed this attitude with these words of caution,

> When you pray, use not vain repetitions, as the heathen do: for they think that they shall be heard for their much speaking. Be not like them: for your Father knows what things you have need of, before you ask Him (Matt. 6:7, 8 AKJV).

This confidence in His grace, mercy and attentiveness to all we have need of, frees us from a morbid self-introspection and preoccupation with our shortcomings, to go forward with the attitude that "I can do all things through Christ who strengthens me" (Phil. 4:13 AKJV). It is that revelation which enables us to address the needs of others and those of our communities.

It is a wise thing to schedule regular meetings with God so that we do not grow cold or indifferent in nurturing intimacy with our Father. When we are in need of physical food, our desire for it increases the longer we are without it. Therefore, the more we eat, the less food we desire. On the contrary, when we neglect "feeding" our spirit with the nourishment that comes through worship and prayer, the awareness of this spiritual starvation lessens over time. Hence, we must be careful that a spiritual lethargy does not overtake us. The more we pray, the more our spiritual "appetite" increases. Our spirits can never get enough of God.

Also, always be mindful that God's Spirit indwells the believer, literally lives within the essence of our spirit being. We can speak with Him along the way, trusting Him in every moment of every day wherever our feet take us, whether within the four walls of a church or on the streets of the inner city.

These sisters of worship and prayer, according to David the Psalmist, are a "shield" and "refuge" as God's Spirit and His warring angels surround and cover the believer. The Devil cannot touch the man or woman who has been properly prepared to deal with evil.

From this intimate and safe place with God, we find a foundation for close relationship with one another. Tozer puts it this way, "Has it ever occurred to you that 100 pianos all tuned to the same fork are automatically tuned to one another?"

This leads us to the next key.

KEY 3: Unity

Jesus, the Son of God, spoke of the "oneness" He shares with His Father,

> My prayer is not for them alone. I pray also for those who will believe in me through their message, that all of them may be one, Father, just as you are in me and I am in you. May they also be in us so that the world may believe that you have sent me (John 17:20, 21).

To convey a degree of understanding about His relationship with God the Father, Jesus said that the Father was *in* him, and he was *in* the Father. This is a concept totally foreign to our natural understanding. The closest we come is in our experience of the intimacy shared between a man and woman through the union of marriage.

What Jesus conveyed is a spirit-state of being that transcends the limitations of the physical. He spoke of two distinct entities that are also one in essence. Jesus also affirmed that the Holy Spirit is one with He and the Father. A Holy Trinity. Three divine personalities, comprising the one true God. Try to separate the coffee, cream, and sugar that have been joined together. The blend is still comprised of three elements but is "one" in substance and influence.

Underscoring the "three-in-one" of the Godhead, Jesus said, "Anyone who has seen me, has seen the Father" (John 14:9), and that He and the Father would "come to them and make our home with them" (John 14:3), speaking of the Holy Spirit that would come to live within the believer upon His return to Heaven.

Jesus also said that men and women may also now be *in us*, He, the Father, and the Holy Spirit. Through the miracle rebirth experienced when we receive Jesus and become alive in spirit, we are joined to God the Father, God the Son, and God the Holy Spirit. God's life is now our life. In being united to God, we have also been joined to one another, co-sharers in the life of God.

If the people of the world are to believe our message that Jesus was truly sent by God, then we must bring forth into the practical aspects of our living, that which exists in the spirit realm. Again, what is a reality in the kingdom must become manifested in the physical sphere of our existence.

This oneness we share, what the Scriptures call "the body of Christ" (1 Cor. 12:27), is revealed to the world as we, by faith, acknowledge our common ground as *forgiven equals* in God's sight. From that place, we commit ourselves to serve and love one another in the manner of Jesus while he was on Earth. As this is done, those who have been united to God will display that fact in increasing measure, with external evidences that will turn the hearts of others to the true and living God. Unity is born of servanthood, and irresistible Spirit power of unity.

Love, the Tie that Binds

Jesus said,

> A new commandment I give you: Love one another. As I have loved you, so also you must love one another. By this everyone will know that you are my disciples, if you love one another (1 John 13: 34, 35).

Jesus was speaking to the disciples of his day. Three times, he emphasized the necessity of love; that they *must* love one another, in the *way* he loved them, if others were to genuinely *know* that they were sent by a living, loving God.

The love of God is a foreign virtue to the culture of the world. The culture of Heaven is counter to that of the world. Heaven thinks and acts "you" and "yours", while the world thinks and acts "me" and "mine". Heaven freely gives while the world keeps and covets.

The reality of the love of God in Heaven, and in *us*, is proven through sacrifice. And our acts of sacrifice must begin with one another. How will the world believe us when we say an invisible God of love exists, that shed his love abroad to humankind, when His people refuse to act with love toward their very visible fellow believers. The proof to others that they can be delivered from the snares of their own sinful nature, is to observe individuals who have encountered a living God who is enabling them to overcome those same bents!

The authority of Jesus and his kingdom will not manifest in and through our lives if there is no bond of love. Remember, God is love. Where God's love is found, there will be the presence of God by His Spirit. And where God makes his home, the Devil is evicted. Without the practice of real love, mankind's various gestures of religious sacrifice are devoid of God's approval, and, hence, the power to dispel darkness.

We are empowered to love one another as we develop a lifestyle that includes worship and prayer. Then we will "see" others through the eyes of God. People will no longer be viewed as obstacles or competitors. The natural judgments we readily make about others will be replaced with a sense of their potential as His unique creation. We are reluctant to judge and condemn others when under the searchlight of Truth.

This directly shapes our perspective concerning our cities. A love and compassion for the communities will be born in our hearts that will motivate us to act on behalf of the destiny of the city in which we live. We cannot love our city if we will not love her people.

The City-Wide Church

Uniting with other local churches in worship and prayer is God's non-negotiable design for driving darkness from our cities. It requires a city-wide collaboration to achieve the ultimate goal.

Together, the body of Christ is the hands, feet, and voice of God within our communities. We are the sole means designed by God through which society will be delivered. We will either contribute to the problem or cooperate in the task of freeing our cities. A greater representation of the united people of God, will result in a corresponding release of Spirit power.

Nothing will silence and immobilize God more than disjointed agendas among the churches of a city, driven by personal ambition. For the body to effectively accomplish its mission, the right hand must work in cooperation with the left.

The Scriptures that detail the acts of the Christian believers that were sent by Jesus into society upon his return to Heaven, are remarkable. We read how they "turned the world upside down "(Acts 17:6 AKJV) with their message. They were effective in upsetting the status quo of secular society because they were "one in heart and mind" (Acts 4:32). The phrase, *one accord*, is used eleven times in the book of Acts, underscoring unity as mandatory if the power of God is to be released in our communities.

God will not honor competition, envy, and self-promotion with His presence. It is when Christ is lifted up that He will draw men and women to Himself. The enemy will be vanquished from society only when the churches of our communities recognize this, join in coordinated efforts and redirect their weapons at the enemy instead of one another.

Until the people of God are united in purpose, clouds of darkness will continue to envelop the city and demonic strongholds will remain undisturbed.

KEY 4: Anointing

We do not know what Jesus' last name was. Contrary to popular assumption, His last name was not Christ. In the cultures of the ancient world, a person would be referred to by the village or town they were from, or by their parentage. In Jesus' case, he was known as "Jesus of Nazareth" (John 18:5) or "Jesus, the son of Joseph" (John 6:42). A person would also be referred to by their vocation or calling. In fact, the word *Christ*, derived from the Greek Χριστός (*christos*), is a translation of the Hebrew *mashiakh* (חשיימ) meaning anointed one, hence, *Jesus the Anointed One*. It was a title denoting his position or function.

Jesus emphasized the key of anointing when declaring his purpose to the Jewish religious leaders of his day. Taking an ancient scroll bearing the words written 750 years earlier by the prophet Isaiah, he read,

> The Spirit of the Sovereign Lord is on me, because the Lord has anointed me to proclaim good news to the poor. He has sent me to bind up the brokenhearted, to proclaim freedom for the captives and release from darkness for the prisoners...to bestow on them a crown of beauty instead of ashes, the oil of joy instead of mourning, and a garment of praise instead of a spirit of despair (Isa. 61:1-3).

So, Jesus was *anointed*. What does that mean? We have talked about the Spirit of God coming and living within the believer, beginning the restoration of the human soul, revitalizing flesh and bone, giving insight and understanding as our Counselor, and bringing forth the nature of God as our fallen nature passes away. However, the dynamic of an individual being anointed by the Spirit of God is a *different* working of the same Holy Spirit.

Jesus said that he was "anointed" and that "the Spirit of the Sovereign Lord is on me." He then lists some of the ways for which this anointing was intended, "to proclaim good news...to bind up the brokenhearted...to proclaim freedom for the captives...release from darkness for the prisoners...beauty instead of ashes...praise instead of a spirit of despair."

Pastor and author Bill Johnson summarizes the two-fold ministry of the Holy Spirit as it relates to the believer, "He is in me for my sake, but He's upon me for yours." The purpose of the anointing is not for ourselves, but for the benefit of others. It is the act of *carrying* the presence of God upon our lives into a dying world to be released against the forces of darkness and for the relief of captive mankind.

Oglethorpe understood what would bring God's presence and blessing upon the new American colony when selecting the moto, *Not for self but for others*. If our focus is on ourselves and not the needs of others, then the Spirit anointing will not rest upon us.

Protected and Enabled

Among the rites of Judaism described in the Old Testament scriptures, was the sprinkling or pouring of oil upon someone chosen by God and *set apart* for God's service. Kings, priests, and prophets were commonly anointed with oil. The use of oil in this rite was symbolic of the Spirit of God, who would protect and enable the individual to accomplish that which he or she was called to do in their service to God and to their nation.

If Jesus was dependent on God's Spirit resting upon him to accomplish the purposes for which he came to Earth, then it is essential that so should we. Without the Holy Spirit resting upon the individual believer and the corporate body of believers, the task of rescuing those in darkness will be void of the necessary presence and power of God.

There can be no anointing upon the life of a man or woman until that individual is set apart to God through receiving Jesus as Savior, and then committed to walk in obedience to His Spirit. It is then that he or she goes confidently forward, knowing that His presence rests upon their life, with demonstrations of power that will vanquish darkness and set human captives free.

This commitment to God does not require that we attain perfection in attitude and conduct before we can be effective in extending God's kingdom on Earth. Only God is perfect and as His children, we will be in His care while maturing throughout eternity.

In the meantime, we trust the Spirit within to smooth the rough edges of our life while we advance the kingdom among mankind. We need not be bogged down with a self-consciousness of our imperfections of character. The Devil is the accuser, not the Spirit of God. As we go about our Father's business, we will gradually experience the inward transformations of our souls!

There is no magic formula for having this anointing. Because only God can know the motives and secrets of the human heart, we often misjudge upon whom the anointing will rest. Our expectation is that the vigorous, charismatic personality would be the prime candidate. However, God frequently uses what secular man considers *foolish* to confound the *wise*, and it is the *weak* in human estimation through whom God will demonstrate His strength. It is not necessarily the person with the good looks and the smooth style, as God looks on the heart. The proof is in the power.

According to the Scriptures, the expectation of anointing upon our lives is through having in operation the first three keys, worship, prayer, and unity. As we carry the presence of God into the four corners of our cities, Jesus assured us that the miraculous will follow.

Now for the remaining three.

KEY 5: Intercession

Earlier we looked at the key of prayer in a general sense and how the intimacy of relationship with God is nurtured as we spend time in His presence. An integral aspect of our prayer life is the activity of *intercession*. The word is defined by Webster as "prayer, petition, or entreaty in favor of another". The practice is commonly referred to as intercessory prayer.

Intercessory prayer involves directing our requests of God specifically on behalf of a person or, in this case, the city as a whole. It is the activity of a *mediator* – taking specific human needs and going before God who stands ready to meet every need through Jesus' sacrifice on the cross.

More of Jesus' words:

> My prayer is not for them alone. I pray also for those who will believe in me through their message (John 17:20).

Jesus didn't say much about this key of intercessory prayer, but often demonstrated it. It was His frequent practice to go before His Father and pray for the welfare of His disciples, Jerusalem, the world's people, and those that would come to believe in Him following His death and resurrection.

In his letter to the early church in Rome, Paul the Apostle makes it clear that Jesus' intercession did not cease once he departed Earth, "Jesus, who died – more than that, who was raised to life – is at the right hand of God and is also interceding for us!" (Rom. 8:34). This is a great confidence booster knowing that, today, Jesus names you and me in His prayers to the Father!

Jesus wasn't just going through the motions. He emphasized that these prayers in accordance with the Father's will are necessary if ground is to be gained in the invisible realm of spirit war. As we exercise our role in the battle, the Holy Spirit is released into action on behalf of those bound in darkness. Angels of the light are empowered in their fight against wicked, malicious spirits. If we are to do as Jesus did, and is now doing, then our engagement in intercession is crucial if our cities are to experience deliverance.

Identification

Our intercession must include our identification with those for whom we pray. As those once lost, now pardoned, we identify with the need of those still held in the Devil's grip. We were humans in need of forgiveness, we are still humans mercifully delivered from our own sin. With humility we extend to our fellow human beings, the grace in Christ we have received.

United prayer offered by those forgiven, for those seeking forgiveness, with humility and repentance, must mark the people of God if deliverance and healing is to visit our cities.

Specific Strategy For Your City

We discussed the concept of spiritual discernment and how we can be recipients of insight given by the Holy Spirit. It is the ability to receive spiritual understanding of activity within the spirit realm and how it is influencing those who live in the visible, physical realm.

Intercessory prayer is an act of spiritual warfare. As we seek the liberation of a city, the Holy Spirit will provide strategy as to how the prison doors can be swung opened. There are numerous scriptures, in both the Old Testament and New Testament that urge those who profess to know Christ, to pray for cities and nations if we are to see His blessing and favor overtake the people of a land.

Paul's protégé, Timothy, points out the relationship between the activity of our intercession for our city leaders and the resultant quality of life within the community. It is a simple formula, "(pray) for kings and all those in authority, that we may live peaceful and quiet lives in all godliness and holiness." Between sowing the seeds of prayer and the blossoming of peace, other acts of faith and obedience are required.

As we go before God on behalf of our communities, we will be given understanding of His intended plan and destiny. This will include "intelligence" as to the nature of the demonic activity and entities that may have a hold over the land and population. It is as we pray in accordance with this insight and knowledge of God's will, that the Holy Spirit moves with power and puts to flight satanic oppression.

Generally, our prayers must precede our proclamation. For people to accept what we say about their eternal state and God's provision for their salvation, the light of the Gospel must be turned on. As we discussed earlier, this only can happen as darkness is driven from the atmosphere over a society, and from the soul of the individual citizen. Only then will the eyes of the man or woman sufficiently "see" so an informed choice can be made to either choose or reject our message concerning the claims of Jesus.

This darkness is not a nebulous, undefined condition. Again, it is the presence of evil demonic entities that blind the individual and keep them in a state of ignorance and darkness. As we identify the enemy and how he has taken hold of our communities, we are enabled to specifically address that entity with kingdom authority, exerted in our intercession and our face-to-face communication.

Binding and Loosing

Binding and loosing are activities of the individual believer or body of believers engaged in addressing the presence of darkness and the effects of sin on mankind, wherever found.

This aspect of intercessory prayer was put forth by Jesus when he said,

> Truly I say to you, Whatever you bind on Earth will be bound in Heaven: and whatever you loose on Earth will be loosed in Heaven (Matt. 18:18).

The expressions to *bind* and *loose* were common Jewish legal phrases meaning to declare something *forbidden* or to declare something *allowed*.

Jesus was saying that that which does not exist in Heaven; death and darkness, afflictions of the mind and body, doubt, fear, and hatred, is what we forbid here on Earth. It is to be bound and rendered powerless. On the other hand, that which exists in Heaven; the life and light of God's presence, the wholeness and perfection of mind and body, the inherent faith, assurance, and love that permeates that domain is what we allow on this earth. It is what we bring and establish among mankind. To bind and loose are actions taken by believers to right the wrongs within society here on Earth. This is the outworking of the authority granted to the believer.

When teaching the disciples to pray, Jesus summarized this objective of His Father, "Your Kingdom come, Your will be done, *on Earth as it is in Heaven*" (Matt. 6:10).

In the New Testament, the Greek word for bind is *deo*, and is frequently used for the idea of *tying something up*. Jesus expressed this when he said, "No one can enter a strong man's house and spoil his goods, except he will first bind the strong man" (Mark 3:27 AKJV). In the context of dealing with evil spirit activity, binding means to restrict the presence and power of evil wherever it exists.

The Greek word for loose is *luo*. It implies the idea *to release*. Jesus spoke this when raising Lazarus from the dead, "Loose him, and let him go" (John 11:44 AKJV). Jesus was disallowing death and releasing the life of Heaven. It is the entrance of kingdom life that releases and frees those held in the Devil's grip.

Jesus used both these words when healing a woman, "Ought not this woman…whom Satan has bound these eighteen years…be loosed from this bond?" (Luke 13:16 AKJV).

This woman approached Jesus, bound in sickness by an evil spirit. As Jesus drove away the spirit of infirmity that had her bound, physical healing and the praise of God that marks Heaven were immediately released into her life!

Jesus demonstrated the prevailing power of the kingdom of Heaven in dealing with evil. The influence of the demonic binds and restricts human beings. However, when the Spirit of God arrives on the scene, the human is set completely free as the evil spirit is bound and rendered powerless!

Jesus only acted in ways that would bring humans into a state of being, consistent with life in Heaven. He pointed us to Heaven as our model. Our first look is into the spirit reality of the kingdom of Heaven to see what exists and what doesn't exist to determine the parameters of our authority. We will only see the Spirit of God move on the earth in those ways consistent with the will of the Father who is in Heaven. That is what is to be established here on Earth by the working of God's Spirit through redeemed humans, now citizens of Heaven.

This is the process by which the kingdom of God is extended on this planet, within and among humanity.

The Nature, Not the Name

There are instances in the scriptures where evil presence is identified by name, as in the case of Jesus confronting "Legion" in Luke 8:30. The word means *many*. This was revealed for *our benefit*, so we would understand the severity of the Devil's affliction over the human victim. However, when dealing with evil, what matters is not the *name*, but the *nature*.

We must always bear in mind that the essence of the demonic entity is evil, and vice versa. There is no rehabilitating an evil spirit. As we discern the nature (the attitude and activities) of the evil presence, we will also gain the understanding of how to apply our authority in Christ. The believers strategic response is in accordance with the *kind* of spirit activity that is present.

Knowing your city's history is an important aspect of our active intercession. Identifying the major events that have taken place, and the key decisions made by city elders are often indicative of the nature or kind of spirit that influenced the circumstances and gained a measure of control.

This is applicable when addressing society on any level, whether an individual human being, a family, or any institution that is part of the greater society. It is also relevant when assessing the entrenched evil presence within a house or any structure in which human activity has occurred, as underscored in our study of Savannah "hauntings".

We will usually discover that what the Devil has sown is the "flip-side" of God's intentions and promises for the city. The Devil perverts God's design and the result is in direct contrast to His will. Knowing this gives us a head-start in understanding how to specifically direct our intercession for an individual or the community.

As we assessed the history of Lady Savannah, we discovered how a city designed to serve others, provide for the less fortunate, and to promote the potential of her citizens, was usurped by the powerful territorial prince of Greed, with its oversight of lower level spirits that harass and exploit the human weaknesses of her citizens.

These lower level spirits fortify the territorial hold of the evil prince. As we expose, confront, and expel these underlings, the grip and control of the territorial prince is weakened. Ours is a systematic dismantling of the demonic authority structures that exist in the spirit world and exert control in the physical sphere of our existence.

The Opposite Spirit

So, in knowing God's design for your city, you can intercede with authority for those aspects of God's intended purpose to be birthed within society. Your practical, outward actions should be in accordance with God's promises to your city. Our activities will therefore be in direct contrast to what the Devil has sown among society. We must confront the enemy in the *opposite spirit*.

This simple truth is put forth in the prayer of Saint Francis of Assisi,

> Lord, make me an instrument of your peace; where there is hatred, let me sow love; where there is injury, pardon; where there is discord, union; where there is doubt, faith; where there is despair, hope; where there is darkness, light; and where there is sadness, joy.

As we confront the powers of darkness and apply this principle as an individual or corporate body of believers, there is a release of corresponding Spirit power. The following is a simple personal example of this truth.

During the missions work I referred to earlier, I was involved with leading a team of young people into the country of Mexico. One of our first days was spent in Tijuana, at the U.S. – Mexico border. We were there to share the promise of citizenship in God's kingdom through Jesus Christ. As was our method, the team dispersed in pairs among a large group of Mexicans, old and young, who were waiting for nightfall and an opportunity to scale a wall onto American soil. We were well aware of the danger that existed as many of those present were driven by their desperate life circumstances.

As the sun dipped below the horizon and a chilling wind kicked up its heels, my teammate and I were approached by a band of four or five men who were clearly unreceptive to what we offered. The apparent leader of the group became more aggressive while shouting in Spanish. I knew that my response of "no comprendo" would not rescue us. Instantaneously, my mind was occupied with just one thought: *Give him your coat.* I didn't have the luxury of time to weigh the idea, so I quickly slipped off my coat and extended it toward my attacker. Immediately, he stopped in his tracks. In a moment, the attitude of this gruff, angry Mexican had completely changed. His facial expression went from one of hostility, to that of perplexity, and his hostile demeanor, to an inquisitive humility. He was briefly silent, received the coat, and then expressed his thankfulness for my gift. My teammate and I were then enabled to extend the infinitely more valuable gift of eternal life through Jesus Christ. St. Francis would've said it this way,

"When one wants to forcibly take, then freely give."

The enemy encourages an attitude of "an eye for an eye", because he knows that his ground is not threatened by our trying to even the score on a human level. However, if we understand that we are addressing the instigating spirit behind a person's actions, then we will not return fire for fire. The ancient proverb of "A gentle answer turns away wrath" will be found true if tested.

Because our battle is foremost against an invisible, spirit enemy, there are times when the most powerful means of addressing our foe is without speaking a word. The simple fact that we usher in the presence of God *with our presence*, the enemy trembles and flees. When an enlightened believer walks onto enemy territory, the Devil knows that the believer knows what God knows: that he is trespassing on ground now rightfully entitled to God's people. As we occupy that territory, the Devil has no choice but to turn and flee.

As we receive insight from God's Spirit concerning the nature of the Devil's inroads to the soul of an individual or a society of people, our opposite, counteractions have the power to *disarm* the demonic presence. The result is that the kingdom of God is advanced as the presence of God's Spirit invades the city landscape and atmosphere.

In defining the next Key, the Gospel, we will look more closely at the active element of our intercession, that of being present on the ground, and moving within the atmosphere over the area for which we are seeking the liberation of the people.

KEY 6: Good News

The cornerstone on which the other keys depend is the Gospel message. It is the one key around which the others revolve. The word gospel comes from the Greek word *euangelion* and means good news. Without it, the other keys have no meaning or purpose.

The disciple John defined this good news in one sentence:

> For God so loved the world that He gave His one and only Son, that whosoever believes in Him, will not perish but have everlasting life (John 3:16).

Jesus announced and underscored the nature of His mission when He said, "I have come into the world as a light, so that no one who believes in me should stay in darkness" (John 12:46). He added that this would be accomplished as He would willingly "Give His life a ransom for many" (Mark 10:45).

This is the Gospel message. It is the most important communication that anyone could ever deliver, or anyone could ever receive; yet in its simplicity, can be understood or explained by a child. It is one that we are to communicate in a straightforward manner, with uncompromised boldness, in both word and deed. And it is a message that won't reach the ears or hearts of those in need if confined within the walls of our churches and our houses.

Earlier, we talked about anointing, the dynamic of God's Spirit resting upon the believer for the sake of those in need, whether it be physically, emotionally, or, most importantly, spiritually. In essence, we carry and deliver the good news that can set them free.

Beautiful Feet

Isaiah concurs,

> How beautiful on the mountains are the feet of those who bring good news, who proclaim peace, who bring good tidings, who proclaim salvation, who say to Zion, "Your God reigns!" (Isa. 52:7)

Replace "Zion" with the name of your city, and it's just as true.

If our communities are to experience release into their unique destiny, then they must hear from you and me that "My God is your God! He is alive and saves! He reigns as King of Kings and Lord of Lords!"

There is an interesting promise contained in the Old Testament book of Deuteronomy. The words are written by Moses who has led the Jews out from their bondage in Egypt and are now camped just outside the land promised them by God. The area is infested with other people groups who, in human terms, are much "greater and mightier" than the Jews. They are devil worshippers and notoriously evil in their conduct. They have settled in and have no intention to relinquish the land. As the Jews prepare to enter, God whispers this to Moses:

> Every place where the soles of your feet tread shall be yours (Deut. 11:24).

This command to go and physically set foot in the land we are repossessing for God's kingdom, is mandatory. God has designed the process by which humankind can receive forgiveness of sin and the promise of eternal life in Heaven, to include your and my involvement.

In the same manner that the Father sent His Son, so the Son sends us. We must carry and deliver the gospel message, as we also carry upon us the anointing of God's Spirit who will confirm that message with displays of unrivaled power.

People will not come to us. We must go to them. The Devil seeks to keep God's people idle, lethargic, and comfy. Whereas, God's Spirit waits patiently for our cooperation, guaranteeing victory if we will carry Him into battle. The Devil knows that when God's people rise up and declare Christ's triumph over the powers of darkness and sin, he must flee as the light of His presence fills the land.

Boots on the Ground in DC

For several decades now, the integrity of the U. S. Constitution has been under attack by certain factions within the nation. This founding document, signed on September 17, 1787 by delegates to the Constitutional Convention in Philadelphia, Pennsylvania, established America's national government and the framework by which it would function. It defines the nations fundamental laws and certain basic rights of its citizens. It has been, as declared in the body of the writing, "the supreme law of the land."

However, those seeking to diminish the authority of the Constitution criticize it as outdated and irrelevant to the realities of today's world. The document is characterized as *fluid* and should be subject to interpretation or alteration based on the predominant views and values of the present society of citizens. While the Constitution is subject to the addition of amendments, as it was in 1865 with the passage of the 13th Amendment that abolished slavery, the laws that it puts forth must not be subject to alteration or deletion.

In essence, the position propagated by detractors of America's founding, assert that there are no absolute rules or laws by which the conduct of past, present, or future generations of citizens should be governed. That the prevailing ethics or lack of them, at a given point in time, should dictate what is or is not acceptable among society. As we discussed earlier, this rejection of God's eternal code of moral conduct leads to chaos and anarchy among a people.

As the veracity of our nation's founding documents came under more blatant attack during the initial decade of the twenty-first century, Elizabeth and I found ourselves leading a charge of like-minded people whose objective was to protect the integrity and identity of the American republic. The group was founded in Savannah, Georgia, and given the name, *13th Colony Patriots*.

This involvement included weekly meetings to hone our purpose, identify threats to our American liberties, and brainstorm ways to hold our elected officials accountable to the will of the people. The group, which grew to the point where it drew local, state, and national attention, also organized periodic, timely visits to the Georgia capitol and Washington D.C., that coincided with those of similar groups that sprouted up throughout the 50 United States, during that season of time.

Two of the more powerful visits to DC were in September 2009 and March 2010.

The 2009 event was a three-day protest to a succession of actions by the Barack Obama administration and a liberal-leaning Congress that were viewed by a large segment of the American population as trespasses against American rule of law and the will of the people. In fact, although a biased mainstream media reported the attendance at "tens of thousands", the more reliable news sources, including the local Capitol Police Department, estimated the crowds at over 1.5 million people. The unity among the participants and the message that was delivered could only be described as divinely inspired.

The 2010 rally was during the weekend that Congress would vote on legalizing Obamacare. This march on the capital was the culmination of two years of diligent and committed efforts to get the attention of Washington's powermongers and convince them to make decisions in accordance with the desires of their constituents, rather than what was personally, politically expedient.

These visits took the form of peaceful, but forceful protests to what has become a fortified system of centralized power that has produced a culture of authoritarians who are more concerned with their own selfish desires than protecting the inalienable rights of the people, endowed by their Creator. Again, Greed rears its monstrous head.

To the naked human eye, the protests would merely be viewed as men, women, and children lifting and shaking signs and raising their voices toward a complex of massive, stone structures, set atop a hill. But to those with spiritual sight, what would be witnessed is a violent quaking in the unseen realm as, in response to the presence of these God-fearing people, angelic warriors of light charged forth with divine power, penetrated the atmosphere and engaged the demonic forces that grip this national institution.

The seeds sown by the freedom fighters during those years have budded and multiplied among American society. An enlightenment has grown among the national populace that has resulted in a greater concerted voice and engagement by citizens who seek to protect what has been entrusted them by God. It is no surprise that this rising tide has been met with a more strenuous and ferocious response from the opposing members of society that subscribe to ideology contrary to the bedrock principles on which America was founded.

At the time of this writing, the destiny of America teeters precariously at a tipping point. It is not for dramatic effect that I say her survival as a free nation will hinge on the choices made and actions taken by her people during this pivotal time.

I believe there are more allies of truth among the citizenry, than those committed to redefining the nation. However, the principles we embrace are impotent unless acted upon. Inaction toward evil is compliance with evil.

A battle for human souls, our cities, and our nation is in progress, right here and right now. It is occurring within our families and within our communities, and our action or inaction has a direct bearing on the outcome. To the degree that we rise up and boldly confront this evil, will be a corresponding measure of empowerment, and souls saved from destruction.

As we deliver the words of Life within our communities, we have nothing to fear. Remember Paul's words, "The weapons we fight with are not carnal (natural), but mighty through God to the tearing down of strongholds."

Key 7: Filling the Void

It is essential to understand that establishing God's kingdom upon this earth is not only the action of tearing down the invisible authority structures of the Evil One and restricting his activities among mankind. It is unfinished business if we do not *fill the void* when the presence of evil is displaced from that which it formerly occupied.

As we repossess that which the enemy has deceived mankind into relinquishing, we must also *occupy*. That applies to the internal capacity of the individual human being as well as the society of people that makeup the fabric of our cities.

We must be prepared to speak divine purpose and promise into the life of an individual or the community of people. God delivers us *out of,* to be released *into*. Purpose must follow repentance. Freedom is merely another word until it is lived out as we walk our intended pathway of destiny.

As we discussed earlier, when we come to know that God has a design for our course in life and understand the unique abilities and gifts built into each of us, then we are "occupied" with direction and purpose. In that place, the Devil can't touch us.

But before an individual or society of individuals can begin to walk their appointed path, one essential human need must be met.

Forgiveness in Place of Judgment

Jesus revealed the Father's intent in sending the Holy Spirit to Earth when He said, "When he comes, he will prove the world to be in the wrong about sin and righteousness and judgment" (John 16:8).

This work of God's Spirit among and within human beings is for the sole purpose of convincing men and women of the corrupted state of their hearts and that they are under the judgment of death by a just God. As the Spirit convinces the individual of their need, then the good news of the Gospel is declared, that the penalty for sin has been satisfied and forgiveness is available through Jesus Christ! The whole of the mission of God's Spirit, and, therefore our mission, is to bring the man or woman to a place of confession so that forgiveness, ready and available, can reach its destination.

Nothing of lasting significance has taken place within a person or within a city if that entity has not confessed their sin and received the forgiveness offered through Jesus Christ.

We examined *confession* in an earlier chapter and discovered that it entails agreeing with what God says about our sin, and then repenting, or, *turning away* from those attitudes, actions, or lifestyle that has us bound. A confession is not valid, or sincere, if not followed by repentance.

Forgiveness is the most fundamental issue confronting mankind. Acknowledging the culpability for having violated God's divine law, and the need for pardon, is the ultimate turning point for the soul of the individual or of the city. Receiving forgiveness through Jesus death and resurrection places the man or woman on their appointed path of destiny.

Repentance can be on an individual level, citywide, or national level. We saw when Jonah brought the message concerning sin, judgment, and forgiveness, an entire society of people turned to God.

As we examine the history of our cities, the sins of the city fathers, perpetuated over time, must be identified. It is from those attitudes and acts that present leaders and citizens must confess and turn.

The Child King

For a moment, let's step back into the seventh century BC. The nation of Israel had been divided because of internal strife and there now existed two kingdoms, Israel to the north, and Judah to the south. The people had lived far from God and devil worship was rampant, including the sacrifice of their children to various demon gods. As King Josiah of Judah, who had ascended the throne at the age of eight, was preparing to have repairs made to their neglected temple in Jerusalem, the Book of the Covenant was found among the rubble. These scriptures spoke of God's promise to bless the nation if the people would keep His commandments, and the surety of judgment and ruin, should they not.

The Scripture tells us that King Josiah was jolted by the knowledge of how far their nation had fallen away from God. In response, he took action,

> (Josiah) went up to the temple of the Lord with . . . all the people from the least to the greatest. He read in their hearing all the words of the Book of the Covenant . . . the King stood by the pillar and renewed the covenant . . . to follow the Lord and keep his commands . . . with all his heart and all his soul . . . Then all the people pledged themselves to the covenant" (2 Kings 23:2, 3).

What followed was an entire housecleaning, including a complete demolishing of the shrines and altars and idols that had been set up throughout the land. The king's dealings with the demonic inroads were ruthless. It is written that he "tore down, smashed to pieces, ground to powder, burned" all the "detestable things" that had been devoted to the demonic forces that had infiltrated their land. Furthermore, there was an institutional purging as he "did away with the idolatrous priests…the mediums and spiritists" that had been appointed by previous kings.

The King also knew that it was crucial to replace the demonic ceremonial practices with worship of the one, true God. The final act of King Josiah detailed in Scripture is that he reinstituted the celebration of the Passover. This was an annual feast, prescribed by God, to acknowledge their release from captivity in Egypt, and their dependence on Him for individual and national freedom and prosperity.

King Josiah is a forerunner of you and me. He came to an understanding of the spiritual state of his nation and its people. He exercised his kingdom authority and called the people to repentance for *their trespasses* and those of *previous generations*, that led to the divine forgiveness that would evict the demonic and bring healing to their land. He then boldly, uncompromisingly, and systematically purged any representation of evil from the cities of the nation and replaced them with what would set them on their pathway of destiny. Vision and purpose had been restored within and over the people. This is what we must do if we are to have God's presence and blessing upon our cities and nation.

A fundamental displacement occurs when a person receives salvation and their spirit regenerated to life. It involves the driving out of demonic presence by the entrance of God's Spirit who is joined to the human spirit.

This passing from death to life involves the eviction of demonic power formerly influencing thought and conduct. The mental and emotional torment of living under judgment and condemnation is vanquished, replaced by a sense of peace. The Holy Spirit has now entered the spirit life of the individual, supplanting the distorted bents of human nature with the desires and sensitivities of compassion and truth.

From that place of liberation, the soul life of the man or woman must be set on a path of purpose as it pertains to all that God has planned for that individual.

This is true of the city. Without moving forward in faith and obedience as the Holy Spirit directs, a whole society of people can become prey to the return and subtle schemes of demonic forces.

Referring back to our commission to bind and loose, as we act to forbid or restrict the presence and works of darkness and the effects of sin in an individual and in our cities, simultaneously we release into that individual or people group God's provision and promise, His will as it exists in Heaven. This is how the kingdom comes to Earth. It is a kingdom that exists, collectively within and among His people wherever they are found.

A Stark Waring

Jesus said,

> When the unclean spirit is gone out of a man, he walks through dry places, seeking rest, and finds none. Then he said, I will return into my house from where I came out; and when he is come, he finds it empty, swept, and garnished. Then he goes and takes with himself seven other spirits more wicked than himself, and they enter

in and dwell there; and the last state of that man is worse than the first (Matt. 12:43-45 AKJV).

Billy Graham was a wise man. He heeded this warning. Whenever Reverend Graham held one of his remarkable crusades, he would make certain that every person who came forward to receive salvation in Christ, was put in touch with someone who could visit and help them on their faith journey. They would be given literature and suggestions of where they could attend meetings with fellow believers. Reverend Graham knew the conniving enemy of their soul would do an about-face and return to that human being with a vicious intent to retake what he had lost. The Devil is a poor loser. Reverend Graham knew the importance of filling the spiritual void so that the enemy would have no place to reoccupy.

When seeking to influence a society city-wide, this is what the united front of believers must do when routing darkness from its hideouts among our communities. Where evil is exposed and sent packing, we bring the specific wisdom and plan of God, a pathway to prosperity and destiny that solidly establishes God's presence and continual blessing among society.

Estonia

Let's again apply this principle on a national level as we revisit Estonia.

Earlier, I gave an overview of the prevailing mood and spirit among the Estonian people during the last decade of the twentieth century, as the pieces of the evil U.S.S.R. empire were falling like dominoes. The invisible structure that held the people captive, undermined by the persevering intercession of God's people, had collapsed to the ground, seemingly, overnight. My observations of the fluid phenomenon that followed were made while headquartered in the city of Narva, an east Estonian city that sits on the western border of Russia.

For several years, during and following the fall of Moscow, I worked with teams from the U.S.A. that united with small, local churches in Estonia. The independent Estonian government had reformed in Tallinn, and the nation, back in infancy, was finding its feet in a world that had, many years ago, moved on without them. With the dismantling of an evil centralized government whose dictates had shaped the mindsets of the mixed population of Estonians and Russians, the gate had swung wide open, and elements of western culture were freely accessing the region.

For decades of time, society had, in essence, been bound. They were told what they could and could not have, do, and think. With the dissolution of this "prison of the peoples", as described by academic Richard Pipes, they were thrust into a precarious, vulnerable position. The fact was that the souls of the people, hence, the soul of the nation, were now laid bare. The focus of the populace was the basic human issues of identity and purpose. Communism had failed miserably. The critical question was, what would now come and occupy the vacant space within their hearts and minds? Inevitably, something would settle in, as it is the nature of the soul to give consent to what will form the basis of feeling and thought. The soul of Estonia, and those of the other former Soviet republics, would be defined by whatever or whomever the people would now give their allegiance.

My team and I spent our time presenting the truths and practical applications of God's Word to segments of the public in several cities, including Narva, Kohtla-Jarve, Tartu, and Tallinn, the capital. Meetings were arranged and conducted with city officials in the civic centers, citywide public gatherings were held with question-and-answer follow-up, and meetings held among professional groups, including doctors and nurses, and educators. These people were not offended by the exercise of public worship and prayer, so we made the most of that opportunity in each venue and setting.

The highlight of this season of ministry was while spending time with the children of the public schools. In the city of Narva we were invited to visit every school with permission to present what we knew to be live-changing Truth. Not once did the chairs of the packed auditoriums remain occupied upon conclusion of the gathering, as the children rushed forward with great energy and emotion, often with shouts of joy, to receive all that Christ offered them.

What marked these precious souls, adults and children alike, was their intense desire for truth and real peace. The openness and readiness to hear and embrace the Gospel presented a huge opportunity to populate God's kingdom.

However, the same opportunity was afforded the Devil, and he has been quick to exploit the situation. During the last three decades, he has had his seducing spirits on the march, working through various religious cults and "isms". At the same time, in the modernized cultures of the west, he attempts to immobilize the Christian element with the entrapments of materialism and self-indulgence.

This being the case, I found my time spent among the Estonian and Russian people, both sweet and bitter. How long would the vast numbers of people in these forgotten cities have to wait to hear the message of Life, because of the lethargy of professed believers, unwilling to rise up and go? The void within their souls, and that of their nation, would come to be occupied by something, whether of the Light or a return to darkness.

It was good that these seeking souls were intrigued by new ideas as long as the Gospel reached their ears. Lies wither and die in the presence of Truth. The tenets of human philosophy and dead religion are no match for the life-changing power of the Gospel.

A Lesson in Switzerland

Not long after I began to walk with God, I was in Switzerland at the end of harvest season. I was among a group that traveled to a farm on the outskirts of Zurich, for the purpose of providing manual labor for the owners who needed the extra hands.

Part of the two-week visit involved the harvesting and baling of hay that covered numerous acres of their land. I remember that an intense storm was approaching, and it was critical that the hay, now scattered in bales throughout the fields, be loaded onto the flat-bed truck and brought into the barn before the deluge struck.

For two long and grueling days, I was one of two lucky workers positioned on the bed of the truck who received and stacked the bales. With the imminent arrival of the storm, time was of the essence. Because of the urgency of the task, it proved to be the most demanding and exhausting work in which I had ever been involved. Literally, I thought I was going to die. But, as I was to discover, it was also the most crucial job that needed to be done. If the bales were not brought into the safety of the barn before the darkness and downpour forced us to cease our efforts, the hay would've become saturated with water and subject to spoil and rot. The months of hard work that went before, would all be lost. There existed a short window of time during which the task could be accomplished. It required a focused, committed team effort to save the hay. We got the job done and I learned a lesson that I've carried with me to this day.

As I had recently embraced Christianity, I thought of those with whom I had crossed paths over time; people who took their time to observe my life, and to address my wandering with a message of forgiveness and hope. What if they hadn't? What if I had been left to my own rebel ways? As my thoughts were gathered, God's message to my heart was clear: Time is drawing to a close. The days in which we live are evil. As the tide of darkness increases, so does the flow of God's grace and mercy. We are each given a few years of life on this planet. In the short time we have it is imperative that every living soul be presented the Good News.

With thoughts of the multitudes of earthbound human souls that sit in darkness awaiting rescue, Jesus lamented, "The harvest is plentiful, but the laborers area few" (Luke 10:2). He also warned that "night is coming when no one can work" (John 9:4). Sobering words.

We'll now lay out a battle plan designed to mobilize God's people so that the "lion" of Truth is let loose and evil chased from our cities.

Chapter 33

The Battle Plan

It is natural to assess the challenge before us and feel inadequate or outmatched to make any real difference. And we would be correct if left to our own understanding and abilities. However, we are not. We are led by the omnipotent Maker of all things, the Creator of the heavens and the Earth. And we conduct our mission equipped with supernatural weapons and abilities that terrify our enemies. Expect to have your mind blown by what you will experience as God demonstrates His power and presence before human and angelic beings.

What follows are practical applications of the principles put forth in previous chapters, with special attention paid to the Seven Keys of the Kingdom. This prescription for the liberation of the city applies to Lady Savannah and to yours, as well.

- Before our *sphere of authority* can expand, our "house" must be in order. We must be committed to God and His purposes, and, dedicated to the prospering of family members entrusted us.

- Those that God sends forth must have hearts that are *set apart*, consecrated to God. No divided affections or straddling the fence will do, for doublemindedness renders one disqualified for God's purposes.

- The mark upon those truly set on pleasing God will be the issuance of Spirit power. God doesn't demand perfection but does require *pure motives* and the *passion* to see human captives set free.

- We must be joined to a group of *like-minded* people. Cities are populated by a variety of groups that worship together. However, not all worship the one true and living God. Remember, Jesus Christ is "the way, the truth, and the life", and "no one comes to the Father" except through Him.

- The church we attend must possess vision for the city disclosed by God. In the absence of vision, leadership must earnestly seek God for revelation and direction. The reason for the frustration of many Christian leaders is they lack a *sense of mission*. Their flock, in turn, is in a state of lethargy as their faith remains unchallenged. That group of believers are useless until they understand they are called to rise up and exert the *kingdom authority* entrusted them.

- *Collaboration* of church leaders, including worship and prayer for vision and purpose is necessary. The human tendency to compete must be replaced by a spirit of servanthood. Nurturing unity is the goal.

- The Spirit will give specific promises for the city that pertain to her destiny. These are to be steadfastly embraced as the leaders take steps to *equip* and *mobilize* the people in their care.

- The local group of believers to which we belong must join ranks with other committed groups to worship and to pray for our cities. Remember, all Christian groups, collectively make up the *one body* of Christ. As such, unity in the Spirit does exist, but that oneness only manifests through our daily, practical cooperation, and in the warfare waged against our common enemy.

- In concert with other mobilized local churches, we aim high, but yield to *spiritual process*. Faith will always consider the mountain, but in spirit reality, we must climb the foothills before we can conquer the summit.

- Generally, the leaders set forth the vision, the purposes and intended goals that pertain to your city of destiny. The people are called to worship and prayer, specifically, for enlightenment, discernment, and empowerment.

- Before we call the city to repentance, we, as the people of God, must confess our sins of lethargy, pride, and worldliness, that has caused us to neglect those bound in darkness. Scripture points out that judgment begins with the house of God, as those accountable to walk in the light we have received.

- Monthly *inter-church meetings* are conducted, led by pastors and elders of the various groups. These are times of reiterating God's mandate and commission for His people and standing on His revealed promises for our city. The unity that exists as members of the body of Christ will increasingly manifest, marked by an anointing of power upon the people.

- Pray for the leaders of your community, by name. The Scriptures directs us to "pray for kings and all who are in authority, so that we may lead tranquil and quiet lives in all godliness and dignity" (1 Tim. 2:2).

- Binding and Loosing principles apply. This element of warfare can be exercised before we set foot into the public places of our communities. God's Spirit does go before us.

- We exert our authority and work *behind the scenes* through intercessory prayer, and *on the scene* by physical setting foot on the ground and location where we are establishing kingdom rule.

- Remember, we must research the history of our city to identify the key events and decisions that have shaped her soul. We can then direct our authority against the specific demonic presence that has gained inroads, as we proclaim God's promise pertaining to the true destiny of our city.

- Whether one person, or a society of people, our desire is to bring others to *repentance*. As people choose Christ, the presence of God will occupy our land in increasing measure, including the homes, businesses, and marketplaces, wherever human activity takes place. Wherever demonic presence is evident, it is there we must go.

- With regard to Savannah and the numerous structures in which demonic entities dwell and exert control, kingdom authority should be exercised *systematically*. As some intercede in prayer, others visit the site and take the land. One by one, these ground-level spirits are vanquished through our actions as God's presence occupies the environment.

- Direct your authority at the spirit enemies that are trespassing on territory rightfully given to the people of God. We are not present to draw people's attention to ourselves, but to enforce God's will and judgment against dark powers of evil.

- As those carrying the Light of God's Truth, we must *infiltrate the territory* where demonic presence has established measures of control.

- In the various institutions where demonic strongholds exist, *godly wisdom* must be obtained in how to infiltrate that area of city culture. We proceed cautiously, but confidently. Intercessory prayer is mandatory in all situations.

- Public meetings are often held by our city's institutions, most commonly the education and government sectors. This allows us the opportunity to speak or sit in attendance and silently exercise authority. Both activities will dispel spirit darkness and bring enlightenment to those present. As we establish control in the spirit realm, what transpires on a physical, human level will reflect that reality.

- Target *key authority figures* within the institutions with intercessory prayer.

- Scheduled meetings with individual or groups of civic and business leaders are effective in changing the course of the community. Often, we will find compatible leaders in agreement with our goals, who will work within the institution for God's purposes. Again, intercession is key in swaying the mind and heart of a person or a group of people.

- We should *expect* the miraculous! Throughout the Bible, those that boldly ventured into battle against evil with the word of God on their lips and compassion in their hearts saw the power of God released. God not only has our backs but goes before us as well. He evicts demonic power with displays of His almighty power that confirms the message delivered by His people.

- We must begin to revolutionize how we *think* and *live*. In essence, we are spirit creatures equipped with supernatural abilities by the Creator of all things. Our mindsets must be retrained so that our expectations of what He will do in and through us are dictated by the infinite Holy Spirit and not our finite humanity.

- We must remain steadfastly *dependent* on God, trusting in His faithfulness to fulfill His promises to each of us and to the cities of which we are a part.

- *Perseverance* is needed if our cities are to be liberated. Rome wasn't built in a day and neither is a God-fearing society of people. Over time, we will see the fruit of victory; a behavioral change within the citizenry, a drop in the crime rate, growth in faith-based organizations, and greater exercise of benevolence and charity. The mindset of the various city institutions will reflect a change in moral principle and ethics.

- As God gives us victory over the works of darkness that have held our city, expect a vicious *counterattack* from the Devil. We must never drop our guard as the battle is continuous. Being sober-minded, alert and vigilant, are the means by which we maintain our ground and continue our advance.

- Perpetual worship and thankfulness to God should mark our lives as those delivered from death into everlasting life.

A Final Word

God's last word for any individual or city is always one of mercy and forgiveness. He is not willing that any soul, whether that of a person, or a collective society of people, be left alone in spiritual darkness, ashamed, confused, and hopeless. Through his grace, He has provided the means by which every human being need not wallow in a place of judgment. Those who refuse His mercy and grace, condemn themselves.

In any city, there are those who cooperate with God and those who resist. Their histories are marked with a *moral fluidity*, as over time the tide of God's grace and mercy advances and then recedes among the society. Enlightenment, like the moon, waxes and wanes. Although this has been the human experience, it does not have to be. As citizens, we need not settle for less than total liberation.

The beauty of Lady Savannah has been obscured, hidden behind a veil of corrupt authority that has given the enemy license to roam her streets, infiltrate her dwellings, and assault her people. The nature of the struggle, and the means to wrench her free is known by the few. However, as those individuals join forces, rise up and move forward with divine authority, the shackles holding Lady Savannah will weaken and crumble to dust, releasing her into destiny.

As God's fountain waters of life flow forth, that which was envisioned by the man James Edward Oglethorpe will come to pass.

As Lady Savannah has received the abundant favor of God, so will she flow with generosity and compassion to the less fortunate, bind the wounds of the broken-hearted, and set them on a pathway to their own fulfilled destiny.

Lady Savannah will perpetually showcase the Creator's existence and magnificence through her inventiveness and originality. As the masses of humanity enter her gates, they will be subject to divine inspiration. As they depart, each man and woman will carry with them a renewed awareness of their own potential as a unique creation of God.

Lady Savannah will be established in the strength and power of the Almighty. Her reliance on God as Protector and the One who trains and equips her to subdue her enemies will attest to His supremacy over Heaven and Earth.

These unique elements of potential for Savannah, and those pertaining to your city, are not just noble, lofty ideals. They are what God intends and destines for the people who comprise the souls of our cities. They are not just wishful goals, but guaranteed realities if we commit ourselves to the One who enables us to do all things by His Spirit.

I will close this writing with a challenge: Will you remain immobilized and indifferent to this spirit battle? Will you bow to the carnal voice of reason that questions, *How can I possibly make any difference in what my city becomes?* Or will you join with Paul and the believers of his day and declare before the hosts of the visible and invisible realms,

> Now to him who is able to do immeasurably more than all we ask or imagine, according to his power that is at work within us, to him be glory in the church and in Christ Jesus throughout all generations, for ever and ever! Amen!

About the Author

Michael Mancha was born and raised in California. He has spent the past fifteen years as a resident of the Deep South, writing and working as an independent private investigator. He is the author of Citizen Warrior: *The Spirit World Battle for the Soul of Your City,* and Three Dog Fright: *The Savannah Ghost Chronicles.* Michael is co-founder of 13th Colony Patriots, a political action group based in Savannah, Georgia, that has drawn national attention while engaged in timely protests in Washington, D.C. As a former missionary, Michael led relief teams to various parts of the world, including the former Soviet Union, Eastern Europe, and Asia. It is from this palette of first-hand experience his writings are conceived.

Visit MichaelMancha.com.

www.ingramcontent.com/pod-product-compliance
Lightning Source LLC
Chambersburg PA
CBHW020514080526
44583CB00013B/600